THE BIG BOOK OF

CHAKRAS AND CHAKRA HEALING

THE BIG BOOK OF

CHAKRAS AND CHAKRA HEALING

**How to Unlock Your
Seven Energy Centers for
Healing, Happiness, and Transformation**

SUSAN SHUMSKY, DD

Foreword by Anodea Judith, author of *Eastern Body, Western Mind*

**WEISER
BOOKS**

This edition first published in 2019
by Weiser Books, an imprint of
Red Wheel/Weiser, LLC
With offices at:
65 Parker Street, Suite 7
Newburyport, MA 01950
www.redwheelweiser.com

ISBN: 978-1-57863-671-6
Library of Congress Cataloging-in-Publication Data available upon request.

Cover and text design by Kathryn Sky-Peck
Interior images by Susan Shumsky

Printed in Canada
SP
10 9 8 7 6 5 4 3 2 1

Dedication

*This book is dedicated to the beauteous kundalini, subtle and radiant
as 10 million suns. To her lotus feet all worshippers bow,
for she invents this mirage by her maya,
and she absorbs it again by her all-consuming flame.*

CONTENTS

PART ONE: UNDERSTANDING SUBTLE ENERGY

PART TWO: AWAKENING YOUR CHAKRAS

PART THREE: AWAKENING KUNDALINI

FOREWORD

The chakra system is an idea whose time has come. Or perhaps I should say "come again," as chakras are elements of an ancient yogic system for spiritual evolution that has roots in the distant past. The revived interest in chakras today is a testament to the need for spiritual systems that are mapped on the body and encompass the full spectrum of human experience, from heaven to earth.

While it's wonderful that so many people are now drawn to learn about the chakra system, the danger of such popularization is that the chakras can become trivialized. The word is bandied about in general conversation, without people understanding its original context as esoteric wisdom for seekers of higher states of consciousness. In my 40 years of working with the chakra system, I have seen chakra dog collars, chakra underwear, chakra chocolates, and of course the usual candles, mugs, cushions, yoga mats, t-shirts, hats, posters, and greeting cards. I've even sold some of these items myself at my workshops!

This popularization does the important service of bringing the chakra system out to the general public, but it only skims the surface. What is missing is the deeper knowledge.

The Big Book of Chakras and Chakra Healing represents that deeper knowledge. With writing that is both friendly to the layperson yet true to a deeper mystery, this is the book to which I refer my students who are interested in the esoteric wisdom and practices of the ancients. While normally it takes intense research with a Sanskrit dictionary and lifetimes of patience to discover these subtle principles and practices, Susan Shumsky has done that work for you, making this information accessible to the average reader.

Where else are you going to find a description of the inner sheaths of the *sushumna,* as well as of the smaller subchakras of the heart and higher chakras? Within these pages you can find descriptions of the meaning of the individual petals, the deities associated with each chakra, and discussion of *mudras* (physical gestures), *bandhas* (inner locks), *pranayama* (breathing practices), and *mantras* (sounds) associated with the chakras.

In addition, she discusses the importance of Shiva/Shakti, the divine couple who represent the polarities of the Tantric tradition, where the chakra system originated, along with the sheaths of the human aura, the *tattvas* of manifestation, and much, much more.

This book is for seekers. It is not for the dabblers but for those interested in serious practice. For behind all the information offered in books and other media, knowledge of the chakras ultimately comes from within oneself, through direct access. But that access takes practice—sustained and consistent effort over many years. Susan Shumsky has done that work as well, and its rewards are hidden within these pages for you to discover through your own practice.

Enjoy the journey!

—Anodea Judith, 2013
Author of *Eastern Body, Western Mind*

INTRODUCTION

There is no doubt the planet has undergone a dramatic transformation in the last 50 years. I was fortunate to participate at the forefront of the spiritual revolution of the 1960s, which changed the world. In 1950s America, there was no "meditation," no "mantra," no "yoga," and certainly no "chakra." These terms did not exist in the West. There were a total of two esoteric bookstores in the United States. Now, half a century later, we see yoga and martial arts studios in strip malls. Esoteric information proliferates on the Internet. Metaphysical books are available in every bookstore. And "chakra" is a term found in magazines at grocery store checkout counters.

Yes, the world has risen to an extraordinary new high in vibrational energy. What used to be on the fringe is now mainstream. Yet there is still a great deal of ignorance about what a "chakra" is. And quite a bit of misinformation gets disseminated in such a democratic medium as the Internet. Because of the confusion about what the subtle energy system is, how it relates to our personal wellbeing, how it fits into the cosmos, and why its importance is vital to recognize, we offer this additional edition of the book known under the titles *Exploring Chakras* and *The Power of Chakras*.

Based upon the ancient Tantric and Vedic scriptures of India, where the most authentic information about the seven major chakras, seven minor chakras, and subtle energy system can be found, this COVR Award–winning, favorably rated, positively reviewed text is now getting a facelift, new name, new cover, larger format, and several improvements. Highly praised by spiritual masters from India as well as thousands of grateful readers, this book has been reviewed as the "quintessential reference on the subject." With this new edition, *The Big Book of Chakras and Chakra Healing,* we hope to reach an even wider audience with the message of wisdom and healing contained in its pages.

My First Kundalini Experience

My own stunning introduction to the human energy field and its elusive *kundalini* energy occurred at age 18. A flower child of the hippie generation, I was attending art college in Oakland, California. The winter of late 1966 was a time of immense discovery. I awoke to Eastern wisdom through Buddhist and Hindu scriptures, readily available in Telegraph Avenue bookstores near the University of California. I consumed as many books about Eastern philosophy as I could lay my hands on.

I came across Alan Watts's *The Way of Zen* and Paramahansa Yogananda's *Autobiography of a Yogi*, which made a profound impression. As I read Tibetan Buddhist scriptures, such as *Bardo Thodal* (Tibetan Book of the Dead) and the story of *Milarepa*, a powerful desire consumed my heart. I wanted desperately to attain the state of consciousness I was reading about: *nirvana*.

I learned that *nirvana*, or its Zen Buddhist equivalent, *satori*, meant the end of suffering: spiritual enlightenment, freedom from the "wheel of birth and death"—the cycles of reincarnation. Something within me knew this was the only goal worth pursuing. Since I read that nirvana could be found by practicing meditation, my heart yearned to learn how. Alan Watts emphasized the importance of a "meditation guide." But, needless to say, in 1966, no yoga or meditation schools could be found in the yellow pages of the telephone directory.

At that time, I lived with some other art students in one of those charming Berkeley, California, redwood-shingled, beamed-ceiling houses. One afternoon, I asked a roommate whether he knew how I could find a meditation guide. He replied, "Have you ever tried to meditate by yourself?"

So I thought I would give it a try. Clearly unaware that I was supposed to sit up while meditating, I entered my bedroom and lay on my back. Because I was clueless about what I was doing, I prayed for an experience of meditation. Without warning, I was suddenly propelled into an ecstatic state! My body felt as if it were plugged into an electric socket. A huge rush of energy bolted from the tips of my toes to the top of my head. I was connected to a powerful cord of energy that continuously pumped through my body like a rocket.

Because I never had experienced anything remotely similar, I figured this must be "meditation." Little did I know, this was not only my first meditation experience, but also my *kundalini* awakening—all at the same time. This atomic explosion of energy was both ecstatic and bewildering.

Under Maharishi's Spell

After my initial meditation, it was not long before I found myself on the banks of the Ganges River in the Himalayan foothills in Rishikesh, India, studying with a spiritual master. I ended up living in his *ashrams* (spiritual communities) for 22 years in the Himalayas, Swiss Alps, and secluded areas of the United States. I was on his personal staff under his close tutelage for six of those years.

His name was Maharishi Mahesh Yogi, founder of Transcendental Meditation (TM) and *guru* (teacher) of the Beatles and of Deepak Chopra. However, I met Maharishi and started TM before these celebrities discovered him. In 1970, I received the unheard-of blessing of staying with Maharishi in his ashram in Rishikesh for six months and remained with him and only eight other disciples for two of those months.

During the 22 years of studying in my guru's ashrams, I meditated up to 20 hours a day. Sometimes I went into my room and did not appear for eight weeks at a time. I observed silence and did not speak to anyone for up to four months at a time. I sometimes fasted for two months at a time, and I observed celibacy for decades.

Under Maharishi's guidance, I experienced *samadhi* daily. Samadhi, a Sanskrit word derived from the roots *sama* (evenness) and *dhi* (deepest part of the intellect), means profound stillness of body along with mental quietude—transcendental consciousness. This experience of samadhi is the goal of Yoga philosophy—what seekers of enlightenment strive to attain.

This experience of *sat-chit-ananda* (absolute-consciousness-bliss) is readily available to anyone. In fact, in this book you will learn a simple meditation to help you attain this higher state of awareness.

Another component of living with a spiritual master is the mysterious experience called *shaktipat*. This blissful transference of energy occurs when enlightened masters put their attention on a disciple. In such cases, the guru acts as an energy conduit for the student in the transmission of kundalini energy.

Maharishi rarely spoke of kundalini experiences, which he pigeonholed as "release of stress." In other words, the phenomena associated with kundalini, such as sensations rushing up the spine, are more precisely defined as blockages to the free flow of kundalini energy. If the channel were clear, there would be no sensations—only the experience of unbounded awareness and bliss consciousness.

Yet, when disciples came into Maharishi's direct presence, the experience of kundalini, in the form of bliss, was automatically transferred to the disciple through

Maharishi's glance, word, or attention. Spiritual masters overflowing with vital energy have the power to transmit this energy in order to heal and uplift people, even bring them to higher consciousness. The mysterious force known as *prana* is key to the secret of divine transmission from *guru* (teacher) to *chela* (student).

Many people think disciples who clamor after gurus are desperate and weak, brainwashed by these cult leaders. In some cases, this is true. Yet one component of being near a spiritual master is often overlooked: the profound transference of energy that occurs in the presence of a true saint. That is why the great spiritual master Ramakrishna Paramahansa said, "Keep holy company; and now and then visit God's devotees and holy men."[1]

When I was studying with Maharishi, I lived for this experience. However, Maharishi's devotees did not call it *shaktipat*. We called it *darshan* (sight)—the blessing of being in the presence of an enlightened master. I tried everything in my power to get near Maharishi as often as possible. For whenever he put his attention on me, I was propelled into a state of sheer delight and ecstasy.

What did kundalini transference feel like? For me, the world stopped. Time and space disappeared. There was nothing but a wave of love on an ocean of bliss. I was knocked over with spiritual energy that poured from my guru's eyes. This energy shot directly from his eyes like a bullet of bliss that blasted into my *aura* (energy field). Rushes of intense power and love throbbed through my body, electrifying and energizing it.

Catapulted into an altered state of consciousness, my mind became expanded, joyous, and free. My body felt ecstatic. My spirit lifted into unbounded awareness. My heart opened. I was filled with light. Nothing existed but the now-ness of now in the eternity of the present. My I-ness dissolved into a sea of love and devotion. Waves of bliss rolled through that sea, and I drowned in complete surrender at my beloved guru's feet.

Throughout the decades, other spiritual masters have graced me with similar experiences of kundalini transference. Notable was Babaji Raman Kumar Bachchan, a Tantric master with whom I studied for a few years. A spiritual healer, he transfers kundalini energy by chanting mantras and then blowing on the person.

Jesus used a similar method when he met his disciples after his resurrection. He "breathed on them, and saith unto them, 'Receive ye the Holy Ghost.'"[2]

A great saint of India, Brahmaveta Shri Devraha Hans Baba, uses his voice to transport people into ecstatic states. A *naga baba* (naked ascetic), he chants devotional songs to the Gods Radha and Krishna in an ancient mysterious language, entirely untranslatable. As he sings, people enter blissful, altered states of consciousness, and, amazingly, they feel compelled to dance as they experience divine love.

Amritananda Mayi, otherwise known as Ammachi, often called the "hugging saint," transfers kundalini energy by hugging her disciples.

In the Judeo-Christian tradition, Moses also used the power of touch as a conduit for kundalini energy: "And Joshua the son of Nun was full of the spirit of wisdom; for Moses had laid his hands upon him."[3]

It's Not Out There but In Here

After more than two decades in the ashram with Maharishi, though I enjoyed so many blissful experiences, I still had not experienced what I was seeking: a true connection and direct relationship with God in a personal way. Luckily, after leaving the ashram, I found a means to connect to Spirit through listening to the "still small voice" of divine guidance and wisdom within—to have direct, two-way "conversations with God."

As a result of this new awakening, I founded a method called Divine Revelation, which offers specific practices to open the mind, heart, and spirit to the riches of direct divine contact and communication. It is a unique, complete, field-proven technology for contacting the divine presence, hearing and testing the inner voice, and receiving clear divine guidance.

What I discovered through more than five decades of spiritual study is that the kingdom of heaven lies within your own heart and soul. You can experience inner shaktipat through your own experiences. You can have direct contact with your inner guru who will bless you with the recognition of ecstasy and bliss within. You can attain spiritual enlightenment by yourself, without looking to others for advice, for energy, for kundalini, or for anything.

You can awaken kundalini through innumerable means, including prayer, devotion, worship, intellectual inquiry, meditation, yoga practices, yoga breathing exercises, willpower, discernment, knowledge, and body purification. In this book, you will discover some of these ways. In fact, any manifestation of spiritual gifts or supernormal powers indicates kundalini is already awake to some degree. This enigmatic kundalini energy, which brings bliss, energy, power, and ecstasy, is definitely worth seeking and finding.

What You'll Learn Here

This book will open the door to the potent, mysterious force called kundalini. It will also uncover the chakra system, a network of energy within your subtle body. Here you will discover the 14 main chakras responsible for physical, mental, and spiritual activity and evolution:

- First chakra: *muladhara,* root lotus

- Second chakra: *svadhishthana,* pelvic lotus

- Third chakra: *manipura,* navel lotus

- Fourth chakra: *anahata,* heart lotus

- Lower fourth chakra: *hrit,* part of heart lotus

- Fifth chakra: *vishuddha,* throat lotus

- Between fifth and sixth: *talu,* palate lotus

- Sixth chakra: *ajna,* brow lotus

- Part of *ajna* sixth chakra: *manas* lotus

- Part of *ajna* sixth chakra: *indu* lotus

- Part of *ajna* sixth chakra: *nirvana* lotus

- Lower seventh chakra: *guru,* part of crown lotus

- Seventh chakra: *sahasrara,* crown lotus

- Upper seventh chakra: supreme *bindu* point

As you delve deeply into the anatomy of this subtle energy system, you will find many keys to unlock the secret of the ages, the mystery of your origin, as well as your destination.

Simply reading this book will elevate your consciousness, because your attention will focus on the subtle chakra and kundalini energies. By reading it more than once, you will comprehend its profound, rich, full depth of meaning. Practicing the simple yoga methods in this book will begin to stir kundalini energies in your body. In addition, in another of my books called *Exploring Meditation,* you can learn to practice yoga *asanas* (postures). These asanas are invaluable tools for awakening kundalini and opening your chakras.

In addition, get out your markers, crayons, paints, or colored pencils to color in the chakra pictures and chakra deities in Part 2 of this book. The correct colors are described in the text near the illustrations. Or order my book *Color Your Chakras* at your local bookstore or an online retailer. Coloring these pictures will help you visualize and experiences the chakra energies.

Let us get started on the path of chakra power now!

Part One

UNDERSTANDING SUBTLE ENERGY

Chapter One

WHAT'S A CHAKRA, ANYWAY?

"The awakening of the inner Kundalini is the true beginning
of the spiritual journey."
—Swami Muktananda[1]

Kundalini is a mysterious, dormant, powerful, cosmic force within your body that, when awakened, is believed to bring spiritual enlightenment. It is also the potent energy within your body understood to be responsible for sexual orgasm. Because of this, much misinformation has been perpetrated in the name of kundalini.

The *chakra* system, consisting of energy centers within your subtle body, is widely explored today through myriad books, seminars, and gurus. Sincere individuals seeking kundalini experiences are led into practices that may or may not produce genuine spiritual evolution.

Many authentic practices yield spectacular results in a short time. Others are erroneous and ineffectual. Methods undertaken sincerely and seriously, with proper training, can lead to spiritual awakening. Others, attempted haphazardly and carelessly, can cause confusion, harm, or, worse, serious physical or mental illness.

After taking a weekend seminar, some misguided people print business cards, put up a shingle, and declare themselves the next "master," "yogi," "sanyasin," "swami," "shaman," or "chakra healer." Suddenly they claim authority in a field that genuine yogis spent lifetimes meditating in caves attempting to master.

Some so-called self-declared experts are sincere yet deluded. Sadly, much confusion is left in their wake.

For this reason, investigating chakras in a reliable, systematic way is vital. Gaining deep understanding about your subtle bodies, energy field, and energy system is essential. Learning beneficial spiritual practices that will not harm your body or confuse your mind is necessary.

By learning from ancient sources that have stood the test of time, you can be assured of deeper comprehension and better experiences. By delving into scriptures of antiquity that have, until recently, been locked in secret hiding places in forests and caves of India, you can uncover new, unexplored, and unrevealed wisdom.

If you are curious about chakras, yet claim no prior knowledge or experience, then it is wise to begin slowly and practice step by step. If you know about chakras, you may want to rethink what you think you already know. Perhaps you can learn deep wisdom from the ancient sages.

Now it is smart to learn and grow spiritually in a safe, precise way. In a phrase: It is time to "practice safe spirituality."

This book will show you how.

What Can This Book Do for You?

Perhaps you picked up this book because of an interest in spiritual development. You may have heard about chakras or kundalini, or previously read about them. Maybe you studied Kundalini Yoga, Tantra Yoga, or Laya Yoga for years, but want to learn more. Or you faced disaster while experimenting with kundalini without supervision.

In every case, this book has something to offer. Beginners as well as advanced students can benefit from the information and methods presented here. This book's authority rests not only on personal experience, but also on ancient scriptural sources.

Through more than five decades of teaching spiritual disciplines, I have often heard the following complaints, to which solutions are found in this book:

1. "I've tried to meditate and awaken kundalini, but it just doesn't work for me." This book provides easy, step-by-step ways to gently awaken kundalini safely, reliably, and systematically, through time-tested, proven yogic practices.

2. "My negative beliefs, mental blockages, and limitations get in the way when I try to meditate or to get spiritual experiences." Here you will learn specific healing affirmations to help you overcome past negative patterns and attain the experiences you seek.

3. "My kundalini experiences are so strange, and no one understands them, including me!" In this book you will find examples and explanations of kundalini, and a road map to your spiritual experiences.

4. "I get totally confused by this energy running through my body. What am I supposed to do with it?" This book provides not only understandings about kundalini energy and chakras, but also methods to help you master the energy.

5. "I get frightened by negative kundalini experiences." This book offers specific ways to handle any situation, no matter how strange or frightening it might be.

6. "I feel overly sensitive to people and influences around me." In this book, you will learn techniques for healing negative influences and for preventing harm from future influences.

7. "I've been deceived by the false promises of gurus." The information in this book helps you become more self-reliant and less dependent on gurus.

8. "I'm offended by rules and regulations, cults, and coercive organizations." The universal techniques offered here impose no restrictions and are compatible with other religious philosophies, lifestyles, and personal beliefs.

9. "I don't want to work at difficult, strict, hard-to-follow disciplines." This book is understandable, logical, and practical, with simple-to-learn methods requiring no previous experience, background, training, skill, or knowledge.

FAQs about Chakras and Kundalini

Perhaps you have already studied subtle energy fields, the aura, prana, chakras, or kundalini. Whether or not you are already familiar with these topics, you might be surprised by what you can learn here. Let us begin with the basics and answer a few questions you may have.

Q: What is subtle energy?

A: Just as physics tells us the universe is made of subtle constituents invisible to the human eye, similarly, your body is made of subtle energy. Let us try an experiment right now. Clench both your fists and place them next to each other, as shown in Figure 1a. Then vigorously rub your left fingers against your right fingers in a washboard motion, back and forth (not up and down), for 45 seconds. Then unclench your fists and face your palms toward each other a few inches apart. You might feel an invisible ball of energy between your palms. This sensation of vibrant activity is subtle energy.

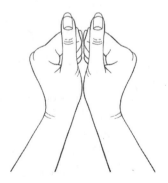

Figure 1a. Buffing Up.

By entering a hospital, a dilapidated house, a prison, a bar, a mental institution, or a crowded bus, you can sense bad vibrations. By hiking in the woods, boating on a lake, hearing inspiring music, or reading uplifting poetry or scriptures, you can feel elated. These are all indications of subtle energy.

In this book you will learn to energize your body, enhance your energy field, heal energy blockages, and prevent energy drain.

Q: What is the aura?

A: The subtle energy field in and around your body is the "aura" (meaning "breath of air" in Greek). Just as the Earth has a magnetic field, your body has an auric field. Your aura consists of several bodies, such as your mental body, emotional body, and subtle bodies that constitute your higher self. Your subtle bodies are invisible to human eyes, but visible to your inner eye or clairvoyant ("clear-seeing" in French) sensory perception. If you stare at a person standing in front of a white wall, you might see energy vibrations or colors around the person's head. By looking into a mirror at night in the dark, you may see a subtle glow around your own head. These experiences are indications that auras exist.

In this book, you will learn about your subtle bodies and auric field.

Q: What is a mental body?

A: Your thoughts and emotions have physical counterparts in your subtle body. These thoughts consist of subtle substances not yet measured by science but visible to clairvoyant sense perception. Thought-forms are habitual thought patterns taking concrete shape in and around your body. You might wear some old, encrusted thoughts like armor. Others might seem like a jail cell. These old thought-forms and habits can be healed. You will learn how in this book.

Q: What does the word "chakra" mean?

A: In the ancient Sanskrit language, in which the scriptures of India were originally written, the word *chakra* (in Sanskrit: चक्र) translates as "wheel." This word is pronounced phonetically as "chukr": chu, as in the English word "chunk," and cr, as in the English word "crumb," but the "r" is rolled. There is no word pronounced "shock-rah" in the Sanskrit or English languages. That pronunciation, though widely used in America, is incorrect. Because chakras are centers of vital energy in your subtle body, they are not observable by your gross senses. However, they can be experienced through subtle sense perception.

Seven main chakras are described in the ancient *tantras* (*tantric* or *agamic* scriptures of India). Each chakra in your spinal column is believed to influence or even govern bodily functions near its region of the spine.

In this book, you will discover and explore these chakras.

Q: What is a kundalini shakti?

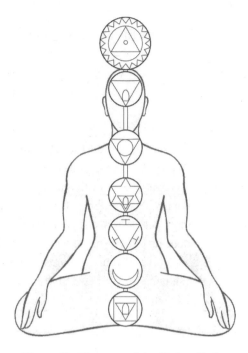

A: *Kundalini shakti* is a spiritual cosmic energy hidden in the human body. The term derives from Sanskrit roots, *kundala* (coiled), *kunda* (pit, depression), and *shakti* (energy). Shakti is also known as the Goddess, the mother of this universe. Kundalini is a vast reservoir of untapped, potential energy, which, when fully awakened, brings self-realization and enlightenment. However, in most people, it lies dormant at the base of the spine near the tailbone, lodged in the subtle body. Kundalini is often called "serpent power," "serpent fire," or "mystic coil," because it resembles a sleeping snake

Figure 1b. Elements of the Major Chakras.

coiled in a spiral shape. Many yoga practitioners attempt to awaken this serpent, uncoil it, and nudge it to rise up toward the brain.

In this book, you will learn about kundalini and how to rouse it.

Q: What is prana?

A: *Prana* is universal energy that breathes life into matter. It is formless, ubiquitous, potent energy that sustains both living individuals and also the cosmic order—the power within everything, animate and inanimate. Individual prana is the vital life-principle in all animate life. Cosmic prana is a universal energy that unifies the living and nonliving in a coordinated whole. Prana, the life force in your breath, is the key to life—electromagnetic fuel that energizes every tissue and cell. Without prana, your body could not function.

Figure 1c. The Sleeping Kundalini.

Gopi Krishna in *The Dawn of a New Science* describes prana as "a living electricity, acting intelligently and purposefully, that controls the activity of every molecule of living matter. It carries the life principle from one place to the other."

In this book, you will discover how prana functions in your body.

Q: What is yoga?

A: The Sanskrit word *yoga* comes from the root *yuj* (to yoke). The purpose of yoga, therefore, is to unite the individual soul with universal Spirit. Each path of yoga takes a different approach to attain this goal. Because the most visible, popular path today is Hatha Yoga, which uses physical postures called *asanas,* most people think yoga is nothing more than physical exercises performed on a floor mat in a gym. However, yoga is not an exercise routine. It is a profound science for experiencing union with the divine. In this book, you will learn how yoga can enhance your life, and you will learn some yogic practices to gently awaken kundalini.

Q: What is the purpose of raising kundalini energy?

A: When kundalini shakti travels up the spine to the brain, the goal of yoga is achieved as *shakti* (female principle or inner Goddess) merges with *shakta* (male principle, the inner God Shiva) in divine union. This results in a state of higher awareness called *nirvikalpa samadhi,* the superconscious state of spiritual enlightenment. Here the individual is fully unified with universal Spirit, and all sense of separateness dissolves. You will learn more about what that means in this book.

Q: What is Kundalini Yoga?

A: Kundalini Yoga, Laya Yoga, and Kriya Yoga are systems of yoga that seek to awaken the slumbering kundalini. Practitioners engage in various methods to rouse the sleeping energy until it moves up the spine, pierces the chakras, moves through the brain, and finally reaches the crown chakra or thousand-petaled lotus above the skull. Kundalini Yoga is an aggressive path of rigorous *asanas* (physical postures), intense *pranayama* (breathing exercises), *bandhas* (muscular locks), *mudras* (gestures), meditation using *mantras* (sacred Sanskrit sounds) and imagery, and strict dietary and behavioral control. Kundalini Yoga masters generally agree that celibacy is essential to this path.

If you are serious about deep involvement with Kundalini Yoga, then study with an enlightened spiritual master who can guide you personally through the sometimes-bizarre experiences that occur when the force of kundalini is unleashed in the body.

In this book, you will learn basic, gentle meditations, physical practices, and breathing techniques to begin your exploration of kundalini energy without the benefit of a teacher. However, you can study a spiritual practice called Divine Revelation or even embark on a serious study of yoga or take a yoga retreat. For more information, visit the websites mentioned on page 280 of this book.

Q: What's the purpose of reading about this stuff?

A: You might think chakras have no bearing on your everyday life. After all, what can they do for you? Learning about the subtle body, chakras, and kundalini can transform your life. You can heal mental, physical, and emotional problems for yourself and others. You can develop intuition, ESP, and subtle sensory perception. You can attain greater sensitivity, manifest extraordinary powers, fulfill your desires, and unfold greater awareness. You can even reach the ultimate goal of self-realization and spiritual enlightenment in cosmic consciousness or higher levels of consciousness.

What You Will Learn

As you dig deeper into this valuable book, you will:

- Discover your subtle bodies and their purpose.

- Learn about prana and how it functions in your body, mind, and spirit.

- Gain understanding of kundalini energy and the chakra system.

- Learn details about the energies and purpose of each chakra.

- Use easy meditation techniques to experience and awaken kundalini.

- Learn how to heal blockages in your subtle body.

- Learn how to maintain the health of your energy field.

- Use gentle yoga practices and breathing methods specifically designed to safely awaken kundalini energy.

- Empower yourself as a multidimensional being.

By practicing the simple, easy-to-learn techniques, you can begin to experience depths of spiritual awareness comparable to what many seekers have sought for generations. You will explore subtle realms of mind, spirit, time, and space, and how they relate to your body. You will chart previously unknown regions of your inner being. A map of your life will emerge—a road map providing deep understanding of yourself and how you fit into the cosmos. You will travel through worlds upon worlds and times beyond time in a multidimensional universe. This is the time for action. So let us get started now!

Chapter Two

WHAT WESTERNERS DON'T KNOW

"When you succeed in awakening the Kundalini, so that it starts to move out of its mere potentiality, you necessarily start a world which is totally different from our world. It is the world of eternity."
—*Carl Jung*[1]

West vs. East

Western medicine looks at your physical body as a mechanic might view a car engine. Medical doctors see a plethora of valves, tubes, pockets, chambers, and sacks, with channels of fluid flowing through them. To most physicians, the body is a piece of machinery. Just as mechanics diagnose an automobile and then fix it, so doctors diagnose and "fix" your body.

According to Western allopathic medicine, the only way to cure disease is purely mechanistic—cut out the tumor, kill the offending cancer cells, destroy the invading predatory virus, chop out the stone-producing gall bladder, obliterate the diseased uterus, delete the swollen prostate, cut and paste the arteries to the heart.

This slice-and-dice method of medical practice is not only viewed as acceptable, it is lauded as miraculous. In our Western culture, doctors attain mystical status. As our holy men and women, "medical deities" hold the power of life and death in their hands, and whatever they say is gospel.

Few brave souls ever question their doctors. Whatever prescriptions given, especially to vulnerable, elderly patients, are taken without objection or inquiry. Few patients take responsibility for their own healthcare. Many ravage their bodies with a fast food diet, improper rest, and a debilitating lifestyle, while imagining that if they fall ill, a medical doctor will rescue them.

There is no doubt that allopathic medicine is highly effective, and amazing cures happen daily. I was certainly grateful for a highly skilled orthopedic surgeon when my leg was fractured. Yet knowing what I do about holistic health and preventative medicine, I wonder what greater healing could occur with physicians trained in skills widely practiced in the Far East—acupuncture, homeopathy, chiropractic, *Qi Gong,* fasting, *Ayurveda,* massage, *marma* therapy, and so forth. More importantly, I imagine what diseases could be prevented with the public educated in self-healing skills.

Oriental medicine has not been added to the repertoire of Western medicine because of the fundamental philosophical difference between West and East.

In the West, we see life as a material object that begins at birth and ends at death. It is made of water, blood, cells, muscles, and other slimy things that dry up and disintegrate once the heart stops pumping. Life ends with the last breath, and nothing else exists.

In contrast, to people of the Far East, their gross physical body is just one of many. Not only do they accept subtle bodies and subtle energy; they might even heal their own bodies through a variety of subtle practices, including meditation, visualization, prayer, and spiritual healing.

Whereas in the West, people only believe what they see, hear, and touch, in the Far East, people learn to experience what they cannot see with eyes, hear with ears, or touch with fingers.

This book is a journey into these subtle realms of existence. It takes you beyond the gross physical body. It opens your eyes to worlds beyond this world and the timeless beyond this time. A new view of the body will emerge to your awareness—an amazing picture of beauty and miracles.

If you could open your eyes to the truth, you would see the power to heal is in your own hands. You can prevent disease, maintain your body in glowing, radiant health, and experience peace of mind daily.

By practicing yogic methods, eating a nourishing diet, and following a healthy lifestyle, you can transform your mind and body to align with divine Spirit.

You Are a Multidimensional Being

Western medical doctors would disagree when I say your physical body is not your only body. In fact, they would probably give me a prescription for one of those antipsychotic drugs. However, I contend that you do have subtle bodies within, around, and above your physical body.

Here you will explore your own subtle bodies and subtle senses. Yes, along with your subtle bodies, you also have subtle senses. Through these you can experience other dimensions, or planes of existence. Indeed, there are other worlds beyond this world and times beyond this time. You can begin to visit them.

Your gross physical body, made of elements on chemistry's periodic table, is not the only one you inhabit. Your identity is greater than you can imagine. Your mind and body extend far beyond this physical plane.

My belief is that you are a multidimensional, unlimited light-being of great magnificence, power, and energy. You are not bound by time or space. You are beautiful beyond words. Your mind is brilliant, heart is open, and body is exquisite. You are divinity itself, incarnated in human flesh.

Does this sound far-fetched? This is how scriptures of all religions describe you. You may not recognize the true magnificence of your being, but divine Spirit does. Let us read what the scriptures say:

"God said, 'Let us make man in our image, after our likeness.'"
(Judeo-Christian)[2]

"Know ye not that ye are the temple of God, and that the Spirit of
God dwelleth in you?" (Christian)[3]

"The kingdom of God cometh not with observation: Neither shall they say, lo
here! or, lo there! For, behold, the kingdom of God is within you." (Christian)[4]

"For man is spirit . . . yea, man is the tabernacle of God, even temples."
(Mormon)[5]

"I have breathed into man of My spirit." (Islam)[6]

"Every being has the Buddha Nature. That is the self." (Buddhist)[7]

"The deity is immanent in man and man is inherent in the deity;
there is neither the divine nor the human; there is no difference in essence
at all between them." (Shinto)[8]

"The living self is the image of the Supreme Being." (Sikh)[9]

"That which is the finest essence—this whole world has that as its Self. That is
Reality. That is the Self. That art thou." (Hindu)[10]

Why don't you see yourself as this divine being? When a veil is drawn over your eyes, you cannot see the truth. This veil of ignorance (called *avidya* in Sanskrit) is a mistaken idea about who you think you are. This shade covers the real you. It casts a shadow on your true self and diminishes your value.

If you could rip open that veil and see the truth, your light would shine with unparalleled radiance, and you would express your true nature of being. You would live the divine purpose for which you were born, and dwell in the heart of Spirit.

The Hum of Life

You are a mighty, beauteous being of great light. Within your true nature lies a seed of enlightenment. When nurtured, this seed sprouts and grows. Eventually it blossoms into a full-blown tree of supreme wisdom and freedom. The tree of life is a trunk with many branches, depicted in the Kabbalah and in India as the subtle body system, including the chakras (see Chapter 8).

Strangely, this same subtle body is depicted as the emblem of Western medicine—the caduceus—yet rare is a medical doctor who knows what that symbol means. By reading this book, you will uncover its hidden meaning.

Figure 2a. The Caduceus.

Your physical body is the gross manifestation of this tree of life. What does this mean? You came into being as a result of mere thought-stuff, which manifested first as sound, then as light. It is said, "In the beginning was the Word, and the Word was with God, and the Word was God."[11] That Word, the everlasting hum of creation, spoken by Spirit, is the progenitor of the cosmos.

How does a hum manifest creation? The latest developments in theoretical physics postulate that the fundamental objects in nature are not point-like (such as bosons, fermions, gluons, or quarks), but rather different vibrational modes of an extended object—a *brane* (from the word "membrane"), which may either be a superstring or a brane with more dimensions.

In this theory, the essential component of this universe is vibration, like violin music. Stretching violin strings to specific degrees of tension produces various musical notes. A note played on a violin might be called an "excitation mode." Similarly, in string theory, the elementary particles observed in particle accelerators are like musical notes—excitation modes of elementary strings.

As with a violin, these elementary strings must be stretched under tension to become excited. Unlike violin strings, however, the average size of an elementary string is approximately the length scale of quantum gravity, called the "Planck length," which is about a millionth of a billionth of a billionth of a billionth of a centimeter.

Superstring theory envisions a 10-dimensional or 11-dimensional space-time with a symmetry that gives every particle that transmits a force (a boson) a partner particle that makes up matter (a fermion). The partner particles are called *superpartners,* and the symmetry between forces and matter is called *supersymmetry.*

String theory unifies in one single quantum theory all known forces and elementary particles. Brian Greene, author of the best-selling book *The Elegant Universe,* describes: "It provides the first way of putting quantum mechanics and general relativity together—that is, merging the laws of the small and the laws of the large—and it does it in such a sleek manner that it is quite breathtaking. And the term elegant really describes that kind of solution."[12]

Long before John Schwarz, Michael Green, and other theoretical superstring physicists existed, the sages of ancient India cognized that the universe is multidimensional. They said it began with a vibrational hum and is sustained by specific variations of that hum. The primordial hum is called *OM, aum,* or *pranava,* and the variations of that hum are the *Vedas,* or hymns of the Veda.

In your own life, your multidimensional body, mind, and spirit are connected to one another by virtue of that hum. And the humming of thoughts in your mind and in humanity's mass mind profoundly affect your body.

The Mind-Body Connection

Western medicine completely ignores the mental component in its treatment of disease. Yet scientific studies show that your mind and body are connected. Even the effects of prayer have been measured.

For example, Dr. Roger Lobo, Columbia University's chairman of obstetrics and gynecology, found highly significant results in a study on pregnancy and prayer at Cha Hospital in Korea, where 199 women underwent in vitro fertilization. Unknown to the patients and their doctors, groups from the United States, Canada, and Australia prayed for some of these women to get pregnant. After three weeks, 50 percent of the women who were "prayed for" got pregnant, whereas only 26 percent of the women who were not prayed for got pregnant—almost a 100-percent increase in the rate of pregnancy!

How can a word, a thought, or a prayer affect pregnancy? Your subtle mind is intimately connected with your gross physical body. In fact, your thoughts, beliefs, and ideas are the progenitors of your body. Whatever you believe to be true about yourself has manifested and continues to manifest in your body.

Let us take the example of body weight. How fat or thin you are is largely a result of your own body image. By obsessively thinking about how fat you are, by constantly harping to others about how fat you are, by thinking "fat" when you look in the mirror, and thus reinforcing your fatness—your fatness is perpetuated.

This example of beliefs in body image can be extended to other areas, such as wellness or disease. In fact, your beliefs apply to every area of your life, such as success, power, money, romance, family, and children. What is in your mind gets perpetuated in your life. Whatever you place your attention on grows stronger. Whatever you ignore tends to disappear.

"All that we are is a result of what we have thought; it is founded on our thoughts, it is made up of our thoughts. If a man speaks or acts with an evil thought, pain follows him, as the wheel follows the foot of the ox that draws the carriage . . . If a man speaks or acts with a pure thought, happiness follows him, like a shadow that never leaves him." —Buddha[13]

Western medicine would call such notions crackpot at best. That is why physicians treat the body as a machine rather than a fluid, ever-changing vehicle of Spirit.

In the Far East, the body is viewed as a microcosm within a macrocosmic universe. It is affected by and affects everyone and everything around it. The body is a multidimensional part of a holistic individual. Mind is not separate from matter. Thoughts affect and are affected by the body.

In this book, our study of the human energy field and chakra system relies on a perspective that Western medicine completely rejects: the notion of a subtle energy system undetectable by our most powerful microscopes. No doctor trained in a respectable medical college would endorse a virtually invisible system of subtle energy pathways and energy centers governing your bodily functioning. Yet the *chakra* and *nadi* system is the basis of all Oriental medicine today, including the well-respected science of acupuncture.

Perhaps Western medicine has not gone far enough in its study of human physiology. They might well look to the East for more knowledge about the workings of the body.

Let us open that exploration now.

Chapter Three

THE KEY TO LIFE: PRANA

*"Indra [the supreme deity] said: 'I am Prana (breath), O
Rishi, thou art Prana, all things are Prana. For it is Prana
who shines in the sun, and I here pervade all regions
under that form."
—The Upanishads[1]*

The enigmatic energy of kundalini is at the source of two life currents: *prana* (vital energy) and *virya* (virile potency). Prana is the expanding aspect of energy, and virya is its adamantine intensity. Thus, virya inspires every kind of fervor, whether mystical, sexual, creative, artistic, political, spiritual, or otherwise. In your physical body, prana and virya are manifestations of *ojas* (inmost vitality). These two, fully awakened and merged together, create *samarasya*—the bliss of merging the mystical with the instinctual life.

Prana is the basic component of your subtle body, your energy field, and the entire chakra system. Therefore, in this chapter you will discover the power of prana—the key to life and source of energy in the universe. The Sanskrit word *prana*, which cannot be readily translated into English, derives from the roots, *pra* (first, primary, before, or forth) and *an* (breathe, move, live). Prana is widely understood to signify "breath." However, prana is much more than the breath flowing in and out of your lungs.

What Is Prana?

Prana is the medium through which consciousness expresses in myriad life forms throughout the cosmos. It is pure, universal, primary energy, which gives life to matter. It is Spirit, and, according to the ancient scriptures called the *Upanishads*, it is the supreme Being, *Brahman* itself.

"This Prana (spirit) is born of the Self. Like the shadow thrown on a man, this (the prana) is spread out over it (the Brahman). By the work of the mind does it come into this body." —Prasna Upanishad, 3:3

Prana is in air, but it is not oxygen nor any other physical constituent of air. It is in every particle of creation, but is not a particle. Prana is entirely non-material. Yet, without prana, your body would have no life, heat, motion, or activity. You could not hear, feel, see, breathe, walk, or talk. Your blood would not rush through your veins.

"When there is prana in the body it is called life; when it leaves the body it results in death." —Hatha Yoga Pradipika[2]

The Womb of Creation

For life to exist, both consciousness and prana must be present. Prana is pure energy, whether mind, body, matter, or any other form of energy. Consciousness is the absolute, omnipresent, inactive principle underlying creation. Prana is the active ingredient of the cosmos, which supports and gives life to consciousness.

Consciousness is often represented by a male deity, such as Lord Shiva. Prana is symbolized by a female deity, such as Shakti, Kali, or Kundalini. Thus, prana is the fertile field where the seed of creation can take root, grow, and manifest the entire phenomenal world.

The purpose of yoga is to reunite Shiva and Shakti within your own awareness, so your consciousness can express itself perfectly through the medium of life energy—prana.

Your Energy Body

The ancient yogis of India say that a subtle energy body, called *pranamaya kosha* (sheath of prana), permeates and surrounds your physical body. This pranic body has many names: "aura," "auric field," "energy field," "energy body," "subtle body," "astral body," "etheric body," "etheric double," "fluidic body," "Beta body," "counterpart body," "pre-physical body," "bioplasmic body," and so forth.

This subtle energy field of prana can be "seen" around your body with clairvoyant sight. It can also be sensed by amputees, who can feel missing arms or legs. Some people claim to actually see these phantom limbs—missing arms or legs in subtle form, still attached to the body.

The phantom limb is also detected by Kirlian high frequency photographic processes. Even if any part of an organism's physical form is cut away, the pranic body remains whole and clearly visible. When this energy body disappears, the plant or animal dies.

Your pranic body is larger than your physical body. Thus, the aura or light radiating around your body is simply the outer edge of this etheric body, which permeates the physical form and extends past its boundaries.

Your Subtle Energy System

Pranic energy flows throughout your pranic sheath via fixed pathways, called *nadis* (conduits, channels, or arteries), derived from the Sanskrit root *nada* or *nala* (motion). So nadi is energy in motion. At various focal points within your pranic body, networks of nadis intersect to form chakras (plexuses of subtle energy centers).

As wireless mediums, the subtle energy tubes (nadis) are not physical nerves or arteries, and the vortexes (chakras) are not physical nerve plexuses. If you dissected a corpse, you would not locate one nadi or chakra anywhere, because they are composed of nonphysical substance. In fact, even under an electron microscope they are undetectable. Yet these subtle energy tubes and centers give the very breath of life to your body. Without them, your heart would not beat and lungs would not move. Because they are not readily discernable for scientific investigation, their existence is rejected by Western medicine. However, the nadi system is the essence of Chinese acupuncture and Indian Ayurvedic medicine.

Why are nadis and chakras discounted as myth? Consider a man who never saw a mobile phone. If you told him this instrument could pick up signals originating from across the world, he would laugh at you. No wire transmits the signal, yet invisible electromagnetic waves carry it.

Similarly, your body is akin to a phone, in that it receives pranic energy. A healthy body receives these energy waves as a clear, unadulterated signal. An unhealthy body is an old dilapidated phone that distorts the signal.

One of the primary aims of yoga is to tune up your physical energy receiver (your body) and your mental energy receiver (your mind). Thereby you can receive and transmit cosmic pranic energies through a clear, pristine vehicle.

In my book *Exploring Meditation*, there are many yoga practices to tune up your body and open the nadis, including a simple practice called "Body Tone-Up," on pages 109–110, which immediately increases overall flow of pranic energy throughout your entire nadi system.

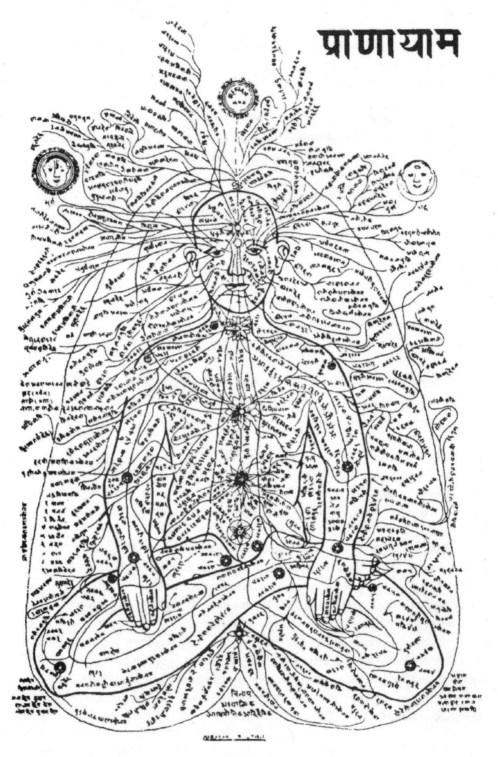

Figure 3a. The Nadi System.

Life Force in Breath

The dormant spiritual force within every individual can be awakened by consciously using prana. Regulating and harmonizing prana within breath brings steadiness of mind. Conversely, stilling your mind through meditation harmonizes and regulates breath. Thought is the most refined, potent form of prana. The movement of the lungs is the weakest. Filling your body with pranic energy brings health and vitality to every cell.

Pranic energy can be transferred. Anyone in proximity to a prana-filled person receives this energy by osmosis. The most powerful speakers, biggest celebrities, greatest politicians, revered prophets, successful businesspeople, captivating movie stars, and alluring women all owe their fame to abundant pranic energy. Magnetic personalities have a knack for influencing others by their speech, even their mere presence.

Pranic healing, used by saints and healers throughout the ages, transmits pranic energy directly from healer to patient. Many natural-born healers and therapists are not even conscious of this energy-transference. However, high-tech photographic methods show intense beams of bioluminescence pouring from healers' hands to their patients, thereby recharging depleted pranic bodies. In Chapter 4 you will discover exciting scientific research on pranic energy.

By practicing ancient yogic methods, you can collect and conserve pranic energy in your navel chakra (*manipura*)—your pranic storage battery. Prana power can increase charisma, willpower, influence, and supernormal powers. Through *pranayama* (yogic breathing), *bandhas* (yogic locks), and meditation, you can tap the vast power of prana to heal yourself and others. Later in this book, you will learn some of these practices.

Conserving the Power in Breath

Yogis believe your life span is predetermined at birth. Your length of life is a contract, counted in breaths, not years. This is one reason yogis are concerned with conservation of prana.

Pranic energy is continually drained by every thought, word, and deed, and replenished by every breath. Other sources of prana are sunlight, water, air, and food. Prana is absorbed by skin from fresh air and daily bathing, by the tongue through prolonged chewing, and by nostrils and lungs through breathing.

Moderate exercise, such as walking, bicycling, swimming, and yoga asanas (postures), along with proper breathing and pranayama, oxygenates blood and revitalizes energy without the strain or oxygen debt of heavy exercise.

Every time you inhale, prana enters your body and gets stored in your energy centers, particularly your navel chakra. The more prana you receive, the more vital you become. Proper breathing prevents disease and increases concentration, self-control, and spiritual awakening.

During deep meditation, breathing automatically becomes slow, regular, and quiet. In the state of *samadhi* (equanimity of mind and body), breath becomes so refined it is imperceptible.

How does meditation cause your breath to settle down to near-nothingness? As mental activity becomes subtle and quiet, physical activity also relaxes and metabolic functions decrease. Energy is conserved. Heart rate slows. Breathing rate slows. The mind and body become quiet and silent, like a still pond without a ripple. Such is samadhi—the goal of yoga.

The Five Pranas

Prana, in its capacity of the life force in breath, takes five separate forms. These five vital forces (*pancha prana*) breathe life into your body. Each of them is responsible for a unique kind of energy movement, body area, and physical activity: inward or outward, upward or downward, horizontal, or circular.

The five pranas work through the sympathetic nerve plexuses to receive or generate *vayus* (currents or impulses of vital air), from the Sanskrit root, *va* (motion). Vayus are functions or motive powers by which prana operates, and each of the five pranas is governed by a vayu.

1. Prana

Prana (up-breathing) is inward and downward. Seated in the heart energy center (anahata chakra), it governs respiration, swallowing, heartbeat, body temperature, and movements of the gullet. Prana moves through the median of the body from base of the throat to navel. It resides in the eyes and ears, operates in the heart and lungs, and moves in and out of the nose.

Prana vayu (forward-moving vital air) is the positive animating life energy, the ability to move and operate. It is responsible for receiving substances into the body, such as food (eating), liquids (drinking), air (inhaling), as well as incoming sense perceptions (seeing, hearing, tasting, smelling, feeling, and mental experiences). It is associated with the element of air.

2. Apana

Apana (down-breathing) is downward and outward motion. Seated in the anus energy center (muladhara chakra), it governs the kidneys, bladder, genitals, colon, and rectum, and it moves between the navel and rectum.

Apana vayu (vital air that moves away) is the capacity to withdraw and is responsible for eliminating, excreting, or expelling substances, such as air (exhaling), feces (defecating), urine (urinating), gas (flatulence), semen (ejaculation and conception), bearing down (childbirth), as well as letting go of mental blocks, such as resentment, fear, and anger. Associated with the earth element, it regulates the sense of smell and makes the body stable.

3. Samana

Samana (on-breathing) is horizontal motion. Seated in the navel energy center (manipura chakra), it maintains digestive fire and regulates the stomach, liver, pancreas, and intestines. It is responsible for oxygen assimilation. Its realm of activity extends from heart to navel. Samana separates nutrients from toxins, carries the grosser product of food to apana for excretion, and brings the subtler material to the extremities. The word *samana* means "equalizing" or "balancing," as it unifies the forces of prana and apana. It controls the ability to balance, hold, and contract. Samana is the force in the mind that makes choices as we discern truth from falsehood, reality from illusion, and beneficial from detrimental.

By developing *samana vayu* (balancing vital air), all parts of the body are properly nourished, and the energy supplied by food is evenly distributed. The ancient scripture *Yoga Sutras* says, "By conquering the vital force called samana, effulgence is acquired."[3] By controlling samana, you gain charisma and a powerful aura. It is said in the scriptures that "seven lights" proceed from samana. It is associated with the element of fire.

4. Udana

Udana (out-breathing) is upward and outward motion. Seated in the throat energy center above the larynx (vishuddha chakra), it regulates falling asleep, bodily growth, ascending, rising upward, and it gives muscular strength to the extremities.

Udana vayu (subtle vital air that carries upward) controls all automatic functions in the head, including sensory function of eyes, ears, and nose, and it maintains body heat. Udana is responsible for speech, music, singing, and humming. At the time of death, udana separates the astral body from the physical body. By controlling udana, levitation can occur. Udana is responsible for kundalini rising up your spine all the way to the seventh chakra. It is associated with the ether element.

Yoga Sutras says, "By conquering the vital force called udana, the chance of immersion in water or mud, or entanglement in the thorns is avoided, and exit from the body at will is assured."[4]

5. Vyana

Vyana (back-breathing) is circular motion, a combination of prana and apana, by which these two are held. All-pervading and moving from the body's center to its periphery, through all the nadis, *vyana vayu* (outward moving of vital air) controls the circulatory, lymphatic, and nervous systems, directs voluntary and involuntary movements and coordination of muscles, joints, tendons, and fascia, and keeps the body balanced, cohesive, and integrated through unconscious reflexes.

Vyana is responsible for blood flow, lymph detoxification, sweating, goosebumps, and other sensations of the skin, and coordination of all systems. It governs the mental feeling of wholeness and integration, as well as the sense of body boundaries. It controls the capacity for self-expression. The word *vyana* means "pervading one." It is associated with the water element and with svadhishthana chakra (pelvic center).

Five Vital Airs

NAME	KNOWN AS	SEATED IN	ELEMENT	CHAKRA
Prana	Up-Breathing	Heart	Air	Anahata
Apana	Down-Breathing	Anus	Earth	Muladhara
Samana	On-Breathing	Navel	Fire	Manipura
Udana	Out-Breathing	Throat	Ether	Vishuddha
Vyana	Back-Breathing	Pelvis	Water	Svadhishthana

According to Ayurvedic medicine, suppressing natural body urges cuts off the natural flow of prana, which causes imbalance and disease. Thirteen urges that allow natural flow of prana are to:

1. Defecate

2. Flatulate

3. Urinate

4. Sneeze

5. Belch

6. Yawn

7. Vomit

8. Eat

9. Drink

10. Cry

11. Sleep

12. Pant after exertion

13. Ejaculate or orgasm

During the practice of *pranayama* (yogic breathing), prana vayu is generated by inhaling, and apana vayu by exhaling. *Prana vayu* is an afferent impulse (going to the brain) and *apana vayu* is an efferent impulse (moving from the brain and nerve centers). While the breath is retained (*kumbhaka*), the two vayus unite in muladhara (root chakra), generating tremendous concentration of prana to awaken kundalini. You will learn methods of yogic breathing in Chapter 22.

Chapter Four

YOUR LUMINOUS AURA

"Life is prana, prana is life. Immortality is prana, prana is immortality. As long
as prana dwells in this body, so long surely there is life. By prana he obtains im-
mortality in the other world, by knowledge true conception."
—The Upanishads[1]

The power of *prana* (vital life force energy) has been studied in many cultures, although India is acknowledged as the source of this knowledge. In this chapter, you will discover scientific investigations and philosophical inquiries into pranic energy through the ages.

Let us now discover the luminous body known as the aura.

Seeing Auras

This gross physical body that you temporarily inhabit is just one of your many bodies. Subtle bodies of pure liquid light, in myriad brilliant crystalline hues, pervade your physical frame and extend beyond it. Clairvoyants can "see" these subtle bodies, also known as your aura, or auric field, with their inner eye.

Many near-death survivors, such as Dannion Brinkley, author of *Saved by the Light,* saw these subtle bodies clearly. When Dannion was struck by lightning, he catapulted out of his body, where he viewed the proceedings from high above his physical form. From this vantage point, he perceived loved ones scurrying about, trying to save his life. Yet Dannion saw more than just their physical, material bodies. They were filled with multicolored radiant light. However, Dannion's body, lying on the floor, was stone-like, with no luminosity. Then Dannion, whose senses were fully functional, even though he was floating up near the ceiling, looked at his own spirit arm, hand, and fingers, as they shimmered with brilliant effulgence.

During reported near-death experiences, the survivor customarily passes through a tunnel and then enters a dazzling light of immeasurable beauty. There the individual meets a divine being, higher self, or deity of limitless love. Such typical near-death experiences indicate that after death your beautiful aura, your subtle light body, flees your lifeless corpse and moves into higher realms of existence.

The Aura in World Cultures

Your aura includes what sages of ancient India called the pranic sheath (*prana-maya kosha*). This luminescent, immortal sheath gives life to your body. At death, pranic energy leaves the physical form. Therefore, a corpse no longer possesses the luminous energy body called the aura.

The concept of a life energy body or human energy field is not unique to the Far East. This pranic sheath has been depicted in various religions and cultures. A few examples are outlined here. In addition, please refer to the chart on pages 30–31, which identifies various names for pranic energy, known throughout the ancient and modern world.

Artistic Representations

The halo is a symbol of the pranic sheath. Christian paintings and sculptures portray a halo around the head of Jesus, apostles, saints, angels, and religious leaders. Similarly, halos radiate from statues and paintings of Buddha and other Gods of the Far East. These halos artistically depict pranic emanations from spiritual beings. In fact, references are made to the human energy field in 97 different cultures, according to John White's book, *Future Science*.

China: Qi Gong

The *Huang-ti Nei Ching* (*Canon of Internal Medicine*), written more than 4,000 years ago in China, describes universal spirit as primordial energy that gives birth to all elements and permeates them. *Chi* (also known as *ki* or *qi)* is primal substance pervading the cosmos and all forms, animate and inanimate. Each individual is intimately linked to this universal powerhouse.

The balanced, harmonious flow of chi energy is critical to health, whether flowing through a human body, home, or city. The power of chi is cultivated in *Qi Gong*, *Tai Chi*, *Kung Fu*, and other martial arts, as well as *Feng Shui* (Chinese architecture) and Chinese medicine. In fact, by using chi, ancient Chinese physicians were so proficient in preventing disease that they received payment from their patients so long as no disease was contracted. If the patient fell ill, the doctor was then obliged to begin paying his ailing patient.

China: Taoism

According to Taoists, the ultimate reality (consciousness) is Tao, comprised of *yin* (female negative force) and *yang* (male positive force). These mutually interacting, eternally changing, complementary principles create matter and manipulate energy. The Chinese medical science of acupuncture is based on this theory.

Unlike modern allopathic physicians, who focus on separate organs and symptoms, the ancient Chinese conceived the entire body as one unit, with each part intimately related to the whole. Mapping specific pathways of *chi* (pranic flow) through the *nadis* (energy tubes known as meridians), they located about 700 points on the skin corresponding to this flow. If the flow is blocked or unbalanced, illness results. Inserting needles into these *deiketsu* or *seiketsu* (acupuncture points) balances pranic flow, thereby preventing or curing disease.

Jesus: Healing Power

Pranic healing was depicted in the Christian Gospels. Here a woman, internally hemorrhaging for 12 years, spent all her money on physicians, to no avail. As Jesus walked through a crowd, she touched the hem of his cloak. Her bleeding suddenly stopped and she was instantaneously cured.

> *"Somebody hath touched me,"* Jesus said,
> *"for I perceive that virtue is gone out of me."*[2]

In another instance, a large group gathered on a plain, asking Jesus for healing:

> *"And the whole multitude sought to touch him:*
> *for there went virtue out of him, and healed them all."*[3]

Such healing through pranic transference has been practiced by yogis of India for eons.

Scientific Theories of Prana

Western scientists or philosophers throughout the ages have postulated an energy field permeating and surrounding your physical body. Most modern scientists either discount or ridicule such ideas. However, the scientific research verifying such an energy field is compelling. In the following section, you will discover researchers who advanced theories about the pranic energy field. Many were persecuted or imprisoned for their beliefs. On pages 34–35 you will find a chart listing many of these brave pioneers.

NAMES OF THE VITAL LIFE ENERGY OR SPIRIT IN THE ANCIENT AND MODERN WORLD

CULTURE	EQUIVALENT NAME
AFRICA	
Central African, Yaos	Mulungu
Central Africa, Sudanese	Mungo
Congo	Elima
Dagara	Energy Body
Gold Coast	Wong
Ituri Pygmies	Megbe
Kalahari Bushman	N/um, Rlun
Nkundu	Elima
Masai	Ngai
Yoruba	Ashe
AUSTRALIA	
Aborigines	Kurunba, Churinga
	Arunquiltha
Torres Strait Tribes	Zogo
ASIA	
China	Ch'I Qi
Japan	Ki, Reiki
India, Hindu	Kundalini, Prana

CULTURE	EQUIVALENT NAME
MIDEAST	
Avicenna (Arabic)	Anima Mundi
Egyptian	Ka, Hike
Hebrew	El, Manna
Jewish Kabbalah	Yesod, Astral Light, Neutral Force
Moroccan, Persian, Sufi	Baraka
Sumeria	Al-ad
Zoroastrian	Asha, Ahura Mazda
NORTH AMERICA	
Algonquin	Manitou, Monedo, Wakantanka
Apache	Dige
Chickasaw	Hullo
Crow	Maxpe
Hopi	Massau'u
Inuit, Eskimos	Sila
Iroquois	Orenda, Oki
Navaho	Digin
Omaha, Sioux	Wakonda

(Asia, Cont.)	
Indonesia	Kerei
Tibet	Tsal
Parsee	The Living Force
Malaya	Badi, Mana
Pali	Eckankar, Ek, Eck
Sumatra	Tondi
Vietnam	Tinh
EUROPE	
Christian	Holy Spirit
Druid	Wouivre, Nwyure
Early Europe	Elàn Vital
Early Europe	Ether
German	Wodan
Greek	Dynamis, Pneuma
Medieval Alchemists	Vital Fluid, Vis Naturalis
Roman	Numen
Radiesthists	Etheric Force

(North America, Cont.)	
Pueblo	Po-Wa-Ha
Sioux	Wakan
Chiropractic Medicine	Universal Intelligence
Allopathic Medicine	Will to live
PACIFIC	
New Guinea	Labuni, Gelaria
Malagasy (Philippines)	Andriamanitra
Maoris	Atua
Palau	Kasinge, Kalit
Polynesian	Huna
Polynesian/Hawaiian	Mana
Ponape	Ani, Han
Sumatra, Bataks	Tondi
Tobi	Yaris
SOUTH AMERICA	
Incan, Peruvian	Huaca
Mayan	Itz, K'awil, Ch'ul, Ch'ulel

Figure 4a. Pranic Energy Worldwide.

Hippocrates: *Medicatrix Naturae*

Hippocrates (born 460 BC), the "Father of Medicine," was a Greek philosopher and writer. To him, the art of medicine consisted of managing a spiritual restorative essence or principle called *vis medicatrix naturae* (natural healing power). In his writings, he described a field of energy as a force flowing from people's hands. Hippocrates believed disease must be treated as subject to natural laws: *"Natural forces are the healers of disease."*

Pythagoras: *Pneuma*

Pythagoras (560–480 BC) was the High Priest of the ancient Orphic mysteries of Crete. In his travels, he studied with priests and healers throughout the ancient world. The wisdom of India, Egypt, Palestine, Persia, and Chaldea laid the foundations for the teachings, philosophy, cosmology, and medicine of his Pythagorean mystery school.

Pythagoras envisioned a dynamic vital force or primordial energy pervading the cosmos, which he called *pneuma*—a central fire in the universe that not only creates physical vitality, but also gives rise to the immortal soul. Its light produces a variety of effects, including physical healing: *"One Universal Soul permeating all things, which in substance resembles light."*

Pythagoras enumerated three bodies occupied by the soul:

1. *Ethereal* (which is radiant and celestial), in which the soul resides in a state of bliss in the stars.

2. *Luminous,* which suffers the punishment of sin after death.

3. *Terrestrial,* which is the vehicle that the soul occupies on this Earth.

Paracelsus: *Ilaster*

For Swiss physician and alchemist Paracelsus (1493–1541), the *prima materia* is made first in two opposing forces—the One and the Other, consisting of vital power and vital substance. Paracelsus calls the One principle *ilaster,* and the Other *aquaster.* The ilaster is a fiery, active, masculine principle; the aquaster a watery, passive, feminine principle. In each human being, both principles are simultaneously at work.

Kepler: Facultas Formatrix

Johannes Kepler (1571–1630) determined that an energy field is responsible for keeping planets in their orbits around the sun. He termed this energy *anima motrix* (motive soul), but later modified it to *vis motrix* (life force). His conjecture was that visible forms arise from a *facultas formatrix* (formative capacity), a ubiquitous force that pervades and shapes everything.

Van Helmont: Aura Vitalist

The notion that magnetism played a significant part in the behavior of organisms was first proposed by Johann Baptista van Helmont (1577–1644), Belgian physician and alchemist. He postulated that all humans radiate a magnetic fluid, *magnale magnum,* a diffused universal magnetic force that could be drawn upon for healing. He believed the agent of the soul is *aura vitalist* or *principal archaeus,* the equivalent of prana, the true vital element.

Mesmer: Animal Magnetism

The Viennese Franz Anton Mesmer (1734–1815), who lived in Paris, postulated that all organic and inorganic bodies respond to each other through an influence called *animal magnetism*—a universally diffused, continuous, incomparably subtle fluid, which naturally receives, propagates, and communicates all motor disturbances. Its action takes place at remote distance, without any intermediary substance.

Hahnemann: Dynamis

Samuel Hahnemann (1755–1843), founder of homeopathy, termed the universal spirit *dynamis* and viewed disease as an imbalance in the vital force. The patient's disease symptoms should be supported, as they are indicative of positive efforts of the vital force to restore health and balance. This philosophy is diametrically opposed to Western allopathic medicine, in which symptoms are suppressed through drugs.

Homeopathic remedies strengthen the vital force by using substances that aggravate similar symptoms, so the natural healing process will be spurred further to overcome disease. Therefore, his first axiom is *similia similibus curentur* (likes are cured by likes), also known as the "Law of Similars." His findings were proven in

NAMES FOR VITAL LIFE ENERGY OR SPIRIT
STUDIED BY THE RESEARCHERS AND PHILOSOPHERS THROUGHOUT THE AGES

RESEARCHER	AREA of STUDY	RESEARCHER	AREA of STUDY
Dr. Albert Abrams	Radio Therapy	Dr. Jessel Kenyon	Biophoton Emissions
Aristotle	Ether, Entelecheia	Johannes Kepler	Anima Motrix, Vis Motrix,
Thomas Aquinas	Life Power		Facultas Formatrix
Cleve Backster	Primary Perception	Walter J. Kilner	Aura
Basilides	Abraxas	Semyon D. Kirlian	Kirlian Energy
Dr. Robert Becker	Biomagnetic Fields	Arthur Koestler	Integrative Tendency
Henri Bergson	Elan Vital	Konstantin G. Korotkov	Electrophotonics
Ludwig von Bertalanffy	Anamorphosis	N. A.Kozyrev	Time Emanation
Marie François Xavier Bichat	Vital Force	Todd R. Knudtso	Pure Nonmanifest Energy
H.P. Blavatsky	Astral Light	Justus, Baron Von Liebig	Vital Force
M. R. Blondolt	N-emanation	Gottfried Wilhelm Leibnitz	Monads
David Bohm	Quantum Field	V. V. Lensky	Multipolar Energy
Niels Bohr	Complimentary	Charles Littlefield	Vital Magnetism
Barbara Brennan	Universal Energy-Field	Sir Oliver Lodge	Ether, Void
T.T. Brown	Electrogravitation	Abraham Maslow	Synergy
Dr. Oscar Brunler	Bio-cosmic Energy	James Clerk Maxwell	Ether, Void
Sir Edward Bulwer-Lytton	Vril	Franz Anton Mesmer	Magnetic Fluid, Animal
Gaston Burridge	Ethertricity		Magnetism
Harold Saxon Burr	L-Fields (Life Fields)	Dr. John V. Milewski	Superlight Energy
	Electrodynamic Field	Johannes Müller	Vital Force
John W. Campbell	Psionics	Dr. T.H. Moray	Radiant Energy
A. L. Chizhevsky	Z-emanation	Dr. Thelma Moss	Bioenergy
Jesus Christ	Virtue	Dr. Hiroshi Motoyama	Prana and Yoga
Dr. William Crookes	Ether, Void	H. Moriyama	X-agent
A.A. Deev	D-field	Charles Muses	Noeric Energy
Dr. Richard Dobrin	Human Energy Field	Gustave Naessens	Somatid
James DeMayo	Negative Entropic Energy	H. A. Nieper	Gravity Field Energy
P.A.A. Dirac	Neutrino Sea	Francis Nixon	Arealoha
Hans Driesch	Entelechy	Paracelsus	Mumia

Name	Energy Name	Name	Energy Name
Ruth Drown	Homo Vibra Ray, Radionic	Robert Pavlita	Psychotronic Energy
Réne Joachim H. Dutrochet	Vital Physico-Organic Force	Drs. John & Eva Pierrakas	Bio-Energy, Core-Energy
L.E. Eeman	X-Force	Plato	Nous
Albert Einstein	Ether	Andrija Puharich	Psi Plasma
Prof. G. Feinberg	Tachyon Field	Pythagoras	Pneuma
Baron Eugene Ferson	Universal Life Force	Dr. Dejan Rakovic	Ionic Structure
Robert Fludd	Spiritus, Space Energy	Wilhelm Reich	Orgone Energy
Sigmund Freud	Libido	Karl von Reichenbach	Od, Odyllic, Odic Force
Galen	Pneuma	Richardson	Nervous Ether
J.G. Gallimore	Neutricity	Dr. Zheng Ronliang	Qigong Vital Force
Luigi Galvani	Life Force	J.B. Rhine	Psi Faculty
George I. Gurdjieff	Hanbledzoin	Erwin Schroedinger	Negative Entropy
Johann Wolfgang von Goethe	Gestaltung	I.M. Shakhparnov	Mon-Emanation
V.S. Grischenko	Bioplasma	Rupert Sheldrake	Morphogenetic Fields
A. G. Gurvich	Mitogenetic Emanation	George Starr	Cosmo-Electric energy
Samuel Hahnemann	Lebenskraft, Dynamis	Rudolf Steiner	Biodynamic Ether
Heraklet	Curative Force	Gustaf Strömberg	Genii
Johann Baptista van Helmont	Aura Vitalist	Dr. Alexander Studitsky	Animal Morphology
	Archaeus Influus	Nikola Tesla	Prana, Creative Force,
	Magnale Magnum		Akasa, Luminiferous Ether
Thomas Galen Hieronymous	Eloptic Energy	Dr. William T. Tiller	Magneto-Electricity
	Eloptic Radiation	Hermes Trismegistus	Telesma
	Logoital Plasma	A.J. Veinik	Chronal Field
B. Hilton	Fluroplasmic Energy	Dr. Gordana Vitaliano	Ionic Structure
Hippocrates	Vis Medicatrix Naturae	Eugene Wallace	Biophoton Emissions
Dr. Valerie Hunt	Biofield	George de la Warr	Biomagnetism
Dr. Victor Inyushin	Bioplasmic Energy Field		Prephysical Energy
Carl Gustav Jung	Synchronicity	Dr. Aubrey T. Westlake	Prephysical Energy
Yu V. Tsz'yan Kanchzhen	Biofield	L.L. Whyte	Life Force
John Ernst Worrell Keely	Latent Neutral	Dr. John Zimmerman	Unitary Principle in Nature
			Biomagnetic Fields

Other names for this pranic energy: Fermi Sea, Primary Energy, Zero Point Energy, Gravity Field Energy, G-Field

Figure 4b. Scientific Research on Vital Energy.

the European cholera epidemic of 1832, where the mortality rate of those treated with allopathic medicine was 70 percent and with homeopathic medicine only 10 percent.

Von Reichenbach: Odic Force

The German industrialist, chemist, and inventor Baron Karl von Reichenbach (1788–1869) conducted thousands of experiments to validate a cosmic force he termed *od, odylic,* or *odic* force. Reichenbach defined *od* as nature's unceasing power, a rapidly penetrating force that flows through everything.

His investigations suggest the odic field is both energetic, like a light wave, and particulate, like a fluid. Conducted great distances by all solid and liquid substances, it is charged or discharged by contact or proximity.

Reichenbach discovered the human body's vital power has a polarity similar to crystals. The left side of the body is negative and the right side is positive—a concept already well known in Taoism and acupuncture.

Kilner: Auric Field

In 1911, Walter J. Kilner, MD, of St. Thomas Hospital in London, reported observing an energy field of three layers, which he called the *aura*. By gazing at lights through glass screens stained with Dicyanine A dye, he trained his eyes to see this luminous oval halo of energy, a mist or cloud of radiation extending from the human body, displaying distinct colors.

Kilner saw this glowing mist in three distinct zones around the body:

1. A one-quarter-inch layer closest to the skin.

2. A more vaporous layer, one inch wide, streaming perpendicularly from the body.

3. A delicate exterior luminosity with indefinite contours, about six inches wide.

Kilner found each aura is unique, depending on age, gender, and mental, emotional, and physical states. Fatigue, disease, or mood altered its size and color. Magnetism, hypnosis, and electricity also affected it.

Because certain illnesses were visible as stains or irregularities, Kilner developed a system of diagnosis based on the color, structure, volume, and general presence of the auric field. He successfully treated many diseases, including epilepsy, liver disease, tumors, appendicitis, and hysteria.

Burr: Electrodynamic Field

In 1935, Dr. Harold Burr, professor of neuroanatomy at Yale University School of Medicine for 43 years, revealed the basic blueprints of life: *electrodynamic fields,* which control all organisms. He measured and mapped these "fields of life," or "L-fields," with standard voltmeters. Because L-field voltages reveal physical and mental conditions, he proposed doctors should diagnose illnesses before symptoms develop.

Thousands of experiments by Burr and colleagues confirmed these fields control the growth, shape, and decay of cells, tissues, and organs, and are influenced by mental disturbances.

Kirlian: High-Frequency Photography

In 1939, Semyon Davidovich Kirlian, an electrical technician at the Research Institute of Krasnodar, in South Russia near the Black Sea, discovered that in a field of high-frequency electrical currents, the human body's brilliantly colored light emanations can be photographed. Kirlian invented high-frequency photography with a specially constructed spark generator of 75,000 to 200,000 electrical oscillations per second.

A tree leaf photographed by Kirlian's method revealed myriad dots of energy. Turquoise and reddish-yellow patterns flared from channels of the leaf. Kirlian's own hand looked like the Milky Way in a starry sky and a fireworks display against a blue and gold background. Yet the lights and movements bore no relationship to the hand's physiological structure or processes.

Light patterns of healthy or diseased organisms differed from one another. Also, mental tension or emotional stress distorted the patterns. By deciphering the photographs, Kirlian diagnosed diseases long before symptoms appeared.

Inanimate objects photographed by Kirlian's process were also permeated with bioluminescent energy, but the light, of constant intensity, lacked the iridescence, movement, and animation of live organisms.

When an organism died, the intensity and orderliness of the luminous energy body slowly oozed out. Blobs of light ejected from the organism until the bioluminescence eventually disappeared altogether.

Through Kirlian photography, Soviet scientists found the flow of bioluminescence corresponds exactly to acupuncture meridian pathways (*nadis*). Acupuncture points, where needles are normally inserted during acupuncture treatment, correspond precisely to brilliant light flashes in Kirlian photographs.

Inyushin: Bioplasmic Energy Field

Since the 1950s, Dr. Victor Inyushin, at Kazakh University in Russia, extensively investigated the human energy field. He postulated that Kirlian's light is not electrical, magnetic, nor heat, but a new energy called *bioplasma*. Its bioluminescence is caused by ionized atomic particles, but not the customary haphazard emission of ionized free protons or electrons. The pattern and structure indicate order and unity.

Inyushin discovered *bioplasmic* particles in continual motion are constantly renewed by cellular chemical processes. The balance of positive and negative particles within the bioplasma remains relatively stable. A severe shift in this balance adversely affects health.

The bioplasmic body emanates its own electromagnetic field, which changes with emotional states and is affected by other fields. This energy body needs continual replenishment from oxygen. Some of the oxygen transfers its surplus electrons and a certain quantum of energy into the bioplasmic body. Breathing charges the entire bioplasmic body, renews reserves of vital energy, and equalizes disturbed energy patterns.

Popov Group: Bioplasma

In 1965, Soviet scientists from the Bioinformation Institute of A.S. Popov began extensive experiments on extrasensory perception (ESP) and telepathy. They found living organisms emit vibrations with a frequency of 300 to 2,000 nanometers. They named this emanation *biofield*. This biofield is stronger in people who are more successful at transferring their bioenergy. The Popov scientists found that the receiving medium of telepathic messages is the bioplasmic body, which acts as a relay station to transmit psychic impressions to conscious perception. Artificial stimulation to specific points in the bioplasmic body increases psychic awareness. These key points exactly correspond to major and minor chakra energy points well known to the yogis of India.

Reich: Orgone Energy

A psychiatrist and scientist, Dr. Wilhelm Reich (1897–1957) studied what he called *orgone,* and founded *orgonomy*—the study of life energy in organisms, the Earth, atmosphere, and outer space. Reich defined orgone as pre-atomic "mass-free primordial power that operates throughout the universe as the basic life force." This energy is present in all living things and its "proper flow" is crucial to maintaining individual health as well as life on earth.

Using a high-power microscope, Reich observed the energy fields of both animate and inanimate objects, including microorganisms and human blood cells. He studied changes of orgone flow in relation to physical and psychological disease, trauma, and neurosis. His work included traditional psychiatric analysis along with other methods of releasing blockages to the free flow of orgone energy.

Reich built an "orgone accumulator" to concentrate orgone energy and speed up natural healing of the body. With the accumulator, he charged a vacuum discharge tube. This tube then conducted a current of electricity at a potential lower than its normal discharge potential.

Becker and Zimmerman: Schumann Resonance

Independent research in the 1980s by Dr. Robert Becker and Dr. John Zimmerman investigated the human energy field during varied healing treatments. Not only do brain wave patterns of healer and patient become synchronized in the alpha band (characteristic of a deeply relaxed, meditative state), but they also pulse at eight Hertz, known as the Schumann Resonance, in unison with the Earth's magnetic field.

The biomagnetic field of the healer's hands increases at least 1,000 percent—not as a result of internal body current. This suggests that healers link their energy field with the earth, drawing on an infinite energy source via the Schumann Resonance.

Hunt: Biofeld

From 1970 to 1990, Dr. Valerie Hunt of UCLA electronically measured the frequency and location of the human *biofield*. Dr. Hunt placed electrodes on the skin to record low millivoltage signals from her subjects. At the same time, clairvoyant aura readers recorded their observations of the color, size, and energy movements of the chakras and auric clouds.

Scientists then mathematically analyzed the wave patterns by Fourier-analysis and sonogram frequency analysis. The waveforms and frequencies reported by the aura readers correlated exactly with specific colors. For example, when the readers saw blue in the aura, the electronic measurements showed the characteristic blue waveform and frequency in the same location. Hunt successfully repeated this experiment with eight aura readers.

For more information about how to see and feel auras, please read my book *The Power of Auras*.

Chinese Researchers: Acupuncture Points

Repeated experiments have proven acupuncture points as scientifically measurable phenomena.

In 2013, researchers from China published a groundbreaking study, using state-of-the-art CT (computerized tomography) imaging, which revealed clear distinctions between non-acupuncture point and acupuncture point anatomical structures. Researchers found an unusually high density of microvessels, complex microvascular structures, and higher density of vascularization of vessels at acupoints. Bifurcated microvascular densities surrounded thick blood vessels. In contrast, non-acupuncture point areas contained few thick blood vessels and none showed fine, high-density structures.

Another Chinese research team took amperometric oxygen microsensor readings and published a study in 2012 that revealed the lung, pericardium, and heart channel acupoints of the distal forearm and wrist crease region displayed high oxygen pressure levels. Non-acupuncture point areas throughout this region did not exhibit this quality. These measurements were natural resting states of acupoints without stimulation by acupuncture needles.

Other researchers used fluorescence microscopy to determine that acupuncture points are structurally defined entities. In 2014, they published findings that epidermal and underlying dermis layers of acupoints contained high densities of "connexins," which are gap junction proteins that provide intercellular communication. They create a pathway for ions and molecules to transfer between the cells.

Another study published in 2014 measured anatomical structures associated with acupuncture points. Researchers found a "vessel-like structure" composed of calcitonin gene related peptide (CGRP)-positive neurofibers, and more CGRP-positive neurofibers in the dermis and hypodermis layers at acupoints, mainly concentrating around the vessel-like structure.[4,5,6]

Korean Researchers: Primo Vascular System

Until recently, no scientific explanation has proven the flow of *chi* (a.k.a. *prana*) through meridians (a.k.a. *nadis*), which informs both traditional Chinese medicine and Ayurveda. Western medicine has not accepted acupuncture because no anatomical foundation supported meridians and acupuncture points. However, a new bodily system was recently discovered.

In 1963, North Korean surgeon Bong-Han Kim presented a biomedical theory that supported meridians and acupuncture points. He found tubular structures (which he named Bonghan ducts or channels) inside and outside blood vessels and lymphatic vessels, on the surface of internal organs, and under the skin.

Since 2003, researchers primarily from Seoul National University (SNU: Seoul, South Korea) have corroborated Kim's findings, published more than 50 articles, and obtained more than 200 citations. They suggested the "primo vascular system" (PVS) and its channels and nodes—"primo vessels" (PV) and "primo nodes" (PN), respectively—provide an anatomical structure for acupuncture points and meridians. The PVS is said to channel the flow of energy and information relayed by biophotons (electromagnetic light waves) and DNA.

The Korean researchers injected a staining dye at acupuncture points, which colored the meridians and revealed thin lines. In contrast, no lines appeared at non-acupuncture points. Researchers found a liquid, which aggregated to form stem cells, flowed through these lines in a duct system.

The PVS has changed our fundamental understanding of biology and medicine, because this system is located throughout the entire body and is believed to regulate and coordinate all biological life processes.[7, 8]

These studies compliment ancient Chinese medicine and Ayurveda with verifiable scientific data. Please read *Awaken Your Third Eye* and *The Power of Auras* to find more research that indicates physical evidence of chakras, nadis, and prana.

Chapter Five

WHAT IS KUNDALINI?

*"Glory, glory to Mother Kundalini, who through her Infinite Grace and Power,
kindly leads the Sadhaka from Chakra to Chakra and illumines his intellect and
makes him realise his identity with the Supreme Brahman."*
—*Sri Swami Sivananda*[1]

As you read in previous chapters, your physical body is just one of many.
Your subtle energy system consists of a vast complex of *nadis* (energy
conduits) and *chakras* (plexuses of subtle energy centers). This system is
like a computer board— intelligence underlying the growth, health, and maintenance of your body.

As you have read, your life force or vital energy is called *prana* (see Chapter
3). In the form of vital currents, prana travels through subtle energy tubes (*nadis*),
energizing every part of your body. Pranic energy is crucial to your body's homeo-
stasis, and if pranic flow is blocked, disease or death occurs.

Gopi Krishna says prana "energizes, overhauls, and purifies the neurons and
maintains the life-giving subtle area [soul] of the body much in the same way as
the blood plasma maintains the grosser part."[2]

Of the 72,000 nadis in your body, the one most vital to pranic energy is
sushumna nadi, the energy conduit through which kundalini travels. The ancient
scriptures call sushumna the "royal road *(rajapath)."*

Your chakras are vortexes of intense pranic energy where many nadis intersect,
like a wheel hub with spokes radiating from it. These chakras organize and regulate the flow of prana through your subtle body. Raising kundalini through the
major chakras progressively awakens consciousness.

As kundalini moves up your spine, it pierces through six of the seven major
chakras: *muladhara* (root chakra), *svadhishthana* (pelvic chakra), *manipura* (navel chakra), *anahata* (heart chakra), *vishuddha* (throat chakra), and *ajna* (brow

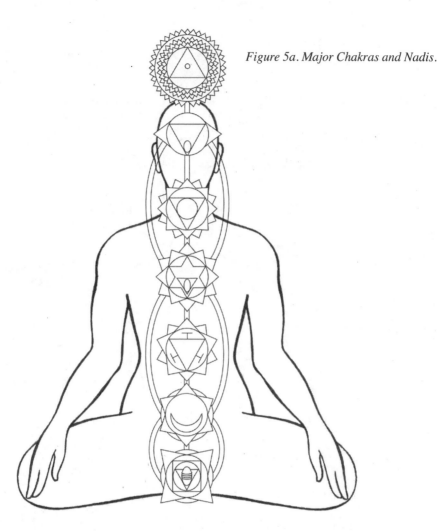

chakra). Finally kundalini reaches *sahasrara* (crown chakra), which is outside su-shumna nadi, above the skull.

Pathway of Kundalini

Usually kundalini is asleep, coiled near the tailbone in *muladhara* (the first or root chakra), in *brahmarandhra mukha* (mouth of God), derived from *mukha* (mouth) and *brahma* (God). This is also termed *brahmadvara,* from the root *dvara* (gate). This doorway, through which kundalini must pass, is at the base of sushumna nadi, which runs through the vertebral column all the way up to the brain.

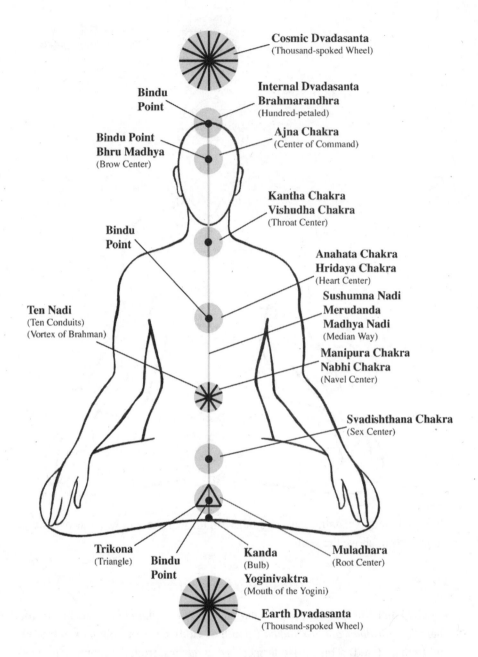

Cosmic Dvadasanta
(Thousand-spoked Wheel)

Bindu Point

Bindu Point Bhru Madhya
(Brow Center)

Internal Dvadasanta Brahmarandhra
(Hundred-petaled)

Ajna Chakra
(Center of Command)

Kantha Chakra Vishudha Chakra
(Throat Center)

Bindu Point

Anahata Chakra Hridaya Chakra
(Heart Center)

Sushumna Nadi Merudanda Madhya Nadi
(Median Way)

Ten Nadi
(Ten Conduits)
(Vortex of Brahman)

Manipura Chakra Nabhi Chakra
(Navel Center)

Svadishthana Chakra
(Sex Center)

Trikona
(Triangle)

Bindu Point

Kanda
(Bulb)

Yoginivaktra
(Mouth of the Yogini)

Muladhara
(Root Center)

Earth Dvadasanta
(Thousand-spoked Wheel)

Figure 5b. Awakening Kundalini.

At its lower end, sushumna nadi arises from a nadi center called *kanda mula* (root bulb), which lies just below muladhara (root chakra), under the lower end of *filum terminale,* below the coccyx (tailbone). Then sushumna ascends up the spine through the filum terminale, central canal of the spinal column, fourth ventricle of the brain, cerebral aqueduct, third ventricle of the brain, telencephalon medium, anterior commissure, fornix, septum pellucidum, corpus callosum, and longitudinal fissure, to reach the central point of the cerebral cortex.

At its top, sushumna nadi reaches *brahmarandhra* (also known as *nirvana chakra),* a pranic complex at the top center of the head. *Brahmarandhra* (hollow of Brahman), believed to be the dwelling place of the human soul, is at the crown of the head called anterior fontanelle, between the parietal and occipital bones—the "soft spot" of a newborn baby.

Sushumna is usually closed at its lower end in kanda mula (root bulb). In most people, no prana ever passes through sushumna, because kundalini remains dormant at the base of sushumna.

Some ways to activate kundalini are devotion, worship, meditation, willpower, discernment, knowledge, and body purification. Any manifestation of spiritual gifts or supernormal powers indicates kundalini is awakened to some degree.

Those with arrested kundalini are awake to the world and asleep to the higher self. Using just a tiny portion of their latent potential, they roam in the dream of waking life, fettered by ego attachment. When kundalini wakes up and rises through the chakras, awareness grows. Those with kundalini fully aroused are asleep to the world and awake to inner enlightenment and higher consciousness. Therefore, kundalini represents the full flowering of human potential.

Sushumna nadi is considered a hollow tube. Inside this outer tube are three more concentric tubes nested within each other. Each of these conduits is more subtle than the surrounding one. The three outer tubes correlate to the three *gunas* (primal attributes or modes of activity) of nature. (See Figure 5c on page 46.)

The nadis corresponding to the three gunas are as follows:

1. *Sushumna nadi*, characteristic of *tamas guna* (the power of destruction), indicates ignorance, laziness, and negativity.

2. *Vajrini nadi*, characteristic of *rajas guna* (the power of action), suggests passion, motion, creativity, and activity.

3. *Chitrini nadi*, characteristic of *sattva guna* (the power of purity), implies purity, harmony, and knowledge.

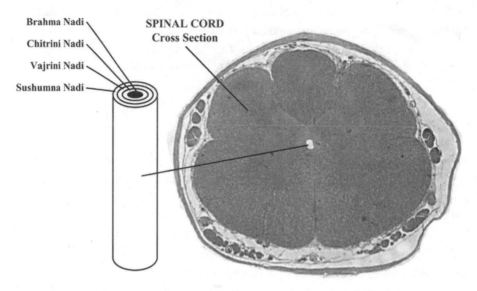

Brahma Nadi

Chitrini Nadi

Vajrini Nadi

Sushumna Nadi

SPINAL CORD
Cross Section

Figure 5c. Major Nadis in Axis of Spinal Canal.

4. *Brahma nadi,* characteristic of pure consciousness, beyond the three gunas, is also called *brahmarandhra.* In order to transmute your tamasic and rajasic energies, represented by sushumna and vajrini nadis, the pranic energy of kundalini must travel through brahma nadi, the most thin, subtle, pure passage, through which only the most delicate, rarified prana can flow.

This refined prana can only flow through your subtle body when your breath reduces in a highly refined level of awareness during deep meditation. As prana flows more freely through the nadis, even the finest, subtlest nadis with the narrowest of passageways, such as brahma nadi (the size of 1000th of a hair), which are normally closed off in average individuals, begin to open and allow the subtlest prana to flow through them.

As your mind and body settle to *samadhi* (stillness of body and mind), your breath becomes so fine that it is suspended between in-breath and out-breath. Amazingly, breathing seems to stop altogether. In fact, breath is not being held; it is in suspension—neither breathing nor not breathing. This most delicate form of breathing, free from any blockages and resistance, increases mental and physical energy. *Kundalini,* the most powerful form of prana, will force open the narrowest nadi passageways when prana gets highly refined.

Three Rivers of Life

Two other major nadis, *ida* and *pingala,* run alongside sushumna nadi, taking a spiral route to the brain. Ida emanates from the left side of muladhara (root chakra) and ends at the left side of the ajna chakra (third eye). Pingala begins at the right side of muladhara and ends at the right side of ajna chakra.

Ida and pingala represent time and duality, while sushumna nadi devours time, as it leads to oneness in timeless eternity. Thus ida and pingala bind you to material life, while sushumna is the path to freedom (*moksha*), full integration, and balance. During meditation, when ida and pingala are balanced and prana enters sushumna, you can enter the timeless state.

IDA NADI	PINGALA NADI
Left side of body	Right side of body
Left nostril breath flow	Right nostril breath flow
Parasympathetic	Sympathetic
Introversion	Extroversion
Awareness	Energy and action
Mental Body	Pranic Body
Moon	Sun
Subjectivity	Objectivity
White	Red
Tha	Ha
Negative	Positive
Cold	Hot
Inactive	Active
Yin	Yang
Feminine	Masculine
Mental thought	Physical activity
Awareness	Energy
Shiva: Consciousness	Shakti: Universal Energy
Purusha: Witness	Prakriti: Action

"One should control the sun (pingala) and moon (ida) because these are the day and night of time; the secret is that the sushumna (passage of kundalini) is the eater of time." —Hatha Yoga Pradipika[3]

Ida, the left nadi, represents the female, moon, and your subjective nature. The right nadi, pingala, symbolizes the male, sun, and your objective side. Refer to the chart on page 47.

Solar and Lunar Breaths

Do you notice at any given moment that one of your nostrils is more open and the other more blocked? You can check this right now by closing one nostril, then the other.

In the course of each day, clear breathing switches from one nostril to the other periodically. If you are in excellent health, this alternation takes place regularly, about every 110 minutes. Right before your predominant breath-flow switches to the other nostril, your breath flows through both nostrils equally for a few minutes.

Yogis of antiquity discovered that when air flows more through the left nostril, then prana flows predominantly through ida nadi. When the flow is greater through the right nostril, prana flows more through pingala nadi. Ida and pingala nadis are conductors of two different poles of pranic energy. Ida is the negative *chandra* (moon) nadi, and pingala is the positive *surya* (sun) nadi.

Your right nostril's breath, connected to pingala nadi, is said to be hot. Called "sun breath," it generates body heat, raises metabolism, and accelerates body activities. Your left nostril's breath, said to be cool, is "moon breath," connected to ida nadi. Its energy cools your body, lowers metabolism, and inhibits body activities.

During periods when the right nostril predominates, you are inclined toward extroversion, physical activities, and work. When the left nostril predominates, you are drawn toward mental activities and feel introverted. During sleep, ida dominates and during waking hours, pingala dominates.

Although pranic flow automatically switches about every two hours, you can manipulate breath to flow through ida or pingala. For instance, if you need to work but feel sleepy, you can curb breath through your left nostril, thereby activating pingala. Or if you are restless and cannot sleep, you can force breath to flow through your left nostril by lying on your right side. When you sleep on your left side, air will flow more through your right nostril. When you sleep on your right side, your left nostril will be more open.

If breath flows through one nostril for more than two hours, the body is un-balanced—too much heat or cold. If ida is overactive, mental activity wanes and lethargy increases. If pingala is overactive, nervous activity rises and mental disturbances result. If breath flows through one nostril for 24 hours, it is a warning of illness. The longer breath continues in one nostril, the more serious the illness will be.

The science of Hatha Yoga seeks to balance these two *vayus* (vital airs). The word *hatha, ha* (sun) and *tha* (moon), means solar and lunar breaths, which are *prana vayu* (positive vital air) and *apana vayu* (negative vital air).

The alternate flow of breath profoundly affects your energy cycle and health. A major aim of all yoga practices is to equalize the flow through both nostrils. In this book, you will learn several methods to do this.

Balancing Your Autonomic Nervous System

Ida and pingala are associated with the parasympathetic and sympathetic aspects of your autonomic nervous system. Pingala and right nostril stimulate sympathetic outflow. Ida and left nostril stimulate parasympathetic outflow. At any given time, either the sympathetic or parasympathetic system is predominant.

The sympathetic, quick-response, mobilizing system is greatly stimulated during fight-or-flight response, which prepares the body for external muscular action and expends energy. It speeds up life processes, such as heartbeat and breathing, and raises temperature.

Conversely, the parasympathetic, slowly activated, dampening system slows down bodily processes, conserves energy, rests the body, and directs energy to internal processes, such as digestion. Without conscious awareness, these two systems are at work day and night, regulating and maintaining equilibrium of various bodily functions automatically.

You may study the functions of the nadis ida and pingala on the following chart. These energy flows govern the sympathetic and parasympathetic systems.

For optimum health, the energies governed by ida and pingala must be balanced. Too much objectivity, dynamism, and physical activity stress the body beyond its limits. This causes hypertension, leading to heart disease. Too much subjectivity, passivity, thought, and internal brooding can cause neurosis, depression, even insanity. Excesses of either ida or pingala lead to selfishness and egotism.

Organ	Ida Function Parasympathetic: Introversion	Pingala Function Sympathetic: Extroversion
Eyes: Pupil (Iris)	Contricts pupil via sphincter muscles: miosis	Dilates pupil via radial muscle: mydriasis
Eyes: Ciliary Muscle	Contracts lens: close vision mode	Relaxes lens: far vision mode
Head: Blood Vessels		Vessel constriction; increases alertness
Salivary Glands	Copious secretion; digestion increases	Slight secretion; digestion decreases
Heart	Heart rate decreases	Heart rate increases
Bronchial Muscle	Constriction; air intake reduces	Dilation; air intake increases
Stomach: Sphincters	Relaxation; increased digestion	Contraction; decreased digestion
Liver	Glycogen synthesis	Gluconeogenesis and glycogenolysis: for emergency energy
Gallbladder	Contraction	Relaxation
Adrenal Medulla		Secretion of epinephrine and norepinephrine: for sudden emergency.
Intestines	Increase of motility and secretions for digestion	Decrease of motility and secretions for digestion
Rectum	Bowels constipate	Bowels evacuate
Urinary Bladder	Bladder contracts; sphincter relaxes	Bladder relaxes; sphincter contracts
Sex Organs	Blood vessel dilation; erection	Blood vessel constriction; ejaculation
Temperature	Reduction	Increase
Blood Vessels to Visceral Organs	Dilation; for internal action	Contraction
Blood Vessels to Limb Muscles	Contraction	Dilation: for physical action
Sweat Glands	Generalized secretion	

Thus it is significant that kundalini, unifier of all divergent energies, rises up sushumna nadi, the middle path, balanced between ida and pingala, inner and outer, absolute and relative, *yin* and *yang, nirvana* and *samsara.*

Figure 5d. Taoist Tai Chi Symbol.

The ancient Chinese understood these positive and negative forces in the body and based the entire healing system of acupuncture on these principles. Thus ida and pingala are represented in Taoism by the well-known *Tai Chi* symbol, representing the balance of yin and yang energies.

Unless kundalini is somehow awakened, prana normally flows through ida and pingala.

However, *pranayama* (yogic breathing exercises) can force prana to withdraw from ida and pingala, open sushumna nadi, flow into it, and travel up the spine, awakening kundalini. (See Chapter 21.)

The Three Knots

Three *granthis* (knots) in your pranic energy body are storage areas for psychic blocks, attachments, and delusions that prevent kundalini from flowing freely through sushumna nadi. These psychic knots are like snares or traps, blocking you from ascending higher and ultimately achieving spiritual enlightenment.

In these three regions, the power of *maya* (illusion), ignorance, and bondage to the material world is particularly strong. The granthis are located at three chakras where ida, pingala, and sushumna meet.

Brahma Granthi in the root center (muladhara chakra) is the knot of attachment to the world of material life *(samsara),* which binds the mind to base desires, physical pleasures, and selfishness. This knot implies the ensnaring power of *tamas guna,* which obscures the truth and restrains the mind. It manifests as indolence, inertia, forgetfulness, negativity, delusion, ignorance, fear, sadness, depression, dullness, inability to meditate, and rejection of spirituality.

Vishnu Granthi in the heart center (anahata chakra) is the knot of attachment to emotions, which binds the mind to love, loyalty, compassion, and pride about a cause. This granthi is connected with *rajas guna,* which makes the mind wander and manifests as passion, anger, hatred, greed, skepticism, obsession, jealousy, opinion, craving, egotism, defensiveness, aggression, and competition.

Rudra Granthi in the brow center (ajna chakra), connected with *sattva guna,* is the knot of attachment to the mental world. It binds the mind to thoughts, spiritual experiences, psychic powers, and supernormal abilities, such as telepathy, prescience, clairvoyance, clairaudience, mind-reading, visions, intuition, and other psychic gifts.

All three knots must be released for kundalini to complete its ascent through the chakras to sahasrara (thousand-petaled lotus), where spiritual enlightenment occurs.

Symbols of Kundalini Worldwide

The ida, pingala, and sushumna energy tubes are represented by the caduceus—the ancient symbol known as the staff of Hermes or Mercury in Greek and Roman mythology. It is also the Staff of Aesculapius, named for the Greek physician Asklepios, revered as the deity of medicine and healing by the ancient Romans. This symbol, first found on a libation vase of King Gudea of Lagash (circa 2000 BC), was later adopted by the medical profession as its emblem (see page 14).

Another ancient symbol for the three primary nadis in the spinal column is the thyrsus—a staff with a pine cone on top, twined with ivy and vine branches, borne by the Roman God of fertility, Dionysus. In India, the symbol is a bamboo shoot with seven knots for the seven major chakras (energy centers). A barber pole, with spiral red and white bands and a knob on top, also symbolizes kundalini. This is widely known to represent the barber's former sideline of surgery. The pagan tree, adapted by Christians as the Christmas tree, represents kundalini, and its lighted ornaments signify the chakra centers.

The Jewish symbol for kundalini is the Kabbalist tree of life (see page 104). In the Biblical story of Adam and Eve, the tree of life in the middle of the Garden of Eden symbolizes sushumna nadi. The serpent is "more subtle than any beast of the field which the Lord God has made."[4] This snake is kundalini, representing consciousness, the most subtle element of nature. Adam and Eve lived in oneness and harmony. But through illusion they were tempted to eat the fruit of the tree of knowledge of good and evil (falling into duality). Because of this, their kundalini descended to the level of muladhara chakra.

Ancient Egyptian priests are depicted wearing a headdress with a snake called *uraeus* placed on the forehead between the eyebrows. This center is called *bhrumadhya* by the yogis and is connected with the ajna chakra (third eye).

Perhaps the oldest book in the world, known as *Bopal Vuh* of the ancient Quiché Maya, pictures the deity Quetzalcoatl wearing a multi-rayed sun as a crown on his head along with a symbolic form of a snake.

The Mother Goddess

In India, kundalini is personified as the Divine Mother: Shakti Ma, Kali Ma, or other Goddesses. She is the feminine power at the base of the spine, which travels up the spine to unite with the masculine power, her consort, Lord Shiva (Shakta), in the seventh chakra, sahasrara. This union of opposites is a powerful symbol depicted in all cultures.

In the ancient scriptures, kundalini is described in three different manifestations. The first is unmanifest cosmic energy: *para-kundalini*. The second is vital energy of the created universe: *prana-kundalini*. The third is consciousness: *shakti-kundalini*, the intermediary between the other two.

Shakti-kundalini is the link to higher awareness, the revealer of all mantras, and the eternal source of bliss flowing from sahasrara (crown chakra). Through her *shristi krama* (process of creation), she creates by descending from sahasrara (crown center) through all the chakras. She sustains by abiding in muladhara chakra (root center). Through her *laya krama* (process of absorption), she destroys or dissolves by ascending and returning to sahasrara.

When Shakti descends to the lower chakras, she is known as *jagan mohini* (world-bewildering) and causes *maya*: delusion, limitation, ignorance, and ensnarement in material life. As she descends, she becomes grosser and loses her power and subtlety.

As kundalini Shakti ascends through the chakras, she becomes subtler. On her pathway upward, she reabsorbs all the creative principles that originally descended from sahasrara. This is called *laya*—absorption. During this homeward journey, Shakti removes the veils of *maya* (illusion), which evaporate like a mirage.

As kundalini ascends through the chakras, mental limitations are gradually removed so consciousness can shine in its pristine glory. Mental fluctuations settle down and the mind becomes serene. Awareness flows smoothly and the mind becomes a vehicle for bliss and happiness.

At sahasrara chakra, kundalini merges with Shiva, who is identical with her. In her formless state she is consciousness. In her creative form she is Shakti, the power of manifestation.

Therefore, kundalini's descent creates increasing ignorance, bondage, and delusion. The same kundalini energy, as it ascends, causes spiritual awakening, freedom, and wisdom.

What's in It for You?

The rising kundalini is understood to stimulate the chakras and awaken dormant supernormal powers. When she finally reaches sahasrara chakra (thousand-petaled lotus), then the goal of yoga (divine union) is achieved, and limits of time, space, and causation are transcended.

The powerful force of kundalini can be used to strengthen your body and enlighten your mind. When used properly, it can promote greater creativity, intelligence, and wisdom. When misused or abused, it can degrade your spirit and bring ruin. Kundalini is described in the ancient *Hatha Yoga Pradipika*: *"It gives liberation to yogis and bondage to fools."*[5]

Forcing sushumna open prematurely, without proper understanding or guidance, can result in frightening experiences, intense physical pain, burning bodily heat, sexual obsession, even severe mental disturbances or mental illness. This is because as kundalini awakens, your mind undergoes purification. Deep mental problems, blockages, and conditioning are brought to the surface and removed.

It takes time to acclimate to increased pranic energy flow through your nadis. Your body is like an electrical system that can safely accommodate a certain voltage. If you plug your 110-volt toaster into a 220-volt socket, it will burn out. Similarly, too great a load on your home's electrical system will blow a fuse. By gradually increasing your internal power station by creating more nadi pathways to channel higher energies, you can safely plug into higher pranic flows. Therefore, to follow this path with sincerity and seriousness, study with a fully realized master.

The simple, gentle techniques recommended in this book can be used safely as long as they are done under the guidance of a qualified yoga teacher and with permission from your medical doctor. Here you will learn exercises to begin your own kundalini awakening in a safe and natural way.

When Kundalini Wakes Up

The experience of the rise of kundalini through your sushumna can be described using various metaphors:

- A lightning bolt.

- An electrical current.

- A rush of liquid fire.

- A tube of liquid light.

- A burning sensation moving up the spine.

- A tube of neon light.

- Water under pressure flowing through a hose.

- Tingling along the spine.

- Ants crawling up the spine.

- A pinball machine shooting a ball up the spine.

- A sledgehammer on a weight that rings a bell at a carnival.

- A freight train rushing up the spine.

- A rocket blasting up the spine.

The awakening of kundalini flings open the floodgates to wondrous mystical, paranormal, and magical vistas. At the same time, it can radically impact your body. Strange physical or mental illnesses can occur. Dramatic lifestyle changes can take place.

According to ancient scriptures, signs of the awakening kundalini fall into three basic categories: mental, vocal, and physical. Mental signs may include visions that can be blissful or even terrifying. Vocal signs may be singing, reciting mantras, or making animal sounds, such as growling or chirping. Physical signs include trembling, shaking, automatic strange breathing patterns, and involuntary movements, yoga postures, or yoga breathing (*pranayama*).

Here are a few of the many experiences that may occur when kundalini is raised:

- Heat or blissful sensations along the spine or in the energy centers, especially the forehead or top of head.

- Hearing celestial sounds, such as flutes, drums, waterfalls, birds, bees, roaring, whooshing, thunder, or ringing.

- Sensing celestial fragrances or subtle tastes.

- Seeing inner celestial visions of deities, symbols, or light.

- Feelings or visions of the chakra system or energy centers.

- Subtle-sensory perception and heightened sensory awareness: clairvoyance, clairaudience, clairsentience.

- Seeing vibrations, colors, or auras around people.

- Past-life memories, prophetic dreams, lucid dreams, and visions.

- Hearing the "still small voice" of divine intuition within.

- Greater creativity, such as music, art, poetry, or writing.

- Greater healing powers.

- Higher states of consciousness, mystical experiences.

- Ecstatic feelings of bliss, joy, love, peace, and compassion.

- Deeper insight, inner wisdom, and cognition of spiritual truths.

- Greater sensitivity to subtle internal and external vibrations.

- Experiences of inspiration, direct knowing, and inner revelation.

- Absolute bliss of transcendental consciousness.

Chapter Six

YOUR MULTIDIMENSIONAL SELF

"Know the Self to be sitting in the chariot, the body to be the chariot, the intellect (buddhi) the charioteer, and the mind the reins."
—The Upanishads[1]

As you explore your subtle body in this chapter, you will realize what a multidimensional, powerful, radiant light-being you truly are. Here you will uncover dimensional realities beyond imagination. The amazing world of your higher self will open as you discover multifarious components of your being.

Let us explore your wondrous subtle energy field now!

Your pranic sheath is not the only subtle body vibrating within and around you. On higher vibrational levels, your indwelling spirit lives in several bodies simultaneously. Why do you have a multitude of bodies? Because your inner divinity desires to express in a symphony of instruments, harmonizing a variety of tone, pitch, resonance, and color. Like an orchestra, where each instrument has a purpose, each of your bodies has a specific function, of which you may not be consciously aware.

Your Threefold Body

According to the wisdom of ancient India, three basic sections of this inner orchestra constitute a threefold body. Their Sanskrit names are *stula sharira* (gross physical body), *sukshma sharira* (subtle body), and *karana sharira* (causal or seed body). Your gross body is visible to the eyes. The other two are invisible to the eyes, but visible to spiritual sight.

Your Fivefold Sheath

Within these three bodies are five sheaths, like specific sections of instruments within your inner orchestra: *annamaya kosha* (physical sheath), *pranamaya kosha* (vital sheath), *manomaya kosha* (mental sheath), *vijnanamaya kosha* (intellect sheath), and *anandamaya kosha* (blissful sheath). These five are termed sheaths because, like veils, they hide your luminous *atman* (higher self).

Your three bodies and five sheaths are not stacked inside or around you. The subtler bodies and sheaths permeate and surround the grosser ones.

Your higher self is your true nature, the unchanging, eternal *atman,* separate from and witness to your various bodies. However, you mistakenly identify yourself as these sheaths. You believe yourself to be your physical body, thoughts, or experiences. Yet this is not who you really are. Indeed, you are the unbounded, undifferentiated radiance of *Brahman*—pure consciousness.

Threefold Body	Fivefold Sheath	Worlds or Realms
Gross Body (*Stula Sharira*) **Waking State**	**Food Sheath** (*Annamaya Kosha*)	**Physical World** (*Bhu Loka*)
Subtle Body (*Sukshma Sharira*) **Dream State**	**Vital Sheath** (*Pranamaya Kosha*)	**Astral World** (*Bhuvah Loka*)
	Mental Sheath (*Manomaya Kosha*)	**Subtle World** (*Svah Loka*)
	Intellect Sheath (*Vijnanamaya Kosha*)	**Middle World** (*Maha Loka*)
Causal Body (*Karana Sharira*) **Deep Sleep State**	**Blissful Sheath** (*Anandamaya Kosha*)	**Causal World** (*Janah Loka*)
"I AM" Body (*Atma Sharira*) **Fourth State** (*Samadhi*)	**"I AM" Self** (*Atman*)	**Mansion of the Beloved** (*Tapah Loka*) or (*Siddha Loka*)
God Body (*Brahma Sharira*) **Cosmic Awareness**	**God Self** (*Brahman*)	**Abode of Truth** (*Satya Loka*)

"When the five sheaths are disowned [as not-self by discriminating the self from them] their witness-consciousness is all that remains. That is the real nature of the self."
—Sri Vidyaranya Swami[2]

Figure 6a. Sheaths in Multidimensions.

Three States of Awareness

Your gross physical body experiences waking awareness (*jagrat*), your subtle body experiences dream state (*svapna*), and your causal body experiences deep dreamless sleep (*sushupti*).

During dream state, your ego and consciousness withdraw from your gross physical body and enter your subtle body. Involuntary bodily functions, such as circulation, respiration, and digestion, continue, due to your ever-vigilant vital sheath (*pranamaya kosha*).

During dreamless sleep, your higher self recedes into your causal body (*karana sharira*). All phenomena dissolve, while you experience nothing. Your ego disappears and loses self-awareness, while your mind remains suspended in subtle seed-like form—absolutely still and silent.

"In this state [dreamless sleep] a father is no father, a mother no mother, the worlds are no worlds, the gods no gods, the Vedas no Vedas. In this state a thief is no thief, the killer of a noble Brahmana is no killer, an outcast no outcast, a hybrid no hybrid, a monk no monk, a hermit no hermit." —Adi Shankaracharya[3]

Upon waking, first your ego arises, because all mental and physical functions and characteristics proceed from ego (*ahamkara*). Then your mind appears and you notice your surroundings.

At death, you leave your gross body behind, but your subtle and causal bodies remain intact throughout all your incarnations. It is dissolved only when you attain final liberation in the state of full enlightenment.

The Seven Worlds

As a multidimensional being, each of your inner bodies dwells in a separate dimension, like various sections of your inner orchestra playing different scores simultaneously: distinct harmonies within the symphony.

The ancient scriptures of India speak of seven cosmic regions (*lokas*), corresponding to your sheaths and major chakras (see Figure 6a on page 58). Of these seven realms, the three highest are *Brahma lokas* (worlds of Brahma). Let us now explore the seven realms:

Your gross body dwells in *bhu* (earth) *loka*, material world, the earthly plane, visible to everyone, realm of gross physical elements.

Your pranic body exists in *bhuvah* (sky) *loka*, astral world, intermediate plane of existence called *shunya* (void), the sphere of invisible subtle matter. This realm is said to extend from the earth to the sun.

Your mental body resides in *svah* (heaven) *loka*, subtle world, celestial plane, sphere of the *mahashunya* (great void), beyond gross and subtle matter. This plane extends from the sun to the polestar.

Your intellect body is in *mahah loka* (middle region), world of balance, beginning of *maya* (illusion), connecting link or doorway between the spiritual and material world.

Your causal body is in *janah loka* (place of rebirths), the causal sphere, where oneness separates into duality and individuality originates. It is called *alakshya* (incomprehensible), because it is impossible for wholeness to split into parts—yet it does.

Tapah loka (mansion of the beloved) is also termed *siddha loka* (world of perfected beings) and *agama* (inaccessible), the unlimited sphere of the Holy Spirit.

Satya loka (abode of truth) is the sphere of God, the only reality and only substance: *sat* (absolute). It is also called *anama* (nameless), because it is without form, time, or cause. It is the absolute Brahman.

Your Gross Physical Body

Your *stula sharira* (gross body) could be compared to the percussion section of your inner orchestra, in continual motion, dancing with the rhythm of the heartbeat and undulation of the lungs.

Your physical material body is called *annamaya kosha* (food sheath). This is your home in this incarnation, your vehicle for experiencing waking life.

Annamaya kosha is made of five elements: earth (*prithivi*), water (*apas*), fire (*tejas*), air (*vayu*), and ether (*akasha*), and uses five organs of sensory perception (ears, skin, eyes, palate, and nose) and five organs of action (tongue, hands, feet, genitals, and anus). However these are not your real organs. Indeed, your true organs are invisible, within your subtle body.

Annamaya kosha is your least durable sheath, perishable and ephemeral, subject to six modifications (*sadbhava vikara*): origination, subsistence, growth, transformation, decay, and destruction. This food sheath is a product of food, requires food, dies without food, and, after death, becomes food for plants and animals.

The ancient *Taittiriya Upanishad* of India describes it as "consisting of the essence of food."

The food sheath is often compared to a city with nine or 11 gates (orifices). These nine gates are the two ears, two eyes, two nostrils, mouth, and two organs of elimination. The last two are the navel and crown of the head. The ruler of this city is *atman* (higher self). Just as a ruler is distinct from a city, so atman is separate from your body. As the ruler governs the city, so atman directs all functions of your body. As a city collapses when its ruler abandons it, so your body disintegrates when atman deserts it.

The ancient sage Kapila (circa 6th century BC), founder of *Samkhya,* the oldest of six major systems of Indian philosophy, said, "The building of the body, the seat of experience, is due to the presence of the indwelling experiencer [the atman]; otherwise its decomposition would result."[4]

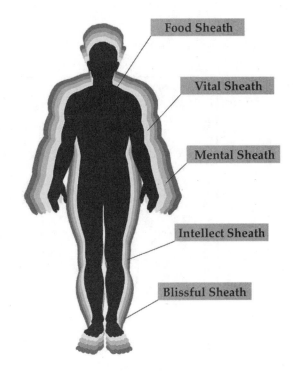

Figure 6b. Fivefold Sheath.

Your Subtle Body

Your *sukshma sharira* (subtle or astral body) is comparable to the brass and wind sections of your inner orchestra, which play a variety of melodies in your mind, from sweet and soft to brash and discordant.

Your subtle body, which is the vehicle of your individual embodied spirit (*jiva*), consists of vital sheath (*pranamaya kosha*), mental sheath (*manomaya kosha*), and intellect sheath (*vijnanamaya kosha*). This subtle body does not change at death. It remains alive throughout all your cycles of incarnation.

According to *Samkhya* (literally "number") philosophy, your subtle body is built of 18 principles: intellect (*buddhi*), ego (*ahamkara*), mind (*manas*), five knowing-senses (*jnana indriyas*), five working-senses (*karma indriyas*), and five sense objects *(tanmatras).*

	Vacuity	Motion	Luminosity	Liquidity	Solidity
Gross Body *(Stula Sharira)* — Organs of Action	Ears	Skin	Eyes	Tongue	Nose
Sense Organs	Voice	Hands	Feet	Genitals	Anus
Gross Elements *(Mahabhutas)*	Ether *(Akasha)*	Air *(Vayu)*	Fire *(Tejas)*	Water *(Apas)*	Earth *(Prithivi)*
Subtle Body *(Sukshma Sharira)* — Subtle Elements *(Tanmatras)*	Sound *(Shabda)*	Touch *(Sparsa)*	Form *(Rupa)*	Flavor *(Rasa)*	Odor *(Gandha)*
Working Senses *(Karma indriyas)*	Express *(Vak)*	Grasp *(Pani)*	Move *(Pada)*	Procreate *(Upastha)*	Excrete *(Payu)*
Knowing Senses *(Jnana indriyas)*	Hear *(Strotra)*	Feel *(Tvak)*	See *(Caksus)*	Taste *(Rasana)*	Smell *(Ghrana)*
Energy Centers *(Chakras)*	Throat *(Vishuddha)*	Heart *(Anahata)*	Navel *(Manipura)*	Sacral *(Svadhishthana)*	Root *(Muladhara)*

Figure 6c. Five Senses, Elements, and Chakras.

THE BIG BOOK OF CHAKRAS AND CHAKRA HEALING

Tanmatras are five sense objects: sound (*sabda*), touch (*sparsa*), form (*rupa*), flavor (*rasa*), and odor (*gandha*). These rudimentary, uncompounded seeds, also called *panch karana* (five instruments), generate the five elements (*mahabhutas*) of your gross physical body. Sound produces the element of ether, touch gives rise to air, form to fire, flavor to water, and odor to earth.

In the same way, your five sense organs (ears, skin, eyes, palate, and nose) and five motor organs (tongue, hands, feet, genitals, and anus) arise from their subtle counterparts, the ten *indriyas* (abstract sense-powers):

- The *jnana indriyas* (five abstract knowing-senses) are the powers of hearing, touch, vision, taste, and smell.

- The *karma indriyas* (five abstract working-senses) are the power of speech (to express and create ideas), grasping (to receive, give, and accept), walking (to move and have mental activity), generation (to procreate and enjoy recreation), and evacuation (to excrete and reject).

What Happens to Subtle Body After Death?

At death, your *jiva* (individual embodied spirit), clothed in your subtle body, abandons your physical body and moves to higher dimensions. When you are ready to reincarnate, you wear the same subtle body that has persisted for lifetimes. Your capacities and tendencies endure after death. Everything you experienced, perceived, thought, felt, and desired is stored in your *samskara chitta* (subconscious mind of indelible impressions). These propensities and latencies of either *punya* (merit—helping others) or *papa* (demerit—harming others) determine your afterlife.

Your subtle body is often named *linga sharira* (index body), because it tabulates previous incarnations and expresses future ones. Your talents or predilections for music, art, writing, cooking, science, math, business, athletics, psychic powers, religion, philosophy, or spirituality were cultivated in previous lives and carry into your next incarnation. Similarly, negative tendencies, such as thievery, dishonesty, addictions, violence, sexual promiscuity, arrogance, or jealousy also transfer from past to future lives. For more information about what happens after death, according to your level of consciousness, read my books *Divine Revelation* and *Ascension*.

Your Vital Sheath

The first of three bodies that comprise your subtle body (*sukshma sharira*) is *pranamaya kosha* (vital sheath). Often called etheric or astral body, it dwells in *bhuvah loka* (astral world). Because the vital sheath appears as an exact replica of the food sheath, it is known as "etheric double." (See chapters 3 and 4.)

The vital sheath consists of five vital airs (*prana, apana, vyana, samana,* and *udana*) and five abstract working-senses (*karma indriyas*), the powers associated with your organs of action: *vak* (speech), *pani* (grasping), *pada* (moving), *upastha* (procreation), and *payu* (excretion).

Pranamaya kosha (vital sheath) breathes life into your physical body (food sheath), animates it, and gives it expression. Your food sheath engages in all activities as if alive, but without the vital sheath, your food sheath would be a corpse. Your food sheath has no inherent life in it. Prana is what gives it life.

> *"Prana (up-breathing) is its [vital sheath's] head. Vyana (back-breathing) is its right arm. Apana (down-breathing) is its left arm. Ether is its trunk. The earth, the seat (the support). The Devas breathe after breath (prana), so do men and cattle. Breath is the life of beings, therefore it is called sarvayusha (all-enlivening)."* —The Upanishads[5]

Interestingly, the vital sheath, not the food sheath, experiences hunger, thirst, heat, and cold. Your body heat, which is maintained by *udana* (outbreathing), remains as long as your vital sheath is present. At death, udana leaves, and the body grows cold.

Although the food and vital sheaths are always connected, they may get partially separated during sleep, or by anesthesia, hypnosis, out-of-body experiences, near-death experiences, certain meditative states, unconscious trances, or psychic mediumship. The vital sheath can travel in *bhuvah loka* (astral world) and leave the gross body behind. This is called astral travel.

What Happens to Vital Sheath After Death

When death approaches, the vital sheath rises out of the food sheath and hovers over the dying body. It is connected to the body by a silver cord attached to the navel. When that cord snaps, the vital sheath withdraws into the mental sheath and abandons the food sheath permanently.

✕ THE BIG BOOK OF CHAKRAS AND CHAKRA HEALING

Your Internal Instrument

The second and third parts of your subtle body (*sukshma sharira*) house your *chitta* (mind or consciousness), which is responsible for all states of awareness, perception, and knowledge. It is the seat of your conscious mind, subconscious mind, and higher states of consciousness.

Chitta includes your threefold mental faculty, called *antahkarana* (internal instrument): *manas* (conscious mind), *buddhi* (intellect), and *ahamkara* (ego). They function through your mental and intellect sheaths, and their interaction creates activity in your life.

Let us now explore the mental and intellect sheaths.

Your Mental Sheath

Your *manomaya kosha* (mental sheath), the second of three aspects of your subtle body (*sukshma sharira*), dwells in *svah loka* (subtle realm) and consists of three parts: lower mind (*manas chitta*), subconscious mind (*sanskara chitta*), and reflexive mind (*vasana chitta*).

> *"Faith is its [mental sheath's] head. What is right is its right arm. What is true is its left arm. Absorption (yoga) is its trunk. The great (intellect) is the seat (the support)."* —The Upanishads[6]

Conscious Mind

Your *manas chitta* (lower, instinctive mind) performs mental functions and directs actions. It has the capacity to think, perceive, deliberate, and experience. It is responsible for attention, selection, reasoning, and sensory perception. *Manas* is undisciplined, empirical, vacillating, and characterized by doubt and delusion.

Subconscious Sensory-Impression Mind

The purpose of your subconscious or sensory-impression mind *(samskara chitta)* is to permanently store all your sensory experiences, memories, impressions, reactions, desires, and feelings. Similar to a computer hard drive, it remembers every bit of data entered.

Subconscious Habit Mind

Your *vasana chitta* (reflexive, patterned mind) is the mind of subliminal traits or subconscious inclinations. Once the mind is set in particular habits, we expect certain results with repetitive, habitual reactions called *vasanas*, which contribute to mental fluctuations (*vritti*). The most complex and emotionally charged vasanas are found in vasana chitta.

Your Intellect Sheath

The *vijnanamaya kosha* (intellect sheath) is the third of three aspects of your subtle body (*sukshma sharira*). It dwells in *maha loka* (middle world) and functions as a semi-permanent vehicle, created millions of years ago, when you first passed from animal incarnation into human form. Its two components are *buddhi* (intellect) and *ahamkara* (ego), which we will now explore.

> *"Understanding [intellect sheath] performs the sacrifice, it performs all sacred acts. All Devas worship understanding as Brahman, as the oldest. If a man knows understanding as Brahman, and if he does not swerve from it, he leaves all evils behind in the body, and attains all his wishes."* —The Upanishads[7]

Your Buddhi (Intellect)

Buddhi is your seat of cognition, intelligence, intuition, and knowledge, with the capacity to discriminate, decide, determine, resolve, discern, generalize, retain concepts, and understand abstract ideas. As the vehicle of higher mind, its properties are imagination, creativity, insight, and super-sensory perception.

The intellect is key to self-mastery. A discriminating intellect serves as an unfailing guide for making wise choices. The real meaning of *buddhi* is an unwavering decision made with conviction, based on right understanding. Your buddhi is fully developed when you can discern between the real and apparent, between eternal and ephemeral, between self and not-self.

Your mind is called *ananta* (infinite) because of its countless modifications and functions. However, cognition underlies them all. You can never feel, will, think, or form an opinion without first knowing the object of perception. Of all aspects of mind, the cognitive (intellect) is the closest reflection of your true luminous higher self (atman). Hence, your intellect is *sattvic* (pure) and radiant.

The great saint of ancient India and founder of *advaita* (nondualism) Vedanta philosophy, Adi Shankaracharya said:

"Buddhi is the instrument for the perception of all objects like a lamp placed in front amid darkness. It has been said, 'It is through the mind that one sees, that one hears.' Indeed, everything is perceived on being invested with the light of buddhi like an object in the dark illuminated by a lamp placed in front. The other organs are but the channels of buddhi."[8]

Your Ahamkara (Ego)

Ahamkara is individual human identity, and its function is to will and demand. Considering itself a separate entity, it accepts or rejects desires made by bodily instincts and impulses. Before spiritual enlightenment, buddhi and ahamkara are mistakenly identified as your real self. Just as white light shining through colored glass appears red, green, or blue, your pure, undifferentiated higher self (atman) appears endowed with properties of the intellect, such as knowledge, decision, and cognition. The true self is not the mind. It is the knower witnessing the mind. Indeed, the true self, *vijnanamaya purusha* (the knower), shines with innate effulgence and dwells in the heart.

> *"All aspects of antahkarana cooperate to produce your every experience. The four cognitive functions of your mind work together: deliberation, recollection, cognition, and ego. Among these sheaths, the intelligent sheath, which is possessed of the power of cognition, is the agent, the mental sheath, which is possessed of the power of volition, is the instrument, and the vital sheath, which is possessed of the power of activity, is the operation."* —Vedanta-Sara[9]

Beyond your fivefold sheath is your higher self (*atman*)—witness of your experiences, neither thinker nor doer. By virtue of atman's reflection, your intellect sheath seems to act as knower and doer. But the reflection cannot function independently of its basis—the true self, atman.

What Happens to Your Internal Instrument After Death?

After death, your *jiva* (individual embodied spirit) dwells in *bhuvah loka* (astral world) in *pranamaya kosha* (vital sheath) as long as warranted for your spiritual evolution. Then your soul retreats to *svah loka* (subtle world) in *manomaya kosha* (mental sheath). After staying in *svah loka* for an allotted period, according to your needs, then manomaya kosha (mental body) breaks apart, and your soul, in its final mental vehicle, *vijnanamaya kosha* (intellect sheath), moves into *mahah loka* (middle world), and finally into *janah loka* (causal plane). According to Adi Shankaracharya, vijnanamaya kosha (intellect sheath) is the cause of your soul to transmigrate into your next body.

Your Causal Body

The *karana sharira* (causal body) is analogous to the string section of your inner orchestra. Here your inner melody becomes refined, harmonious, and lyrical, with a smooth, velvety, pleasing delicacy.

The causal body is the seed of beginningless indescribable ignorance, because it causes both gross and subtle bodies to exist by virtue of something called *maya* (literally "measure" and figuratively "that which is not" or "illusion"—what does not exist). Thus *avidya* (ignorance) is the seed of "I-ness" or ego, from which all experiences arise.

Your Blissful Sheath

Only one sheath comprises your *karana sharira* (causal body): *anandamaya kosha* (blissful sheath), which emits the blissfulness of the higher self (atman), yet covers atman like a veil. The blissful sheath resides in *janah loka* (causal world). In this body, happiness, peace, joy, pleasure, and contentment are experienced.

> *"Joy is its [causal body's] head. Satisfaction its right arm. Great satisfaction is its left arm. Bliss is its trunk. Brahman is the seat (the support)."*
> —*The Upanishads*[10]

Your so-called blissful sheath is not intrinsically blissful. In the state of deep sleep, your mind becomes silent. Then the absolute bliss of your higher self (atman) shines through your blissful sheath. Thus you might remark, "I slept peacefully and blissfully."

The bliss of deep sleep is more refined than the joy derived from desirable objects in waking or dream states. Every variety of delight is a display of the supreme bliss of atman through different channels.

> *"The blissful sheath is that modification of ajnana (ignorance) which manifests itself catching a reflection of the atman that is Bliss Absolute; whose attributes are joy and the rest. . . . The blissful sheath has its fullest play during profound sleep."* —*Adi Shankaracharya*[11]

Your Higher Bodies

"I AM" Body

The *atman sharira* ("I AM" body) or spiritual body dwells in a realm called *satyam loka* (world of truth). Atman is your higher self, the mighty "I AM" presence, your true nature. Very few people ever recognize or experience this body, because it is where *moksha* (liberation) takes place.

"This self-effulgent atman; distinct from the five sheaths; the Witness of the three states [waking; dream; and dreamless sleep]; the Real; the Changeless; the Untainted; the ever-lasting Bliss; is to be realized by the wise person as one's own Self." —Adi Shankaracharya[12]

God Body

The *brahma sharira* (God body) is the cosmic body, which abides in *brahma loka* (abode of God). Once your "I AM" body is realized, then it is natural to seek God. Direct experience of God takes place in this unbounded body of pure light and unconditional love. Rare is the individual who realizes the God body, because it supports the state of God-realization.

"In the highest golden sheath there is the Brahman without passions and without parts. That is pure, that is the light of lights, that is it which they know who know the Self. The sun does not shine there, nor the moon and the stars, nor these lightnings, and much less this fire. When he shines, everything shines after him; by his light all this is lighted." —The Upanishads[13]

Absolute Body

The *nirvana sharira* (absolute body) is not a body and dwells in no world or plane of existence. It is the absolute—without form, phenomena, or boundaries. In this bodiless body, both atman and brahma disappear. Singularity, oneness, and wholeness remain. Here you merge with Brahman in supreme enlightenment and absolute truth. You are free from all bondage and attain the highest beatitude.

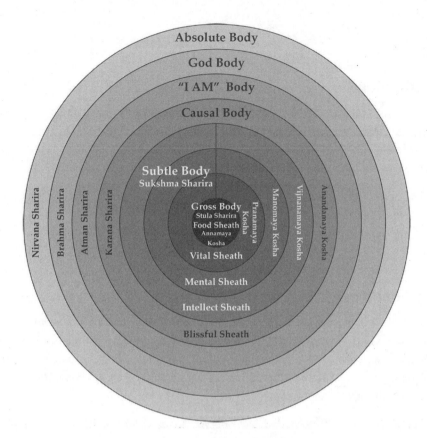

Figure 6d. Bodies and Sheaths.

By distinguishing your higher self (atman) from the threefold body and five-fold sheaths, you ultimately achieve the goal-less goal, the cessation of all striving, the ultimate reality. Here you realize your true nature and its essential unity and identity with the supreme self, Brahman, even while living in a human body.

"This is indeed the Self, who seeming to be filled with desires, and seeming to be overcome by bright or dark fruits of action, wanders about in every body (himself remaining free)." —The Upanishads[14]

✡   THE BIG BOOK OF CHAKRAS AND CHAKRA HEALING

Chapter Seven

AS ABOVE, SO BELOW

"In the beginning this was non-existent (not yet defined by form and name).
From it was born what exists. That made itself its Self, therefore it is called the
'Self-made.' That which is Self-made is a flavour (can be tasted), for only after
perceiving a flavour can any one perceive pleasure. Who could breathe, who
could breathe forth, if that bliss (Brahman) existed not in the ether (in the heart)?
For he alone causes blessedness."
—The Upanishads[1]

On the Emerald Tablet of the Egyptian Hermes Trismegistus the words "As above, so below" are inscribed. This ancient aphorism says that your individual life is a reflection of cosmic life. In this chapter, you will explore this relationship.

Here you will discover how this phenomenal world was created and how it is repeatedly destroyed and recreated. By virtue of *pralaya* (cosmic dissolution), the universe periodically retreats into the absolute. You will also explore how your individuality came to be and how it is dissolved. By virtue of *laya* (absorption), your ego is dissolved, you merge with the absolute, and you become spiritually enlightened.

What follows is the exploration of *laya* (individual absorption) and *pralaya* (cosmic absorption), where you will find a secret golden passkey to unlock the entire chakra system and, thereby, solve the riddle of life.

Lord Shiva's Philosophy

The ancient *Shaivas* (Shaivite scriptural texts) are believed to be direct revelations, dialogues between Lord Shiva and his consort Shakti. When Shakti asks questions and Shiva answers, the scripture is called *agama*. When Shakti answers, the scripture is *nigama*. Twenty-eight texts of Shaivism (Shiva sect) were revealed by Sadashiva, the five-headed aspect of Shiva, through his five mouths.

By the eighth century in India, dualistic and pluralistic philosophies threatened to annihilate monotheism (one God). In order to preserve ancient monotheistic principles, the sage Vasugupta (late AD 700s–early AD 800s) wrote *Shiva Sutra* and *Spanda Karika*. Encompassing both Kashmiri Shaivism and Samkhya philosophy (founded about 8,000 years ago by the sage Kapila), *Shiva Sutra* is lauded as the greatest masterpiece of Indian philosophy. Interestingly, Kashmiri Shaivism is based on a Holy Trinity of God, soul, and matter, called *triksansana, trikasastra,* or *trika.* In Shaivism, the absolute supreme Being is both transcendental and immanent, static (represented by Lord Shiva) and dynamic (symbolized by Goddess Shakti). This entire cosmos is thus a play of Shakti *(lila shakti).*

The absolute eternally alternates two phases: rest and activity, unmanifest and manifest, passive and active. The passive phase is called *mahapralaya* (great cosmic dissolution and absorption), in which the universe retreats like a seed into latency. After this latent period, the seed germinates and consciousness becomes active. The active phase is *sristi* (creation) or *abhasha* (to appear or shine).

Kala Chakra (Wheel of Time)

According to ancient Vedic scriptures, humans have existed an immensely longer time than modern science believes. In India, the universe is perceived as ever-changing, ever-cycling creation and dissolution, with gigantic spans of activity and equally enormous periods of rest.

Steven Hawking's idea of nonlinear, circular space-time is compatible with the Indian view, which states that creation repeatedly cycles through four aeons or *yugas*. These yugas are depicted in the figure "Duration of the Four Yugas" on page 73. Each of these has a *sandhya* (transitional period at the beginning of each yuga) and *sandhyamsa* (transitional period at the end of each yuga).

The ancient scriptures of India state that *Satya Yuga* consists of 4,800 years (4,000 years plus 800 years for sandhya and sandhyamsa). *Treta Yuga* lasts 3,600 years (3,000 plus 600 for sandhya and sandhyamsa). *Dwapara yuga* is 2,400 years (2,000 plus 400). *Kali Yuga* is 1200 (1000 plus 200) years. All the yugas combined total a 12,000-year period, known as *mahayuga* (great age), *chaturyuga* (four ages), or *daiva yuga* (age of the Gods). Two mahayugas span 24,000 years.

This ancient time-map roughly corresponds with modern astronomy. I am about to remind you of somewhat complicated astronomy that you probably learned in school. But simply put, we people on planet Earth experience a different

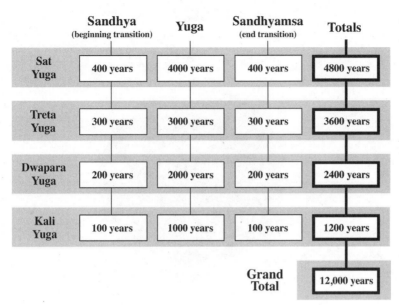

	Sandhya (beginning transition)	Yuga	Sandhyamsa (end transition)	Totals
Sat Yuga	400 years	4000 years	400 years	4800 years
Treta Yuga	300 years	3000 years	300 years	3600 years
Dwapara Yuga	200 years	2000 years	200 years	2400 years
Kali Yuga	100 years	1000 years	100 years	1200 years
Grand Total				12,000 years

Figure 7a. Duration of the Four Yugas.

relationship with our calendar of days and seasons, determined by our orbit around the Sun, than with the actual location of stars and their constellations.

Please refer to Figure 7b on page 74, "Celestial and Ecliptic Planes."[2] The "ecliptic" is a great circle on an imaginary celestial sphere, on the same plane as the Earth's orbit around the Sun. In contrast, the "celestial equator" is a great circle on an imaginary celestial sphere, on the same plane as the Earth's equator and perpendicular to the Earth's rotation axis. The celestial equator is inclined by 23.4° with respect to the ecliptic plane. This inclination is known as Earth's axial tilt or obliquity. This tilt gives us different seasons at different times of the year and in different hemispheres.

The points where the ecliptic and the celestial equator intersect are the vernal (March) and autumnal (September) equinox points. That is where the solar path appears to cross the celestial equator (see figure 7b on page 74).

As the Earth rotates on its axis, it wobbles like a spinning top around its north and south celestial poles, due to varying gravitational forces of the Sun and Moon, which causes the equator to bulge slightly. This wobble causes the equinoctial points to shift westward along the ecliptic. Thus our view of the fixed stars from Earth shifts slightly year after year.

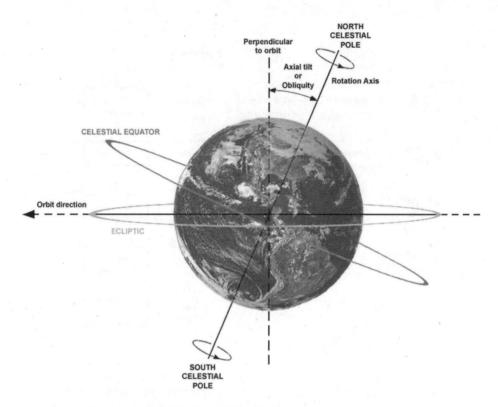

Figure 7b. Celestial and Ecliptic Planes.

Earth's rotational axis moves roughly one degree every 70 years and takes about 25,200 years to finish a complete cycle of this 360-degree wobble—about 2,100 years per zodiacal sign (constellations viewed from Earth along the ecliptic). This phenomenon of backward shift of the equinoctial points around the zodiac is called "precession of the equinoxes" or "Earth's precession."

Modern astronomy tells us the Sun orbits in a wavelike motion (not a circular motion) around the center of the Milky Way, and its entire orbit takes approximately 250 million years. Ancient Indian astronomy calls this center *Vishnunabhi* or *Brahma,* the seat of creative power, which upholds and sustains divine purpose and truth *(dharma).* The Sun comes closest to Vishnunabhi about every 24,000 years, whenever the constellation Aries is on the horizon at sunrise of the September equinox, and the constellation Libra is on the horizon at sunrise of the March equinox. At that time, humans can easily comprehend mysteries of Spirit.

About 12,000 years later, the Sun is farthest away from Vishnunabhi, when the constellation Aries is on the horizon at sunrise of the March equinox and the constellation Libra is on the horizon at sunrise of the September equinox. In this era of greatest decay, humans cannot grasp anything beyond material life.

The precession of the equinoxes moves approximately 12,000 years in an ascending arc into an age of enlightenment, then 12,000 years in a descending arc into an age of ignorance. The entire cycle is illustrated on the chart "Precession of the Equinoxes and Arcs of the Yugas."

Precession of the Equinoxes and Arcs of the Yugas

The development of dharma (divine purpose and truth) waxes and wanes during each 12,000-year period. For the 1,200 years of Kali Yuga, dharma is one-quarter developed. During 2,400 years of Dwapara Yuga, dharma is one-half developed. For 3,600 years of Treta Yuga, dharma is three-quarters developed. During 4,800 years of Satya Yuga, dharma is fully developed.

If you looked out your window toward the east at sunrise of the September equinox in the year 11501 BC, the Sun was on the first degree of Aries: the fixed star Revati. That was the height of Satya Yuga, when humanity could comprehend spiritual knowledge beyond this visible world. Then, from 11501 BC to 6701 BC, as the Sun moved away from Vishnunabhi, humanity's intellectual power gradually diminished until the ability to grasp spiritual knowledge was lost.

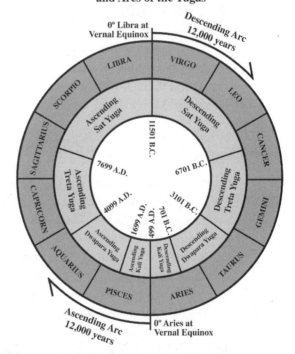

Precession of the Equinoxes and Arcs of the Yugas

From 6701 BC until 3101 BC, as Treta Yuga descended, gradually humanity lost its ability to understand divine magnetism, the source of the four forces of the physical world.

From 3101 BC to 701 BC, as Dwapara Yuga descended, humanity gradually lost its power to comprehend the fine matter of atoms, electrons and other invisible particles.

From 701 BC to 499 AD, the Sun passed through the descending phase of Kali Yuga and reached the point farthest from Vishnunabhi. Humanity's intellectual power diminished and could no longer comprehend invisible particles. It only grasped the three-dimensional world.

In 499 AD at sunrise on the September equinox, the Sun was at the first degree of Libra, and on the March equinox of the same year, the Sun was at the first degree of Aries. This was the darkest time of Kali Yuga, and of the entire cycle of 24,000 years. Disease was rampant, and humans had a shortened lifespan. The Dark Ages in Europe saw great oppression, slavery, wars, and ignorance.

From AD 499 to AD 1699, during the 1,200 years of ascending Kali Yuga, the human intellect gradually started to develop again. During the 100 years of the sandhyamsa (transition) at the end of the kali age, from 1599 to 1699, the existence of finer particles was discovered and political peace began to be established during the Renaissance.

From 1699 to 1899, the 200 years of the sandhya (transition) at the beginning of the ascending Dwapara age, there were great advances in science, spiraling exponentially in the 1800s. After 1899, when Dwapara sandhya (transition) was completed and ascending Dwapara Yuga began, discoveries about invisible realms of nature brought the greatest expansion of scientific knowledge in recorded history. The next 2,200 years of the ascending Dwapara Yuga will continue to bring tremendous knowledge of invisible particles.

What Is the "Age of Aquarius"?

Tropical astrology (the form of astrology Westerners are familiar with) is based on the tropical year: 365 days, 5 hours, 48 minutes, and 46 seconds of mean solar time. The tropical system is based solely upon the Sun's position in relation to the Earth along the ecliptic. Though Western astrologers believe the Sun begins its passage through the constellation of Aries every March equinox, heralding springtime, this hasn't been true since 499 AD due to the precession of the equinoxes. The tropical system of astrology arbitrarily cuts the sky into twelve sections—the Tropical Zodiac, which no longer coincides with the actual location of the constellations.

The Vedic system of astrology is based on the sidereal year, which lasts 365 days, 6 hours, 9 minutes, and 9.54 seconds of mean solar time: the true period of the Earth's orbit around the Sun, using the constellations of fixed stars as a reference frame. The disparity between the tropical and sidereal year is due to Earth's precession.

Please refer to the chart, "Precession of the Equinoxes and Arcs of the Yugas" on page 75. Because of the precession of the equinoxes, in the year 2000 AD, at sunrise on the March equinox, the Sun was actually located in the fixed-star constellation of Pisces—not Aries. That is why it is said we are now in the "Piscean Age" and the "Aquarian Age" is coming.

What signifies the "Dawning of the Age of Aquarius"? It is when, at sunrise on the March equinox, we observe the Sun entering the actual location of the fixed constellation of Aquarius. Sorry to have to inform all of you who think we are now in the "Aquarian Age," but the truth is that, according to actual astronomical calculations, this will not take place until 2438 AD.

Earth Years vs. God Years

Just in case you are already familiar with the yugas, and therefore you think my timespans are wrong, here is where I got my calculations: Current Indian astronomers believe the "years" constituting the yugas, which are described in Vedic scriptures, are "years of the Gods." According to this system, one Earth year is one God-day, and 360 Earth years is one God-year. Therefore Indian scholars contend that Kali Yuga lasts 432,000 years (1,200 Earth years times 360 God-days) and that the age began in 3100 BC. This would means that, as of 2000 AD, only 5,100 of the 432,000 years have passed since Kali Yuga began. According to this theory, the world is sinking into an age of darkest ignorance and has about 426,900 years to go until the nadir is reached. A dark future indeed for humanity!

This theory makes no sense, given the supposed quality of life in Kali Yuga described in the scriptures. In the past few centuries, human life span has increased, not decreased, particularly during the twentieth century, when life expectancy doubled. Humans are getting taller and smarter, not shorter and dumber. Tremendous breakthroughs have occurred in medicine, physics, and other branches of human knowledge. Understanding of the invisible realms is on the rise, not the decline.

In the book *The Holy Science,* Swami Sri Yukteswar, mentor of Paramahansa Yogananda, presents a very convincing argument that the "years" mentioned in the scriptures are actual Earth-years and that, under the dark cloud of Kali Yuga during the Middle Ages, scholars mistakenly invented the concept of "years of the Gods." Yukteswar believes that about 701 BC, wise men foresaw the coming Kali age and retreated to the Himalayas. With no one left in the courts to accurately calculate the calendar, the beginning of Kali Yuga was mistakenly counted from the beginning of the actual Dwapara age, about 3101 BC.

A Day in the Life of the Universe

According to the scriptures of ancient India, one thousand mahayugas (which I calculate to be 12,000,000 Earth years) constitute one day in the life of Lord Brahma, creator of the universe. This period is called a *kalpa*. During each night of Brahma (another 12,000,000 years), the entire universe is absorbed into Brahma's belly while he sleeps. This period is called *naimittika* (occasional) *pralaya* (dissolution)—an annihilation of the physical (*bhu*) and subtle (*svah*) worlds. Only the causal (*janah*) world remains. At the night's end, the physical and subtle worlds wake up again and continue another day of Brahma.

One day of Brahma is divided into fourteen *Manus*. Each Manu lasts 71.5 mahayugas, or about 858,000 years. During each of these periods, called *manvantaras*, a Manu holds power. Vaivasvata Manu is the Manu of the present manvantara, the seventh manvantara in the present kalpa.

One year of Brahma is 360 kalpas (days of Brahma), 4,320,000,000 Earth years. One lifetime of Brahma is called a *mahakalpa* (100 years of Brahma), 432,000,000,000 Earth years. One-half of Brahma's life is called a *parardha*. The first parardha of Brahma's current life span has expired and the second is now running. It commenced with the current kalpa. Brahma has lived 50 years of his present life and is on his 51st year. The present kalpa is called *Swata Varaha Kalpa*, the opening kalpa of the second parardha.

When Brahma's life is over, during a period called *mahapralaya* (great dissolution), also called *prakritic pralaya*, all the causal principles and three gunas are absorbed into Prakriti (primal matter) and return to a state of equilibrium (see pages 85–86).

The period of two parardhas (one lifetime of Brahma) is but a twinkling in the eye of the immutable, immortal, beginningless Lord, the soul of the universe. The absolute Brahman cyclically creates, sustains, and then reabsorbs the universe incessantly. The *sristi* (active creation) process systematically unfolds layers of creation, from subtle to gross. During mahapralaya, these layers fold back into their respective sources. Then the primal soul, father-mother God, remains in deep *samadhi* (transcendent state) for 432,000,000,000 Earth years, until the universe again emanates through the divine cosmic dance.

Both phases, creation and dissolution, are two aspects of one reality—absolute consciousness, never changing, transcendent and undiminished, just as a candle lit from another candle does not diminish the first candle's light.

"Nothingness is the building blocks of the universe." —*John Archibald Wheeler*

Cosmic Evolution

Tattvas (that-ness, truth, reality, or essential nature) can be defined as primary principles, states, or building blocks through which Lord Brahma, the creator God, constructs the universe. At the end of Brahma's lifetime, mahapralaya absorbs all 36 tattvas into their former causes.

In the Shaivite scriptural texts, Lord Shiva reveals to Shakti these 36 tattvas (principles) of cosmic and human evolution—the most complete analysis of nature yet devised by any philosophical system. The lower 25 categories are the same as Kapila's Samkhya system. The higher 11 are unique to Shaivism. Let us explore the tattvas now, as we discover how this universe comes to be.

Paramashiva

Our first consideration, beyond the realm of tattvas, is transcendental absolute consciousness, the ultimate reality, *parasamvit,* otherwise known as *Brahman* or *Paramashiva* (supreme auspiciousness).

Because something cannot come from nothing, the absolute must contain all things in fullness. Thus, its nature is:

Universal consciousness (*chit*).

Universal bliss (*ananda*).

Universal desire (*iccha*).

Universal intelligence (*jnana*).

Universal action (*kriya*).

> *"That (the invisible Brahman) is full, this (the visible Brahman) is full. This full (visible Brahman) proceeds from that full (invisible Brahman). On grasping the fullness of this full (visible Brahman) there is left that full (invisible Brahman)."*
> *—The Upanishads[3]*

The absolute is *sat-chit-ananda* (being-consciousness-bliss), without parts (*niskala*), therefore unproduced, indestructible, and motionless. It is without attributes (*nirguna*), therefore beyond space, time, and mind. It is oneness, without subject or object, realizable by ecstatic spiritual illumination.

> *"Only that which is, was in the beginning, one only, without a second. It thought, may I be many, may I grow forth." —The Upanishads[4]*

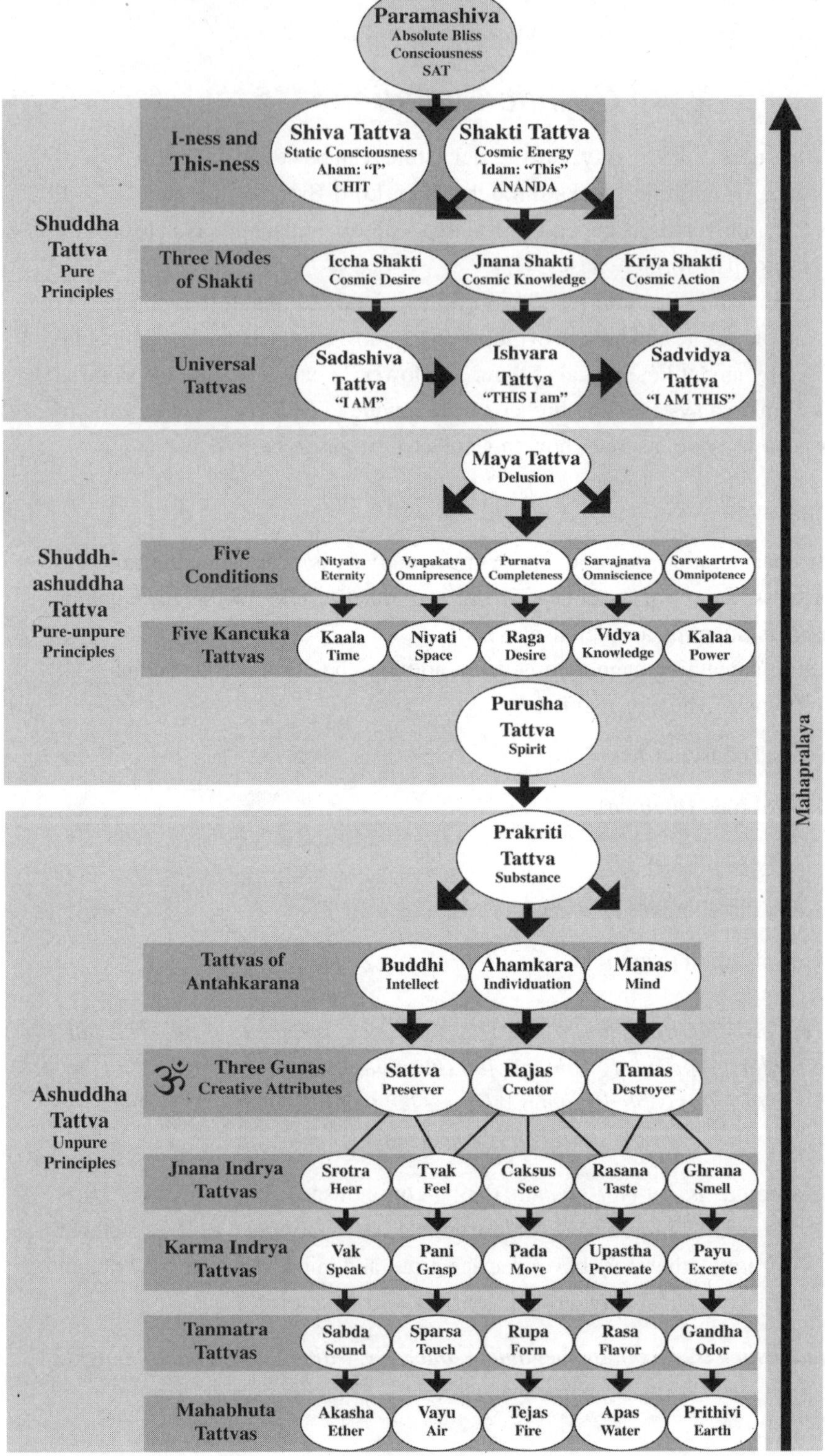

Paramashiva
Absolute Bliss
Consciousness
SAT

Shuddha Tattva Pure Principles

| I-ness and This-ness | **Shiva Tattva** Static Consciousness Aham: "I" CHIT | **Shakti Tattva** Cosmic Energy Idam: "This" ANANDA |

Three Modes of Shakti — **Iccha Shakti** Cosmic Desire — **Jnana Shakti** Cosmic Knowledge — **Kriya Shakti** Cosmic Action

Universal Tattvas — **Sadashiva Tattva** "I AM" — **Ishvara Tattva** "THIS I am" — **Sadvidya Tattva** "I AM THIS"

Maya Tattva Delusion

Shuddh-ashuddha Tattva Pure-unpure Principles

Five Conditions — **Nityatva** Eternity — **Vyapakatva** Omnipresence — **Purnatva** Completeness — **Sarvajnatva** Omniscience — **Sarvakartrtva** Omnipotence

Five Kancuka Tattvas — **Kaala** Time — **Niyati** Space — **Raga** Desire — **Vidya** Knowledge — **Kalaa** Power

Purusha Tattva Spirit

Prakriti Tattva Substance

Ashuddha Tattva Unpure Principles

Tattvas of Antahkarana — **Buddhi** Intellect — **Ahamkara** Individuation — **Manas** Mind

ॐ Three Gunas Creative Attributes — **Sattva** Preserver — **Rajas** Creator — **Tamas** Destroyer

Jnana Indrya Tattvas — **Srotra** Hear — **Tvak** Feel — **Caksus** See — **Rasana** Taste — **Ghrana** Smell

Karma Indrya Tattvas — **Vak** Speak — **Pani** Grasp — **Pada** Move — **Upastha** Procreate — **Payu** Excrete

Tanmatra Tattvas — **Sabda** Sound — **Sparsa** Touch — **Rupa** Form — **Rasa** Flavor — **Gandha** Odor

Mahabhuta Tattvas — **Akasha** Ether — **Vayu** Air — **Tejas** Fire — **Apas** Water — **Prithivi** Earth

Mahapralaya

Figure 7c. Cosmic Manifestation and Dissolution.

I-ness and This-ness

During the *sristi* (creation) phase, the universe appears as a wave on the surface of the ocean of consciousness. For universal mind to perceive the wave, a subject and object must exist. The subject (consciousness) is called *aham* (I AM) and object (power of consciousness) is *idam* (this). One cannot exist without the other. Whether manifest as sristi or unmanifest during pralaya, they are ever the same. During pralaya, they remain in latent equilibrium, ever ready to manifest. When the balance is disturbed, they emerge and cosmic evolution begins.

Shiva tattva is the subject (aham), and *shakti tattva* is the object (idam). Shakti is the force that causes duality by polarizing consciousness into positive and negative, aham and idam, subject and object.

Similarly, in the Bible, the primal man Adam is aham (shiva tattva) and primal woman Eve is idam (shakti tattva), who live in blissful oneness in Eden, until their primal balance is upset and duality arises when they eat the fruit of the tree of knowledge of good and evil (duality—the illusion of separation and identification with the ego). In this story, Eve, like Shakti, is responsible for eating the apple of that tree. Let us explore the principles—cosmic and human evolution—of the 36 tattvas:

1. Shiva Tattva

In *sat-chit-ananda,* Shiva is *chit* (superconsciousness), mind of God, the subject, knower, experiencer, center, and support of all. He pervades all other 35 tattvas. Shiva, the subject (aham), is passive and static, therefore dependent on Shakti (idam) for creation to occur.

Shiva is the seat of *para nada* (beyond sound, primal soundless sound). Though defined as sound, *nada* is actually movement, the first impulse or vibration arising from the perfect quiescence of the motionless absolute.

2. Shakti Tattva

Shakti, from the root *shak* (be capable of), is the kinetic aspect of consciousness, responsible for all activity. She is the object (idam), the mother of the universe, cause of motion and change. Shakti is the *ananda* (bliss) portion of sat-chit-ananda, the cause of form.

From Shakti issues *nada,* the initial stir of movement, which culminates as *shabdabrahman* or Brahman as sound. From nada proceeds *para bindu* (primal nucleus), through which consciousness expresses as form. Para bindu divides into three subsidiary bindus: *karyabindu,* white bindu (cosmic sperm), of the nature of

Shiva (consciousness); *bija*, red bindu (cosmic egg), of the nature of Shakti (creative energy); and *nada*, mixed bindu (conception), Shiva and Shakti together. These three bindus form a triangle called *kamakalaa* (divine desire for manifestation).

Nada (mixed), *bindu* (white), and *kalaa* (red) are states of Shakti, manifesting herself as three principal modes: *iccha shakti* (power of will), *jnana shakti* (power of knowledge), and *kriya shakti* (power of action). These three modes give rise to the next three tattvas.

3. Sadashiva Tattva

The term *sadashiva* derives from the roots, *sada* (always) and *shiva* (happy or prosperous). Sadashiva tattva is the first product or child of consciousness, the first thing with a cause. Thus it is the last product dissolved at the time of *mahapralaya* (great dissolution). Because sadashiva tattva is produced, it is destructible and not eternal. Only that which is without cause, and therefore beginningless and endless, can be indestructible and eternal.

Sadashiva consists of *aham* and *idam:* "I am this," with emphasis on "I." The subject aham becomes aware of itself in relation to the object idam. Here, universal desire *iccha shakti* (power of will) manifests.

4. Ishvara Tattva

Ishvara (God) tattva accounts for the subject *aham* recognizing the object *idam:* "THIS am I," with emphasis on "this" (idam). This is the stage of complete self-identification, as though waking from deep sleep. Here idam emerges into full view, and the divine glory of her being is recognized. Ishvara tattva arises from *jnana shakti* (power of knowledge).

5. Sadvidya Tattva

The word *sadvidya* consists of the roots *sat* (true) and *vid* (to know). It is the complete unity of the dual relationship "I AM THIS," without emphasizing the subject *aham* or object *idam*. Sadvidya tattva is the element deriving from *kriya shakti* (power of action).

Pure Tattvas

The previous five tattvas, from Shiva to Sadvidya, are classified as *shudha tattva* (pure tattvas), the realm of pure consciousness. In these five tattvas, subject and object remain one single unit, with the object viewed as part of the subject, just as the wave is part of the ocean.

6. Maya Tattva

The term *maya* (delusion) is derived from the root *ma* (measure), so it calculates, limits, separates, and divides. It severs "I" from "this" and splits oneness into duality.

Maya tattva accounts for the formless taking form, the infinite becoming finite. It "measures" and limits the infinite universal consciousness and brings mind and matter into being. Because maya tattva is uncaused and eternal, during mahapralaya, it persists in dormancy. During *sristi* (manifest creation), it appears as five sheaths (*pancha kancuka*) of *Purusha*.

7-11. Five Kancuka Tattvas

The five products of maya are called kancukas, from the Sanskrit root *kanj* (bind). These five kancukas derive from five universal modes of consciousness: *chit, ananda, iccha, jnana,* and *kriya*.

These five modes, each of which is displayed in one of the first five tattvas of *shiva, shakti, sadasiva, ishvara,* and *sadvidya,* give rise to the five universal, nondual conditions: *nityatva* (eternal existence or endlessness), *vyapakatva* (all-pervasiveness or omnipresence), *purnatva* (all-completeness), *sarvajnatva* (all-knowledge), and *sarvakartrtva* (all-powerfulness or omnipotence).

The five universal, limitless conditions, when "measured" or limited by maya, create five kancukas. By virtue of the paradoxical activity of the kancukas, the impossible becomes possible. Though the inviolate absolute can never divide, the infinite does become finite.

1. *Kaala* (time) limits the condition of beginningless, endless universal eternity. Therefore, it originates time, dividing into past, present, and future. Thus "time" limits "infinite eternity."

2. *Niyati* (to regulate, restrain) reduces the freedom and pervasiveness of omnipresent, unbounded universal consciousness. Therefore, it limits space, cause, and form. Thus "space" limits "infinite omnipresence."

3. *Raga* (to color) limits the totality of all-completeness and all-satisfaction. Therefore, it creates lack and originates desire and attachment, causing the objective world. Thus "desire" limits "infinite fulfillment."

4. *Vidya* (to know) limits the universal omniscience of all-knowingness. Therefore it is the origin of limited knowledge. Thus "knowledge" limits "infinite omniscience."

5. *Kalaa* (small part) limits the omnipotent universal power and authorship. Therefore it is the origin of limited power, creativity, aptitude, and skill. Thus "power" limits "infinite omnipotence."

You can better see these relationships in the following chart:

Tattva	Shakti	Guna	Infinite Experience	Kangula	Finite Experience
Shiva	Chit		Eternity (*Nityatva*)	Kaala	Time
Shakti	Ananda		All-Pervasiveness (*Vyapakatva*)	Niyati	Space
Sadashiva	Iccha	Sattva	All-Completeness (*Purnatva*)	Raga	Desire
Ishvara	Jnana	Tamas	All-Knowledge (*Sarvajnatva*)	Vidya	Limited Knowledge
Sadvidya	Kriya	Rajas	All-Powerfulness (*Sarvakartrtva*)	Kalaa	Limited Power

When maya and its products, the kancukas, sever *aham* (subject) from *idam* (object), then aham and idam view each other as the dual partners *Purusha* and *Prakriti* (see Human Evolution, below).

Pure-Impure Tattvas

In the previous six *shuddh-ashuddha* (pure-impure) *tattvas,* from *maya tattva* to *Purusha tattva,* the subject is separate from the object. These tattvas represent the condition that exists between pure unity (*shuddha tattva*) and the world of impure duality, composed of the remaining 24 tattvas.

Human Evolution

The third group of tattvas comprises 24 *ashuddha* (impure) *tattvas,* briefly outlined following. Please read my book *Exploring Meditation* for more details about these tattvas. The ancient Samkhya philosophy, founded by the seer Kapila, analyzes 25 principles of human evolution. Two uncaused realities, Purusha and Prakriti (stepped-down versions of aham and idam), account for all experience in the cosmos. They are not recognized as dual objects until *maya shakti* (power of illusion) separates aham from idam. Purusha is the uncaused spirit and Prakriti is the uncaused substance.

"Know that Prakriti and Purusha are both without beginning."
—*Lord Krishna*[5]

12. The Masculine Spirit: Purusha

Through *maya shakti* (power of illusion), Shiva's universal, infinite knowledge and power become Purusha, the universal subjectivity or spirit, the "I-ness" of the universe, the knower by which all is known, the silent witness that maintains continuity, the static background of the cosmos.

Purusha is cosmic Spirit, the uncaused that is not the cause of any new mode of being, the unevolved that does not evolve. The absolute, ultimate reality, the knower by which all is known, the silent witness, the static background that brings continuity to creation, Purusha is like the vacuum of outer space, with no gaseous material in it and no forces acting upon it. Purusha could be likened to "Father God."

13. The Feminine Substance: Prakriti

Whereas Purusha is the experiencer, Prakriti is what is experienced. She is Shiva's objective manifestation, cosmic substance, primary source, the actual creator of the phenomenal world. The roots of the word *Prakriti* are *pra* (before or first) and *kr* (to make or produce). The original substance from which life arises, she is primal nature and life energy.

Prakriti is cosmic Substance, the uncaused that is the cause of the entire manifest creation, the unevolved that evolves. Primal nature or energy, it is the original substance from which all life arises, into which all returns. It doesn't create anything new but manifests what it already is. It could be likened to "Mother Nature," "Mother God," "The Goddess," or "Shekinah."

Purusha and Prakriti never operate independently. They are soul and substance of creation, and all life arises from their relationship. Purusha has no vehicle to act independently, and Prakriti has no desire to act, because it is inanimate. Only by their marriage does creation occur.

Prakriti's Three Gunas

Prakriti embodies three modes of operation, called *gunas,* which give rise to the physical universe. Each has its own function to perform, and, for life to exist, all three must work together. The three gunas are *sattva* (stable maintaining, preserving aspect), *rajas* (active creating aspect), and *tamas* (destructive disassembling aspect). These gunas are stepped-down versions of the shaktis previously described: Tamas arises from *jnana shakti*, sattva from *iccha shakti*, and rajas from *kriya shakti*. (See Figure 7c on page 80.)

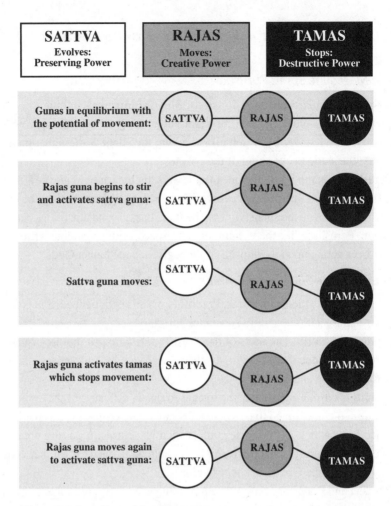

| SATTVA
Evolves:
Preserving Power | RAJAS
Moves:
Creative Power | TAMAS
Stops:
Destructive Power |

Gunas in equilibrium with the potential of movement: SATTVA — RAJAS — TAMAS

Rajas guna begins to stir and activates sattva guna: SATTVA — RAJAS — TAMAS

Sattva guna moves: SATTVA — RAJAS — TAMAS

Rajas guna activates tamas which stops movement: SATTVA — RAJAS — TAMAS

Rajas guna moves again to activate sattva guna: SATTVA — RAJAS — TAMAS

Figure 7d. Interplay of the Gunas.

Sattva guna personifies tranquility and purity, and it corresponds to the fifth and sixth chakras (*vishuddha* and *ajna*). Rajas guna causes motion and restlessness and corresponds to the third and fourth chakras (*manipura* and *anahata*). Tamas guna, the embodiment of inertia and dullness, corresponds to the first and second chakras (*muladhara* and *svadhishthana*).

During *pralaya* (dissolution), in primordial Prakriti's balanced state of equilibrium, the three gunas are in perfect equipoise, yet they maintain their discreet natures. Never do they merge into one. Always in subtle continual motion, even when unmanifest, they retain their latent potential to manifest. Prakriti is like a calm ocean with potential to produce waves but silent, until a force of nature starts the waves

THE BIG BOOK OF CHAKRAS AND CHAKRA HEALING

rolling. No outside cause is needed for the first stir of activity. The inherent subtle movement of the gunas, along with Purusha's desire for creation, is enough.

When the perfect balance gets disturbed, the phenomenal world appears by virtue of the gunas. Every aspect of creation has one guna predominant and the other two subordinate. The three gunas always operate together. Never can one guna exist alone or function separately.

Please refer to the chart "Interplay of the Gunas" on page 86. During the initial spur of the gunas, rajas generates the activity that initiates the role of sattva, which maintains that activity as it expands and evolves into a new stage. Then that activity is stopped by the inertia of tamas, which checks what has been created. Then rajas again kicks in to develop it into a new stage.

The cycle of creation, maintenance and destruction occurs by the cooperation of the gunas. Sattva and tamas govern the direction of the movement, while rajas provides energy for the movement. In short, everything in nature is born, lives, dies, and then transforms into a new state in the eternal dance of life, death, and rebirth.

"The fourfold order was created by Me according to the division of gunas and actions. Though I am its author, know Me to be the non-doer, immutable."
—Lord Krishna[6]

The Pranava (OM: ॐ)

These three gunas are personified by *OM* or *aum*: ॐ, the parent of all sounds. "AUM" contains all other vibrations by nature of its structure. The "A" sound represents sattva and the two upper chakras, the "U" represents rajas and the two middle chakras, and "M" represents tamas and the two lower chakras. When you speak the sound "A," your mouth, throat, and vocal chords open completely in a sound of utter expansion, representing sattva. When you speak "U," your lips thrust forward into a tight circle, representing continuous activity, signifying rajas. The sound "M" is formed by pressing the lips together, creating a humming sound. Your mouth closes completely and stops the expansion of sound altogether, symbolic of complete contraction, representing tamas. In this way, the entire range of sounds is embodied by "A-U-M."

"As an immortal principle, I am formless and as Creator, I possess a form. As an eternal principle, I have no beginning, middle or end; my name is OM."
—The Upanishads[7]

ENERGY CENTER (Chakra)	ROOT (Muladhara)	PELVIC (Svadhishthana)	NAVEL (Manipura)	HEART (Anahata)	THROAT (Vishuddha)
Abstract Knowing Sense (Jnana Indriya)	Smell (Ghrana)	Taste (Rasana)	See (Caksus)	Feel (Tvak)	Hear (Strotra)
Abstract Working Sense (Karma Indriya)	Excrete (Payu)	Procreate (Upastha)	Move (Pada)	Grasp (Pani)	Express (Vak)
Subtle Element (Tanmatra)	Odor (Gandha)	Flavor (Rasa)	Form (Rupa)	Touch (Sparsa)	Sound (Shabda)
Gross Element (Mahabhuta)	Earth (Prithivi)	Water (Apas)	Fire (Tejas)	Air (Vayu)	Ether (Akasha)
Sense Organ (Jnana Indriya)	Nose	Tongue	Eyes	Skin	Ears
Organ of Action (Karma Indriya)	Anus	Genitals	Feet	Hands	Voice
Sheath (Kosha)	Food (Annamaya)	Vital (Pranamaya)	Mental (Manomaya)	Intellect (Vijnanamaya)	Blissful (Anandamaya)
Body (Sharira)	Gross (Stula)	Subtle (Sukshma)	Subtle (Sukshma)	Subtle (Sukshma)	Causal (Karana)
World (Loka)	Material (Bhu)	Astral (Bhuvah)	Subtle (Svahah)	Middle (Maha)	Causal (Janah)
Attribute (Guna)	Inertia (Tamas)	Inertia (Tamas)	Activity (Rajas)	Activity (Rajas)	Purity (Sattva)
Absorption (Laya)	→				

Figure 7e. The Five Elemental Chakras.

THE BIG BOOK OF CHAKRAS AND CHAKRA HEALING

14-36. Tattvas

Through the action of the three gunas, Prakriti differentiates into the tattvas of *mahat* (cosmic intelligence), *ahamkara* (cosmic individuality), *manas* (cosmic mind), 10 *indriyas* (five abstract knowing-senses and five abstract working-senses), five *tanmatras* (sense objects), and five *mahabhutas* (elements). We have already explored some of these tattvas in the last chapter. They are explained in detail in Chapter 16 of *Exploring Meditation*. Therefore, that information is not repeated here.

Putting It All Together

Familiarity with these tattvas (principles) underlying both individual and cosmic life is essential to understanding the chakras. Let us take a moment to examine how the chakra system relates to the principles (*tattvas*), three bodies (*shariras*), and five sheath (*koshas*). Although there are hundreds of chakras in your body, in this book, we will explore the 14 most essential to life and spiritual awakening.

How do these chakras relate to the principles (tattvas) that comprise the universe? In fact, each of the 36 tattvas has its primary residence in one of the chakras. Let us discover these relationships now.

The Five Elemental Chakras

The first five chakras are connected with the fundamental constituents of matter. Therefore, each of them is associated with one of the five senses and five elements. They are also traditionally allied with the three gunas, threefold body, fivefold sheath, and five worlds. Figure 7e on page 88 clearly delineates these relationships.

The Seven Cerebral Chakras

The seven cerebral chakras, associated with your mental and spiritual faculties, are located in your head or above the skull. You will find some of the same sheaths and bodies allied with these chakras as with the lower five chakras. Please, do not let these associations confuse you. All the chakras, cerebral and elemental, are part of *sukshma sharira* (subtle body). The correlations with these cerebral chakras are explored in Figure 7f on page 90.

ENERGY CENTER (Chakra)	BROW (Ajna)	MIND (Manas)	MOON (Indu)	CAUSAL (Nirvana)	LIGHT (Guru)	CROWN (Sahasrara)	SUPREME (Bindu)
Principle (Tattva)	Mind (Chitta)	Sense Mind (Manas)	Intellect (Buddhi)	Ego (Ahamkara)	High Self (Atman)	God (Shiva)	Absolute (Brahman)
Sheath (Kosha)	Vital (Pranamaya)	Mental (Manomaya)	Intellect (Vijnanamaya)	Blissful (Anandamaya)	"I AM" (Atman)	God (Brahma)	Absolute (Nirvana)
Body (Sharira)	Subtle (Sukshma)	Subtle (Sukshma)	Subtle (Sukshma)	Causal (Karana)	"I AM" (Atman)	God (Brahma)	Absolute (Nirvana)
World (Loka)	Perfect (Tapah)	Perfect (Tapah)	Perfect (Tapah)	Perfect (Tapah)	Truth (Satyam)	Truth (Satyam)	Truth (Satyam)
Attribute (Guna)	Purity (Sattva)	Purity (Sattva)	Purity (Sattva)	Purity (Sattva)	Beyond Gunas	Beyond Gunas	Beyond Gunas
Absorption (Laya)							

Figure 7f. The Seven Cerebral Chakras.

Laya: Absorption

The purpose of Laya Yoga is attaining *samadhi* (transcendence) through *laya* (absorption). This process awakens the luminous kundalini and spiritualizes consciousness by absorbing all 36 tattvas (principles) stage by stage. This frees awareness from all that is unspiritual and leads to Brahman.

"Laya yoga is that in which chitta (sense-consciousness) undergoes laya, that is, becomes absorbed in deep concentration; there are many methods of achieving this: but the most effective is dhyana (deep meditation) on God in form, which can be done also while walking, standing, eating, and resting.
This is Laya Yoga." —Goswami[8]

In the first stage of laya (absorption), your mind is transformed through deep meditation using mantras—Sanskrit syllables that embody your personal deity (*ishtadevata*), in whatever form you believe that to be. This practice curtails mental fluctuations and sensory input, because your mind withdraws from sense objects as you move progressively deeper into meditation. Thereby your mind becomes highly refined and transforms into higher consciousness, *samprajnata samadhi* (transcendental superconsciousness).

In the second and final stage, called *asamprajnata samadhi,* even this superconsciousness is absorbed. Here your embodied spirit (*jiva*) unites with supreme Spirit *(Brahman),* and consciousness is completely absorbed.

The external world is composed of cosmic pranic energy, which has centers of operation in each stratum of existence. Consciousness is the link between all pranic energies, cosmic and earthly. Through cosmic mind (*mahat*), the outer world is known. The price of acquiring this knowledge is the masking of spiritual knowledge (as in the story of Adam and Eve, where "the knowledge of good and evil" is gained).

Spiritual knowledge can be regained (Adam and Eve can return to the Garden of Eden) when your mind, which has been tainted and diversified by sensory objects, withdraws from these objects and attains one-pointedness (inner concentration)—*bindu*.

Kundalini is supreme spiritual power. But when this eternal energy is entangled in the finite realm, she remains coiled at *muladhara* (root chakra). The upward movement of kundalini toward Paramashiva effects a spiritual flow to God in consciousness as the cosmic principles are systematically absorbed. In other words, as kundalini travels up the spine, piercing each chakra, she dissolves the tattvas in every chakra.

The tattvas are absorbed in reverse order from the sequence in which they initially manifested. In other words, absorption begins at muladhara, where kundalini absorbs the earth element, smell and excretion principles, *bija mantra* (seed sound) *lam,* deity Brahma and Shakti Dakini. (See Chapter 9.)

Similarly, kundalini travels up sushumna nadi, continuing to absorb all the elements of the first five chakras. Then, at the sixth chakra (ajna), she absorbs the lower mind. In manas chakra, she absorbs the sense consciousness. In indu chakra, she absorbs the intellect. In nirvana chakra, she absorbs the ego. This is her last phase of absorption on the sensory-mental level.

After the tattvas are absorbed, kundalini moves toward sahasrara (thousand-petaled lotus). There, spiritual consciousness is itself absorbed by kundalini and becomes *mahat*—superconsciousness fully illumined by kundalini, free from limiting elements. This is *samprajnata samadhi.*

Finally, kundalini is herself absorbed into supreme Spirit when she unites with Paramashiva and becomes one and the same as he. This is *mahalaya* (great absorption), the final stage of *asamprajnata samadhi,* the highest state of spiritual enlightenment and end of all seeking.

The cosmic phantom show of this universe comes into being by *maya* (that which does not exist, and which limits the limitless by "measuring") and is absorbed by *pralaya* (dissolution)—at the end of time, and time after time. The specter of your individual life is generated by the hallucination of *avidya* (ignorance) and is absorbed by *laya* (absorption) as kundalini moves upward, piercing your chakras—at the end of your evolutionary cycle, the final act of your final show.

Later in this book, you will study details of the chakras and their elements (tattvas) and thereby gain greater understanding of this absorption process.

"He wished, may I be many, may I grow forth. He brooded over himself (like a man performing penance). After he had thus brooded, he sent forth (created) all, whatever there is. Having sent forth, he entered into it. Having entered it, he became sat (what is manifest) and tyat (what is not manifest), defined and undefined, supported and not supported, (endowed with) knowledge and without knowledge (as stones), real and unreal. The Sattya (true) became all this whatsoever, and therefore the wise call it (the Brahman) Sattya (the true)."
—*The Upanishads*[9]

Chapter Eight

DISCOVERING YOUR CHAKRAS

"And he dreamed, and behold a ladder set up on the earth,
and the top of it reached to heaven: and behold the angels of God
ascending and descending on it."
—Judeo-Christian Bible[1]

Y our chakras are *pranic* (vital energy) centers in your subtle body (*sukshma sharira*)—hubs where many *nadis* (conduits of prana) intersect. These are called *chakras* (wheels) because they appear as vortexes of pranic energy at specific points in your subtle body. Their function is to control pranic circulation throughout your system.

The ancient scriptures count hundreds of such energy centers. However, seven primary chakras are responsible for maintaining life in your body and for sense perception, mental activity, and higher awareness:

> *Muladhara* (root chakra)
>
> *Svadhishthana* (pelvic chakra)
>
> *Manipura* (navel chakra)
>
> *Anahata* (heart chakra)
>
> *Vishuddha* (throat chakra)
>
> *Ajna* (brow chakra)
>
> *Sahasrara* (crown chakra)

In addition to these seven major chakras, seven other important chakras exist in your subtle body: *hrit chakra* in the lower part of your heart, *talu chakra* in your palate, *manas chakra* in your pineal area, *indu chakra* in your brain, *nirvana chakra* at the top of your skull, *guru chakra* in the lower part of *sahasrara,* and *supreme bindu* in the upper center of *sahasrara.*

Below muladhara (root chakra) are seven lower chakras: *atala* (at the hips, governing fear and lust), *vitala* (thighs: anger, resentment, blame), *sutala* (knees: jealousy, inadequacy), *talatala* (calves: confusion, willfulness, greed, deceit), *rasatala* (ankles: selfishness, animalistic nature), *mahatala* (feet: without conscience, inner blindness), and the lowest, *patala* (soles of feet: malice, murder, torture, hatred). Just as the seven major chakras are associated with the seven heavens, these seven lower chakras are associated with netherworlds below the earth plane, which share the same names as these lower chakras. These realms are inhabited by beings of lower evolution than humans.

Location of the Chakras

Eleven of these 14 chakras are located along the corridor of the energy tube *chitrini nadi*, nested within *sushumna nadi*, the main conduit of pranic energy in your *sukshma sharira* (subtle body). (See Figure 5c on page 46.) The other three chakras are above your skull.

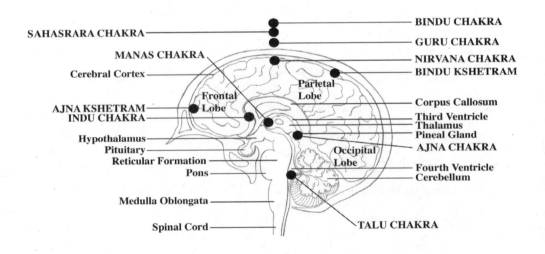

Figure 8a. Chakra Points and Kshetram in Brain.

THE BIG BOOK OF CHAKRAS AND CHAKRA HEALING

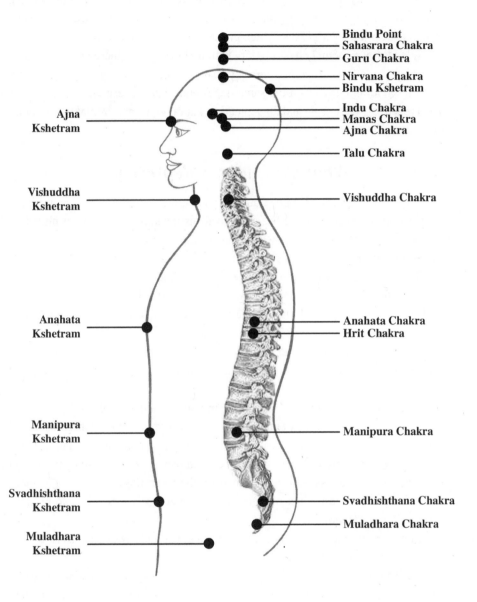

Bindu Point
Sahasrara Chakra
Guru Chakra
Nirvana Chakra
Bindu Kshetram
Indu Chakra
Manas Chakra
Ajna Chakra
Talu Chakra
Vishuddha Chakra
Anahata Chakra
Hrit Chakra
Manipura Chakra
Svadhishthana Chakra
Muladhara Chakra

Ajna Kshetram
Vishuddha Kshetram
Anahata Kshetram
Manipura Kshetram
Svadhishthana Kshetram
Muladhara Kshetram

Figure 8b. Location of Chakra Points and Kshetram.

Your chakras are generally encased by your vertebral column or brain near the area governing the activity represented by that chakra. For instance, your navel chakra is near the solar plexus, which governs digestive functions.

In addition to actual chakra points within chitrini nadi, there are frontal trigger points called *chakra kshetram,* physical counterparts lying directly in front of corresponding chakras on the same horizontal plane. These are used in Kriya Yoga practices. Figures 8a and 8b depict the chakra points and frontal trigger point locations.

What Do Chakras Represent?

Each chakra indicates specific subtle frequency levels and progressively higher states of consciousness, from basic survival instincts, associated with muladhara (root chakra), to intuitive powers in ajna (third eye area), and finally spiritual enlightenment in sahasrara (crown chakra).

Thus, the three lower chakras (root, pelvic, and navel) are concerned with material life and bodily survival. The upper chakras (throat, third eye, and crown) deal with spiritual life and higher creative expression. The key that unlocks this entire system is the middle chakra—heart chakra.

The chakras embody your spiritual path. These seven gates to higher consciousness open your ascent from limited awareness to expressing your full potential.

The first three states are sleep, dreaming, and waking, depicted by the three lower chakras. The transcendental state, *turiya* (fourth), is pure consciousness—the key to unlocking spiritual awakening. This is seated in the heart chakra. Three higher states of consciousness—cosmic consciousness, God consciousness, and Brahman consciousness—are represented by the three upper chakras. For more information about these states of consciousness, read my books *Divine Revelation* and *Exploring Meditation.*

Figure 8c outlines the connection between upper and lower chakras as well as their correlation with states of consciousness.

Activating pranic energy in your chakras induces corresponding states of awareness. In turn, specific levels of consciousness cause prana to predominate in particular chakras. Therefore, stimulating your chakras through yogic practices transforms awareness, widens vision, and awakens your true nature. Later in this book you will learn how.

	CHAKRA NAMES	FUNCTION	DRIVE	LEVEL OF CONSCIOUSNESS
Lower Chakras	Root: Muladhara	Lower Emotion: Instinct	Basic Survival	Deep Sleep State
	Pelvic: Svadhisthana	Lower Creativity: Sexual	Physical Procreation	Dream State
	Navel: Manipura	Lower Self: Egoism	Will Power	Waking State
Gateway	Heart: Anahata	Opening to Spirituality	Awakening	Transcendental Consciousness
Upper Chakras	Throat: Vishuddha	Higher Creativity: Artistic	Creative Expression	Cosmic Consciousness
	Third Eye: Ajna	Higher Emotion: Perception	Higher Knowledge	God Consciousness
	Crown: Sahasrara	Higher Self: Altruism	Union with God	Unity Consciousness

Figure 8c. Chakras and Levels of Consciousness.

Chakra Symbolism Worldwide

The seven major chakras have been depicted in many traditions and cultures. According to Judeo-Christianity, the world was created in seven days, and there are seven days in the week. The tabernacle, a symbol of spiritual enlightenment, is built in seven months. Christian scriptures count seven stars, seven candlesticks, seven angels, and seven churches.[2]

The Hindus speak of seven levels of consciousness, seven sisters (stars in the Pleiades), seven *rishis* (holy seers), and seven planets in *Jyotish* (Hindu astrology). The Islamic religion recounts Mohammed passing through seven heavenly realms on his journey to Allah (God).

According to Pythagoras, seven celestial spirits control humans. Ptolemy symbolized the chakras as seven spheres rotating around planet earth, which represents sahasrara (crown chakra), the *crystallinum primum* (crystal heaven). Shakespeare speaks of seven ages through which humans must pass.[3] According to numerology, the number seven represents humanity.

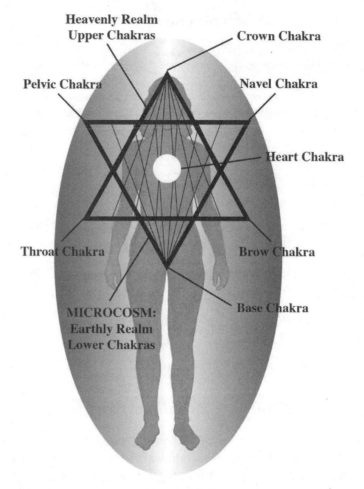

Heavenly Realm
Upper Chakras

Crown Chakra

Pelvic Chakra

Navel Chakra

Heart Chakra

Throat Chakra

Brow Chakra

MICROCOSM:
Earthly Realm
Lower Chakras

Base Chakra

Figure 8d. Star of David and Seven Rays: Heaven on Earth.

The seven chakras or energy centers are symbolized in Judaism by the menorah, a candlestick with seven lights. The Jewish Star of David symbol is made of two triangles. One with apex pointed upward represents the three higher chakras (heaven, the macrocosm, consciousness), and the lord of light, the white Jehovah.

The other triangle, with apex downward, represents the three lower chakras (earth, the microcosm, humankind), and the lord of reflections, the black Jehovah.

This symbol, therefore, indicates the relationship between higher and lower worlds, macrocosm and microcosm, heaven and earth, spirituality and material-

THE BIG BOOK OF CHAKRAS AND CHAKRA HEALING

ism. This same hexagonal star represents the element of air in anahata (heart chakra).

Seven creative powers or rays emanate from the upper white Jehovah (consciousness). These represent seven levels of awareness associated with the seven energy centers arising from the fountainhead, the bindu point at crown chakra.

The seven rays diverge from the source, giving rise to the universe. They then converge back to a point of focus in humankind.

Often, chakras are symbolized by lotus flowers, representing the ascent of human consciousness from ignorance to enlightenment. The lotus first grows in mud, representing ignorance. It seeks to grow out of the water through effort and aspiration. Finally, the lotus reaches the direct sunlight, symbolizing illumination. When the lotus blossoms, even though mud is all around, the flower remains untouched. This is higher awareness, unsullied by the mud of material life.

Chakras and Evolution

Your gross and subtle bodies, explored in Chapter 6, correspond to specific chakras as well as stages of individual and group spiritual evolution. These evolutionary levels are like rungs of a ladder with seven years between each rung. Let us look at the relationship between the chakras and your gross and subtle bodies (shariras), sheaths (koshas), and evolutionary phases.

1. Muladhara: Annamaya Kosha

Muladhara (root chakra) means "root support," the foundation of your expression as an individual. Entirely focused on personal survival, muladhara's motive is obtaining food, drink, shelter, and other basic needs. This chakra is self-centered, and its predominant drive is attaining security by continuing the family line and acquiring material objects, money, friends, and property. The outer world is seen as a means to obtain security.

The main focus of your first seven years of life is experience of *stula sharira* (gross body) and muladhara chakra. Bodily growth forms the foundation for health during those first seven years. If your food sheath does not fully develop, you will be sickly throughout life.

Many people never progress beyond *annamaya kosha* (food sheath) and muladhara. Obsessed with survival and security, their interests never exceed eating, drinking, and other instincts. They give no credence to the spiritual world and are incapable of subtle experiences.

Civilizations are obsessed with food, drink, survival, and basic subsistence when the majority of the population is arrested in muladhara chakra.

2. Svadhishthana: Pranamaya Kosha

Svadhishthana (pelvic chakra) means "abode of the self " and is the basis of birth in human form. It is associated with your subconscious storehouse of latent impressions called *samskaras*. Without these seeds of desire, you would never take human birth. Svadhishthana is the seat of instinctive drives and cravings welling up from unconscious depths. Thus, this chakra is associated with seeking pleasures and sensations through sensory stimuli and sexual contact. This chakra views the world according to how much pleasure it can bring.

Svadhishthana is associated with *pranamaya kosha* (etheric sheath), which develops during the period from ages seven to 14, when the emotions are foremost and puberty arises.

Today most people never mature beyond this stage. Engulfed in emotional needs and oblivious to reasoning or insight, their need for enjoyment of physical pleasures outweighs all other considerations.

When emotions do not fully develop by age 14, problems associated with this chakra will develop.

Those societies with the majority of the population stuck in svadhishthana are centered on sexual pleasures, including their artistic and cultural expressions in books, paintings, film, poetry, and clothing.

3. Manipura: Manomaya Kosha

Manipura (navel chakra), which means "city of lustrous jewels," is the hub of an incredibly complex network of nadis (energy conduits) that conduct pranic energy throughout your body and control bodily functions. Therefore it is an important center of vital energy.

Manipura is the center of self-assertion and domination, which satisfies needs by controlling and manipulating situations and people. This is expressed in motives to gain wealth, prestige, power, status, and recognition. Manipura is focused on external activities, where the world is seen as an object to provide personal power and fulfill worldly ambitions.

This chakra is associated with *manomaya kosha* (sheath of the lower mind). Between ages 14 and 21, its greatest development occurs. At this stage, individuals learn to use logic and reasoning to make choices. Once they become adults, they are expected to be responsible. Now they are allowed to vote, drink liquor, and drive. Few people evolve past this level. Those stuck in manipura have no awareness of Spirit and discredit experiences of higher consciousness.

A nation in which most people have developed their mental sheath will emphasize the power of reasoning, as did the ancient Greeks.

4. Anahata: Vijnanamaya Kosha

Anahata (heart chakra), meaning "unstruck sound," is the center of human consciousness (*jivatama*). Considered the best chakra for meditation, anahata purifies and transmutes emotions into intense devotion.

Anahata chakra accepts and loves others unconditionally. Each person is viewed as a unique embodiment of perfection, acting according to his or her own nature. Anahata accepts both positive and negative qualities.

As the seat of consciousness, this chakra is the gateway to higher awareness. It is allied with *vijnanamaya kosha* (intellect sheath), key to spiritual discernment and opening higher consciousness. This opening is effected by unconditional love, understanding, and acceptance without the emotional coloration characteristic of manomaya kosha (lower mind).

Your vijnanamaya kosha (intellect sheath) should theoretically develop from age 21 to 28, the best period to expand awareness, develop psychic abilities, and begin a spiritual path. However, most people do not avail themselves of this opportunity.

When many individuals fully develop their intellect sheath, such a civilization focuses on acquiring supernormal powers and intuitive knowledge. However, intuition can be deceptive, because it is subject to individual interpretation, imagination, or wishful thinking.

5. Vishuddha: Anandamaya Kosha

Vishuddha (throat chakra), meaning "purification," the center that purifies and harmonizes all opposites, brings understanding, balance, equanimity, and perfection.

Vishuddha chakra is the stage of awareness where all experiences are welcomed without judgment. Rather than resisting negative experiences, you relax, let go, and accept all circumstances, no matter how difficult. This integrated awareness raises consciousness to a blissful state.

Anandamaya kosha (bliss body) is the sheath associated with vishuddha. Through this body, the world becomes a heavenly experience. By age 35, the anandamaya kosha should be completely developed and awareness fully established in cosmic consciousness.

6. Ajna: Atman Sharira

The ajna (eyebrow chakra), meaning "command," is the center of wisdom, higher consciousness, self-realization, and self-authority. Here, awareness opens to the divine. Ajna develops intuition, insight, super-sensory perception, direct revelation, higher voice, and *siddhis* (perfections)—supernormal powers. It is the center of telepathy.

The third eye chakra is widely depicted in many cultures. The medieval mystic Eckhart stated, "The eye with which I see the supreme is the same as that with which it sees me."[4] The Greek philosopher Plato wrote, "In all men there is the eye of the soul, which can be re-awakened by the correct means. It is far more precious than ten thousand physical eyes."[5]

The Eye of Providence is on the back of the one dollar bill as the capstone of a pyramid. And the All-Seeing Eye is a symbol associated with freemasonry. It is seen in myths and fables as Cyclops. It is represented in the Kabbalah as *Ain Soph,* a closed eye directed inward toward higher awareness.

In statues of Buddha and other deities, a jewel is placed between the eyebrows. Hindu deities are portrayed with a *tilaka* (spot of red *kumkum* powder) on the forehead. Married women in India are traditionally required to wear the tilaka. Now it is fashionable for unmarried women also.

Because ajna is the seat of purified *buddhi* (subtle intellect), when it opens, mental fickleness and fluctuations disappear. The mind becomes a perfect instrument of discernment. In this elevated state of awareness, vestiges of imperfection burn away.

Ajna is associated with *atman sharira* ("I AM" body), which brings God-realization. This should ideally be fully developed by age 42 in an enlightened civilization.

To learn more about the ajna chakra and how to develop it, please read my book *Awaken Your Third Eye*.

7. Sahasrara: Brahma Sharira

Sahasrara (crown chakra) means "thousandfold," the awareness of universality, bringing Unity Consciousness, oneness with universality, totality of the inexpressible infinite. This chakra is the crown of expanded consciousness, culmination of the spiritual journey, full realization of supreme knowledge in spiritual enlightenment.

In this state, the experiencer, experience, and experienced are one and the same. Therefore sahasrara transcends experience. Shiva and Shakti live in eternal union. Subject (*aham*) and object (*idam*) merge in wholeness.

This chakra represents the totality of Brahman, the center of everything in infinite nothingness. It is both formless (*nirakara*) and in form (*akara*), yet transcends both. It is beyond the beyond (*paratparam*), yet right here now. It is named *nirvana, satori, kaivalya, turiya, samadhi, baqua, Ain Soph, Tao,* heaven, and others.

The *Brahma sharira* (Brahma body), associated with full illumination and liberation in sahasrara, should theoretically develop by age 49.

8. Supreme Bindu: Nirvana Sharira

The final body, called *nirvana sharira,* beyond the phenomenal world, is associated with supreme bindu point in upper sahasrara, source of all other chakras.

Bindu (to split or divide) is the center where oneness splits into duality, unifying the infinite with the finite. Therefore it is the ultimate cosmic seed origin of the universe. A void without dimension, the gateway to nothingness with full potential of becoming everything, bindu is an infinitesimal point of infinite potential, abstract, inexplicable, and incomprehensible, a mysterious focal point where infinity and zero, fullness and nothingness, coexist.

> *"Nature is an infinite sphere in which the center is everywhere,*
> *the circumference is nowhere." —Blaise Pascal[6]*

Bindu is symbolized by both a full moon and crescent moon. In the Sanskrit language the bindu point is a dot above the letters, as in the mantra OM: ॐ. This dot is called *visarga* (drop). The crescent moon *(nada)* under the point represents one of the moon's *kalas* (phases), of which there are 16.

Bindu is often called *bindu visarga* (falling drop), indicating drops of ambrosia continually trickling from sahasrara, the fountainhead of *amrit* (nectar), which flows down sushumna nadi. Because amrit is bliss, bindu is the abode of uninterrupted bliss. By balancing ida and pingala, bindu floods the sushumna passage with nectar, often signified by the Ganges (nectar) river flowing from the crescent moon on top of Lord Shiva's head (at his bindu trigger point—see Figure 11c on page 139).

Myriad objects in the universe appear when the potential of underlying consciousness accumulates at bindu points. Every object, large or small, has a bindu

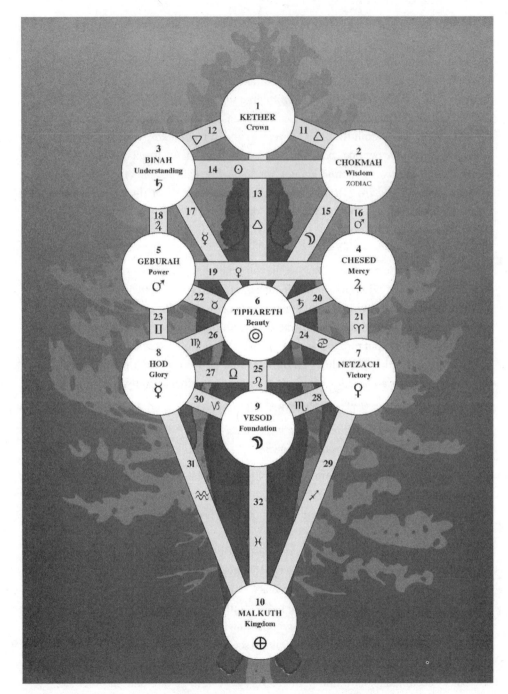

Figure 8e. The Sephiroth.

seed from which it arises. The cosmic bindu is *hiranyagarbha* (golden egg, womb of creation). Bindu is the means of both expressing and limiting consciousness. The shapeless assumes shape through bindu, which determines the pattern and characteristics of each object.

Thus, every object is intimately tied to consciousness through the intermediary of bindu. Each object evolves into material form at *sristi* (creation) through bindu and withdraws back to the source at *pralaya* (dissolution) through bindu. *Yoga* (union) means returning to the source by merging Shakti (individual) with Shiva (consciousness) through bindu in sahasrara.

In Kabbalah, bindu is called "I AM." This is the *kether* (crown), because it creates all things and links the manifest with the unmanifest. Known as the primordial dot, all things emanate through it.

"When the concealed of the concealed wished to reveal himself, he first of all made a single point; the infinite was entirely unknown, and spread no light until the luminous point violently broke into manifested reality." —Kabbalah[7]

According to Kabbalah, nine *sephiroth* evolve from kether (bindu). These sephiroth are the chakra points on the tree of life. Thus kether is the source of the light of consciousness, which progressively filters down to the other sephiroth (chakras).

The key to spiritual enlightenment is to return to bindu. Rather than continually vacillating in sensory perceptions, your mind draws inward and returns to concentrated focus of such intense one-pointedness that it becomes a point (bindu). When all mental fluctuations (internal chatter) cease, then yoga (integration) is attained.

"Yoga is the suppression of modifications of the mind." —Sage Patanjali[8]

Nada Yoga

Nada Yoga is a distinct path of yoga, founded by the ancient sage Gorakhnath. The term *nada* (flow) means the flow of subtle vibration through which consciousness expresses itself. However, *nada* usually translates as "sound."

Nada is also called *shabda* or *surat* (sound), *nama* (name), *akashvani* (sound of the ether), *dhun* (tune), *nad-I-asmani* (heavenly harmony), *vani* (word), the Word, Logos, and so forth. The Zoroastrians call it *sraosha*. The "music of the spheres" of Pythagoras is played by the universe as one chord with a single string connected at the lower end to matter, the upper end to pure consciousness, and in between all layers of subtle energy or nada. Socrates and other Greek mystics used nada as a means to transcendence.

According to ancient yogis, *nada brahman* (transcendental sound) is the source of the entire manifested world. From Brahman (the absolute) through its own power *(Shakti)*, *nada* or vibration (The Word) is emitted. From the Word or name *(nama)*, the form *(rupa)* arises.

> *"In the beginning was the Word, and the Word was with God,*
> *and the Word was God." —Apostle John*[9]

The modern field of theoretical physics, with superstring, brane, and M-theories, now postulates the universe consists of solidified vibration of various frequencies. This reality was known by the sages of ancient India, who believed the "three bindus," *kalaa* (limitation), *bindu* (seed), and *nada* (subtle vibration), work together to form the universe. Bindu is derived from *Shiva maya*, kalaa derives from *Shakti maya*, and nada comes from *Shiva-Shakti* maya.

Kalaa causes the infinite potential of consciousness to contract and accumulate in a bindu (seed) of every object. Nada flows through bindu to each object. Because nada links consciousness to all objects, by tracing nada back to its source, you can return to the infinite through bindu. When you withdraw your attention from sensory objects, and your awareness is absorbed by bindu, then samadhi is experienced.

Four basic levels of nada are discussed in the ancient scriptures:

Vaikhari (gross audible sound): heard by your ears and created by objects struck together. Vaikhari is the plane of the spoken word.

Madhyama (in the middle): rarified form of sound, halfway between gross and subtle nada. At this stage, nada begins to crystallize from formless nada. The Yoni Mudra practice on page 225 can help you sense subtle madhyama sounds.

Pashyanti (radiant sound): nada (sound) with specific colors that are seen with inner vision but not heard. The seat of pashyanti is in deep levels beyond audible nada. My books *Divine Revelation, Awaken Your Divine Intuition,* and *The Power of Auras* can help you experience pashyanti.

Para (beyond): transcendent or unmanifest sound, the source of nada, heard in higher states of consciousness, beyond normal perception. Para nada's high rates of vibration are associated with samadhi. The silent *anahata nada* (unstruck sound) is seated in anahata chakra.

Mantras are used in meditation as vehicles for the mind to travel from the gross level of nada to subtler nada, until even the subtlest level is transcended and the mind stands alone in pure consciousness. To experience para nada, you may use the Divine Revelation Guided Meditation CD or mp3, available from *www.drsusan.org*.

Mantras of the Chakras

Because chakras are similar to wheels, radiating energies like spokes from their centers, they are compared to lotus flowers, with petals radiating from the central pistils. In each chakra, the petals are arranged in a specific order. The first petal is always in the northeast (upper right) corner.

The petals of the first six major chakras vibrate with resonant frequencies called *bija mantras* (seed sounds)—letters of the Sanskrit alphabet. All 50 letters appear on the 50 petals of these chakras: The first chakra (muladhara) has four petals, the second (svadhishthana) has six petals, the third (manipura) has 10, the fourth (anahata) has 12, the fifth (vishuddha) has 16, and the sixth (ajna) has two.

These 50 letters ultimately descend from sahasrara chakra, where all seed sounds arise from Pranava—the sound *OM* or *aum*: ॐ—the vibration from which the entire universe springs. Thus, in guru chakra, in lower sahasrara, all 50 letters are embedded. These 50 letters are also strung like beads on the thread of kundalini, the energy that rises up the spine, as it activates the chakras, vibrating the energy of the 50 mantras.

Sound in the form of mantras is used extensively in Tantra Yoga to raise kundalini. The cosmic sound "AUM" symbolizes *kundalini shakti* (power of kundalini). This transcendental sound arises in sahasrara and descends through the chakras to muladhara, where it manifests as gross matter. The letter "A" represents *sattva guna* and the upper chakras, "U" indicates *rajas guna* and the middle chakras, and "M" symbolizes *tamas guna* and the lower chakras, "AUM" represents the raising of kundalini through the chakras.

In the symbol *OM*: ॐ, the dot or bindu represents the bindu trigger point at *brahmarandhra,* the aperture at the top of the skull (see pages 44, 94, and 109), which symbolizes transcendent nada (para). The crescent moon represents the ethereal nada (pashyanti) from brow chakra to throat chakra. The upper curve

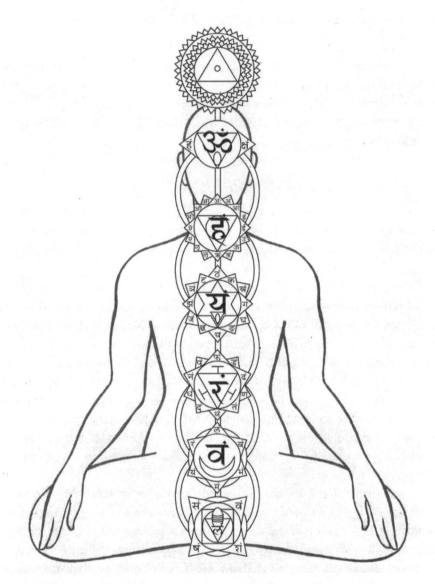

Figure 8f. Sanskrit Mantras in Chakra Lotuses.

THE BIG BOOK OF CHAKRAS AND CHAKRA HEALING

Chakras 3 and 4:
Madhyama

Chakras 1 and 2:
Vaikhari

Bindu Point: Para

Chakras 5 and 6:
Pashyanti

Figure 8g. The Temple of God: Vibrational Levels of Nada.

represents subtle nada (madhyama) from throat to navel chakra. The lower curve represents gross nada (vaikhari) from navel chakra to root chakra. The entire universe is in the spinal cord. Thus it is the temple of God.

All the syllables of the Sanskrit alphabet end with the letter ṁ. That letter translates as "within myself." Thus these 50 letters vibrate within your subtle body's chakra system. The alphabet begins with the subtlest vibration and ends with the grossest. This is the same order in which babies learn to produce sounds, and it reflects how consciousness descends to manifest the universe.

The Sanskrit alphabet starts with vowels and then continues with consonants pronounced in different tongue positions, in this order: guttural, palatal, cerebral, dental, and finally labial. The tongue is the endpoint of a nadi called saraswati nadi, which runs from root chakra through the spine along sushumna nadi. The practice of khechari mudra (see page 223) opens this nadi for spiritual development.

In Vedic astrology, *nakshatras* are considered *shaktis* (powers) of the moon: 27 segments of the ecliptic through which the Moon passes as it orbits the Earth. Figure 8h on page 110 lists the 50 vibrational sounds on the chakra petals, in alphabetical order, connected to the nakshatras (appearing along the ecliptic in the same sequence) and their related planets. A Vedic astrologer can cast your horoscope to find your *nakshatra* (birth star). Then in Figure 8h, you can discover your corresponding mantra. You are connected to the universe: As above, so below!

CHARKA	MANTRAS ON PETALS	NAKSHATRA: "BIRTH STAR"	PLANET
Ajna OM: ॐ Third Eye	ham: हं	Uttara Bhadrapada: "Latter Auspicious One"	Saturn
	ksham: क्षं	Revati: "Wealthy"	Mercury
Vishuddha ham: हं Throat Chakra	am: आं ah: अः	Revati: "Wealthy"	Mercury
	a: अ aa: आ	Ashwini: "Owning Horses"	Ketu
	e: इ ee: ई	Bharani: "To Bear"	Venus
	u: उ uu: ऊ	Krittika: "Razor, Cutter"	Sun
	kre: ऋ kree: ॠ lre: ऌ lree: ॡ	Rohini: "The Growing, The Red"	Moon
	ye: ए	Mrigashira: "The Deer's Head, Hunting"	Mars
	yai: ऐ	Ardra: "The Moist One"	Rahu
	o: ओ ow: औ	Punarvasu: "Return to Goodness and Light"	Jupiter
Anahata yam: यं Heart Chakra	kam: कं	Pushya: "Nourishing, The Flower"	Saturn
	kham: खं gam: गं	Ashlesha: "Entwiner, Embracer"	Mercury
	gham: घं nam: ङं	Magha: "The Great One"	Ketu
	cham: चं	Purva Phalguni: "The Former Red One"	Venus
	chcham: छं	Uttara Phalguni: "The Latter Red One"	Sun
	jam: जं jham: झं nam: ञं	Hasta: "The Hand"	Moon
	tam: टं tham: ठं	Citra: "The Bright, The Distinguished"	Mars

Figure 8h. Chakra-Petal Mantras, Nakshatras, and Planets.

CHAKRA	MANTRAS ON PETALS	NAKSHATRA: "BIRTH STAR"	PLANET
Manipura ram: रं Navel Chakra	dam: डं	Swati: "The Independent One"	Rahu
	dham: दं nam: णं	Vishakha: "The Forked One"	Jupiter
	tam: तं tham: थं dam: दं	Anuradha: "Additional Radha"	Saturn
	dham: धं	Jyeshtha: "The Eldest"	Mercury
	nam: नं pam: पं pham: फं	Mula: "The Root"	Ketu
Svadishthana vam: वं Pelvic Chakra	bam: बं	Purva Ashadha: "The Former Undefeated"	Venus
	bham: भं	Uttara Ashadha: "The Latter Undefeated"	Sun
	mam: मं	Shravana: "The Ear"	Moon
	yam: यं ram: रं	Dhanishtha: "The Wealthiest"	Mars
	lam: लं	Shatabhisha: "Possessing 100 Physicians"	Rahu
Muladhara lam: लं Root Chakra	vam: वं sham: शं	Purva Bhadrapada: "Former Auspicious One"	Jupiter
	shham: षं sam: सं	Uttara Bhadrapada: "Latter Auspicious One"	Saturn

Figure 8h. Continued

The Six Shivas

Every sound or vibration in the universe is the precursor of a corresponding form. Thus, from each Sanskrit letter sound or mantra, a corresponding deity form arises. In the hub of each chakra are Sanskrit *bija mantras* (seed sounds), progenitors of presiding deities within that chakra.

Six forms of Lord Shiva preside over the first six chakra centers. Beyond these six is Paramashiva, residing in sahasrara (crown chakra).

Absolute pure consciousness, the oneness of Brahman (not to be confused with Brahma, the creator God), has three aspects: gross, subtle, and supreme. Its gross aspect as Brahman in form (*vairaja*) assumes the shape of the first five Shivas, each of which governs one the five elements (*mahabhutas*):

1. Brahma, in the first chakra, muladhara, is the deity of earth element.

2. Vishnu, in the second chakra, svadhishthana, is deity of water.

3. Rudra, in the third chakra, manipura, is deity of fire.

4. Ishvara or Isha, in the fourth chakra, anahata, is deity of air.

5. Sadashiva, in the fifth chakra, vishuddha, is deity of ether.

6. Shiva in the sixth chakra, ajna, Parashiva, represents the subtle form of Brahman. It is *hiranyagarbha,* golden egg of creation, characterized by the bija mantra OM: ॐ.

7. The seventh Shiva, Paramashiva, in the seventh chakra, sahasrara, is the supreme aspect of Brahman, absolute bliss consciousness (*satchitananda*)—beyond name, form, and phenomena; unbounded; pure; unmanifest; undefinable; immutable; eternal; and perfect.

The Shaktis

The power (*shakti*) of the supreme Being (Brahman) is eternal, omnipotent, and one with *satchitananda.* Her conscious power (*iccha shakti*) appears in three different forms:

1. The power of divine union (*yogashakti*) operates when the yogi is in higher awareness, samadhi.

2. Power in the material world (*bhogashakti*) functions while the yogi is engaged in worship, charity, or humanitarian activities.

3. Heroic power (*virashakti*) operates when shakti displays eight mystical powers (*aishvarya*) as a presiding female deity in each chakra, where she appears as Goddesses (*devis*) named Dakini in muladhara, Rakini in svadhishthana, Lakini in manipura, Kakini in anahata, Shakini in vishuddha, Hakini in ajna, and Shankhini in sahasrara.

These shaktis are doorkeepers of the chakras, because they control the chakras and only admit practitioners who are qualified to experience them. The fierce appearance of the shaktis is a deterrent for the neophyte. The shaktis in the chakras are various forms of kundalini.

Overview of Chakras

The charts on pages 114 through 117 provide a complete overview of the chakras and their correspondences.

	Lower Chakras			Gateway	
CHAKRA NAME	Muladhara (Root Chakra)	Svadhishthana (Sacral Chakra)	Manipura (Navel Chakra)	Hrit (Heart Chakra)	Anahata (Heart Chakra)
CHAKRA NUMBER	First	Second	Third		Fourth
ASSOCIATED AREA	Perineum	Pelvis	Navel	Lower Heart	Heart
TATTVA (PRINCIPLE)	Earth (Prithivi)	Water (Apas)	Fire (Tejas)	Air (Vayu)	Air (Vayu)
KOSHA (SHEATH)	Annamaya (Food)	Pranamaya (Vital Air)	Manomaya (Mental)	Vijnanamaya (Intellect)	Vijnanamaya (Intellect)
LOKA (REALM)	Bhu (Material)	Bhuvah (Astral)	Svah (Subtle)	Bhakti (Devotion)	Maha (Balance)
ASSOCIATED GLAND	Adrenal	Gonads	Pancreas	Thymus	Thymus
ASSOCIATED PLEXUS	Coccygeal	Sacral	Lumbar	Cardiac	Cardiac
NUMBER PETALS	Four	Six	Ten	Eight	Twelve
BIJA MANTRA (SEED SOUND)	lam ऌ	vam व	ram र	hung हुं	yam य
DEITY	Brahma	Vishnu	Rudra	Narayana	Isha
KUNDALINI	Kula Kundalini	Vahni Kundalini	Vahni Kundalini	Surya Kundalini	Surya Kundalini
MAIN GUNA	Tamas	Tamas	Rajas	Rajas	Rajas
SHAKTI	Dakini	Rakini	Lakini	Lakshmi	Kakini
SOUND VIBRATION	Vaikhari (Acoustic)	Vaikhari (Acoustic)	Madhyama (Subliminal)	Madhyama (Subliminal)	Madhyama (Subliminal)

THE BIG BOOK OF CHAKRAS AND CHAKRA HEALING

CHAKRA NAME	Lower Chakras			Gateway	
	Muladhara (Root Chakra)	Svadhishthana (Sacral Chakra)	Manipura (Navel Chakra)	Hrit (Heart Chakra)	Anahata (Heart Chakra)
WESTERN MUSICAL NOTE	do	re	mi		fa
GRANTHI (KNOT)	Brahma				Vishnu
LINGA (MARK)	Svayambhu Linga				Bana Linga
KEIKETSU (ACUPUNCTURE)	Chugyohn	Kangen	Chukan		Danchu
KYUSHO (JUDO)	Tsurigane	Myojo	Suigetsu		Kyototsu
ESOTERIC PLANET	Mars	Moon	Sun	Jupiter	Saturn
ESOTERIC DAY OF WEEK	Tuesday	Monday	Sunday		Saturday
ESOTERIC GEM	Red Coral	Pearl	Ruby	Yellow Sapphire	Blue Sapphire
ESOTERIC COLOR	Yellow	Orange	Red	Blue	Violet
EXOTERIC COLOR	Red	Orange	Yellow	Green	Green
SHAPE OF MANDALA	Square	Crescent Moon	Triangle	Round	Hexagon
PRESIDING PRANA	Apana	Apana	Samana	Prana	Prana

Higher Chakras | Absolute Being

CHAKRA NAME	Vishuddha (Throat Chakra)	Talu (Nectar Chakra)	Ajna (Brow Chakra)	Manas (Mind Chakra)	Indu (Moon Chakra)	Nirvana (Causal Chakra)	Guru (Light Chakra)	Sahasrara (Crown Chakra)	Supreme Bindu (Absolute Void)
CHAKRA NUMBER	Fifth		Sixth					Seventh	
ASSOCIATED AREA	Neck	Palate	Forehead	Forehead	Brain	Top of Skull	Lower Sahasrara	Above Head	Upper Sahasrara
TATTVA (PRINCIPLE)	Ether (Akasha)	Ether (Akasha)	Chitta (Mind)	Manas (Mind)	Buddhi (Intellect)	Ahamkara (Ego)	Atman (Higher Self)	Brahman (Supreme)	Absolute (Unmanifest)
KOSHA (SHEATH)	Anandamaya (Blissful)	Anandamaya (Blissful)	Atman (Higher Self)	Manomaya (Mental)	Vijnanamaya (Intellect)	Anandamaya (Blissful)	Atman (Higher Self)	Brahma (God)	Nirvana (Absolute)
LOKA (REALM)	Janah (Causal)	Janah (Causal)	Tapah (Perfected)	Tapah (Perfected)	Tapah (Perfected)	Tapah (Perfected)	Satyam (Truth)	Brahma (God)	Absolute (Unmanifest)
ASSOCIATED GLAND	Thyroid	Carotid Sinuses Salivary Tonsils	Pineal	Pineal	Pineal	Pituitary	Pituitary	Pituitary	None
ASSOCIATED PLEXUS	Cervical	Medulla Oblongata	Cavernous	Telecephalon	Telecephalon	Cerebral Cortex	Above Head	Above Head	Above Head
NUMBER PETALS	Sixteen	Twelve	Two	Six	Sixteen	One Hundred	Twelve	One Thousand	Absolute (Unmanifest)
BIJA MANTRA (SEED SOUND)	ham हं		om ॐ		hang हं	gang गं	aing ऐं	All Mantras	Beyond Sound
DEITY	Sadashiva	Soma	Parashiva	Chitta	Parashiva	Shiva	Guru	Paramashiva	Paramashiva
KUNDALINI	Surya Kundalini	Surya Kundalini	Chandra Kundalini	Chandra Kundalini	Chandra Kundalini	Turya Kundalini	Turya Kundalini	Nirvana Shakti	Nirvana Shakti
MAIN GUNA (ATTRIBUTE)	Sattva	Sattva	Sattva	Sattva	Sattva	Sattva	Beyond Gunas	Beyond Gunas	Beyond Gunas
SHAKTI	Shakini	Mohini	Hakini	none	Siddhakali	none	Shakti	Shankini	Shankini

SOUND VIBRATION	Pashyanti (Radiant)	Pashyanti (Radiant)	Pashyanti (Radiant)	Pashyanti (Radiant)	Pashyanti (Radiant)	Pashyanti (Radiant)	Para (Supreme)	Para (Supreme)	Shabdha Brahman
SANSKRIT MUSICAL NOTE	pa प		dha ध					sa स	ni नि
WESTERN MUSICAL NOTE	so		la					do	ti
GRANTHI (KNOT)			Rudra						
LINGA (MARK)			Itara Linga					Jyotir Linga	Supreme Bindu
KEIKETSU (ACUPUNCTURE)	Diatsui								
KYUSHO (JUDO)	Hichu								
ESOTERIC PLANET	Venus	Moon	Jupiter	Mercury	Uranus	Neptune	Jupiter	Mercury	Pluto
ESOTERIC DAY OF WEEK	Friday		Thursday					Wednesday	
ESOTERIC GEM	Diamond	Pearl	Yellow Topaz	Emerald	Amethyst	Aquamarine	Emerald	Emerald	Onyx
ESOTERIC COLOR	Indigo	Orange	Blue	Blue	Blue	Blue	Green	Green	Black
EXOTERIC COLOR	Blue	Blue	Indigo	Indigo	Indigo	Indigo	Violet	Violet	Violet
SHAPE OF MANDALA	Round	Crescent Moon	Round	Round	Nine Sides	Round	Triangle	Triangle	Round
PRESIDING PRANA	Udana	Udana	Udana	Udana	Udana	Udana	Udana	Udana	Udana

Part Two

AWAKENING
YOUR CHAKRAS

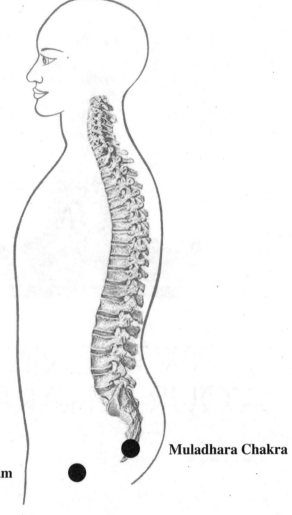

Muladhara Chakra

Muladhara Kshetram

Root Lotus: Center of Primal Energy

Chapter Nine

CHAKRA 1: MULADHARA

"Over it [Svayambhu-Linga] shines the sleeping Kundalini, fine as the fibre of the lotus-stalk . . . It is She who maintains all the beings of the world by means of inspiration and expiration, and shines in the cavity of the root (Mula) Lotus like a chain of brilliant lights." —Purnananda[1]

The center of primal life energy and survival, the first chakra or base chakra, *muladhara* derives its name from Sanskrit roots: *moola* (root, base) and *adhara* (support). This root lotus is said to govern memory, time, and space. Its esoteric color is yellow, and its day of the week is Tuesday. This chakra is ruled by the planet Mars, which governs male potency, basic survival instincts, forcefulness, war, and aggression. In astrology, muladhara is associated with the first house and the sign Aries, indicating survival and security.

Location of Muladhara

Muladhara chakra is the coccygeal point at the base of your spine, in the area of segment II of your coccyx (tailbone). This chakra is seated at the base of *filum terminale,* a threadlike connective tissue that links the bottom of your spinal cord to your coccyx. (Your spinal cord does not extend all the way down to the coccyx; it terminates in the lumbar region.)

Muladhara chakra is just above *kanda mula* (root bulb), the base of the major internally-nested *nadis* that run up your spinal column (see pages 45 and 46).

In the male, the location of muladhara chakra *kshetram* (corresponding trigger point) is in the perineum, between the legs, midway between the anus and penis, one centimeter underneath the surface of the skin. In the female, it is near the cervix, where the vagina meets the uterus.

Opening Muladhara

To locate and awaken muladhara, practice *moola bandha* (page 221) for the kshetram point and *ashvini mudra* (page 221) for the chakra point in the coccyx. Also, practice *Siddha Asana* (Figure 21a on page 219 and page 222) as well as the following exercises in my book *Exploring Meditation*: "Developing the power of the mystic coil," page 105; "Wind-relieving pose," page 111; *Matsyasana,* page 116; *Bhujangasana,* page 117; *Shalabhasana,* page 118; *Mayurasana,* page 119; *Ardha Matsyendrasana,* page 121. In addition, cleanse your anus with water after each bowel movement. Take a rectal enema and a vaginal douche (for women) at least once a week. Engage in periodic fasting and get colonics. (Remember to consult your doctor before starting any new exercises or practices.)

To open this chakra, close your eyes and imagine a cord of energy stretching downward from your perineum to a radiant sun deep in the earth called *earth dvadasanta* (see Figure 5b on page 44). Imagine this cord getting progressively wider, as the energy in muladhara is growing stronger. Say the following affirmation aloud:

"I AM one with Mother Earth, who fills and surrounds me with love.
I AM one with the power of Shakti. I AM the divine Mother.
I AM the power of kundalini.
I AM at peace. Thank you God, and SO IT IS."

Earth Element

The first chakra is associated with earth element (*prithivi mahabhuta*), represented by a yellow square surrounded by eight shining spears (*shulas*). The structure of earth element is maintained by the continuous spinning of the petals of muladhara chakra, radiating red rays. Muladhara, associated with coccygeal plexus, is allied with the organs of excretion and the sense object of odor (*gandha tanmatra),* which is of luminous yellow color.

Because the muladhara chakra is a wheel with four radiations from the central hub, it is likened to a lotus with four petals. These petals are described as either blood color or shining gold. The first petal is in the northeast (upper right) corner, the second in the southeast (lower right) corner, the third in the southwest (lower left), and the forth in the northwest (upper left).

The number of *mantra* letters in each chakra indicates the measure of power concentrated in the chakra. The Sanskrit letters (*varnas*) on the petals of muladhara are the semi-vowel: *vam:* वं and sibilants: *sham, shham, sam:* शं षं सं. Or the mantras *vang, shang, shhang, sang:* वँ शँ षँ सँ. These letters are said to blaze with brilliant golden light.

The petals of each chakra are embedded with specific qualities called *vrittis,* which are thought-forms or emotions held in the chakra. The four vrittis in muladhara are four kinds of bliss:

Figure 9a. Muladhara Chakra.

1. Greatest or highest bliss (*paramananda*).

2. Innate or natural bliss (*sahajananda*).

3. Heroic bliss in the control of desires (*virananda*).

4. Bliss of divine union in meditation (*yogananda*).

Bija Mantra Lam (Lang)

In the center of muladhara's yellow square, is the *dhara bija* or *aindra bija* (earth seed) mantra *lam:* लं or lang: लँ. Because every mantra sound gives rise to a form, Indra, the Vedic king of the Gods and embodiment of earth element, is the equivalent form of this *bija* (seed or germ) mantra *lam.*

The form *(rupa)* of the mantra, in the embodiment of Indra, is described as bright yellow, dazzling as lightning, four-armed, and mounted on the king of elephants, a white, seven-tusked elephant named Airavata—Indra's vehicle. With 1,000 fully awakened spiritual eyes, Indra holds a thunderbolt (*vajra*) and blue lotus. His other two hands make gestures (*mudras*) of dispelling fear (*abhaya mudra*) and granting boons (*vara mudra*).

Indra's thunderbolt (vajra) gives rise to *vajroli*—the power of steadfast discipline and control over the intense desire for erotic pleasure. Vajroli transmutes sexual energy into divine energy by using mental sexual energy for meditation and higher creative endeavors.

The power of *vajra* (thunderbolt), which manifests from the bija mantra *lam,* transforms the subtle level of sound (*madhyama*) into audible sound (*vaikhari*). The spiritual light of vajra represents the illumination of divine consciousness.

Indra's white elephant represents physical strength as well as spiritual development. White reflects bodily purity, mental clarity, radiant health, spirituality, guilelessness, vitality, and well-being.

Figure 9b. Indra.

Lord Brahma in Bindu

On the lap of *lam* is seated a child—Brahma, the splendorous creator God, the presiding deity (*adhidevata*) of muladhara chakra. Brahma, the first of six Shivas residing in the chakras, shines red like the morning sun, with four heads, beautiful as lotuses, facing every direction, three beautiful eyes in each face, and four arms.

The four faces of Brahma represent the four forms of sound, from subtle to gross: *para* (unmanifest), *pashyanti* (radiant), *madhyama* (subtle), and *vaikhari* (audible). The third eye in Brahma's forehead sees with supernormal clairvoyant vision and insight.

Brahma wears the sacred thread (*brahma sutra* or *aksha sutra*) over his shoulder, on which are strung the 50 mantra letters of the Sanskrit alphabet, from *a:* अ to *ksha:* क्ष . This thread of kundalini, stringing all words, is the "Tie of Brahman," which is within all beings and awakens Brahman. This sacred thread is known as a cord of three strands worn over the left shoulder of Hindus. Boys from age five to eight are invested during a Sacred Thread ceremony (*upanayana*) where they become "twice-born" (*dvija*).

Lord Brahma holds a staff (*danda*)—indicative of control over latent impressions (*samskaras*).

THE BIG BOOK OF CHAKRAS AND CHAKRA HEALING

Brahma also holds a rosary (*mala*) of *rudraksha*—a seed sacred to Lord Shiva. The *rudraksha* mala, also called *aksha mala* (seed rosary), represents the 50 mantra letters, from *a* to *ksha*.

The sacred water pot (*kamandalu*) of Lord Brahma symbolizes control of the inherent life force in water, because it is confined to an enclosed space. The water pot also holds the nectar of immortality (*amrit*).

With his forth hand, Brahma imparts spiritual strength to dispel fear in his gesture *abhaya mudra*.

Lord Brahma is seated on a swan (*hamsah or hangsah*), which goes everywhere and pervades everything. *Hamsah,* which connotes inward/outward breath and also Shiva/Shakti, is described as "one without a second"; hence it represents the supreme Being—Brahman.

Figure 9c. Brahma.

Above the Sanskrit letter *la:* ल is the dot or point (*bindu*): लं. Lord Brahma resides within that bindu point. While Brahma rests in bindu, he is unmanifest. When the mantra gets aroused, Brahma emerges from bindu, becomes manifest, and begins to create the universe.

Thus the creator as bindu reposes in unmanifest Prakriti, mother of the entire cosmos, where the three *gunas* of *sattva, rajas,* and *tamas* are in equilibrium, until they get disturbed and cause the universe to appear.

Doorkeeper Dakini

Lord Brahma's power (shakti) or consort is Dakini, also called Brahmi or Brahmani. Her body is described as deep red, agile, dazzling, radiant as many brilliant suns, with four beautiful arms, three bright red eyes, face exquisite as the moon, and fierce teeth. She carries divine knowledge and light to impart to the yogis. Dressed in an antelope skin and adorned with ornaments, she is the mother of wealth. In one of her right hands, Dakini holds a skull staff of death, which can be conquered with the nectar of immortality *(amrita),* which she holds

Figure 9d. Dakini.

in a goblet with her left hand. She cuts through worldliness and ignorance with her sword of divine truth. With her trident, she removes three forms of pain: bodily pain, pain from external influences, and pain from invisible sources.

Tripura Triangle

At the base of the nadis *vajra, sushumna,* and *chitrini* is a triangle *(trikona)* called *tripura* (see Figure 9a on page 123), described as brilliant as lightning and magnificent. A vital air *(vayu)* named *kandarpa* (an aspect of *apana vayu)* is the energy associated with sexual desire *(kama* or *madana)*. Controller of all embodied beings, *kandarpa,* deep red, shining like 10 million suns, is the presiding force in the triangle. *Kandarpa,* always in motion, is also termed fire force *(vahni vayu)* or place of fire *(vahni kunda)*. When stimulated, it brings sexual arousal.

The triangle, also called *yoni* (seat of sexual desire), consists of three lines that form its shape: *vama, jyeshtha,* and *roudri,* representing will, knowledge, and action. Within the triangle resides kundalini. There the radiating desire force *(kama vayu)* vibrates as the desire seed mantra *(kama bija mantra): kling:* क्लीँ . The form of this mantra *(kama rupa)* has the property of fulfilling desire and is associated with the deity Kamadeva, God of romantic love, like Cupid.

Svayambhu Linga

Svayambhu linga is seated in the triangle (see Figure 1c on page 7). Svayambhu (one who exists by himself) is an epithet of Lord Shiva, who represents Parameshvara (the supreme Being). He is self-existing and not dependent on anything else.

The *Shiva linga* (phallus of Shiva) is worshipped in India as Shiva's form, the source of everything. As the linga form gets subtler, it eventually becomes a point (bindu), into which the entire cosmos is absorbed.

Svayambhu linga, also called *mahalinga* (great linga, an epithet of Shiva), is said to be a flawless void *(chidakasha)* with Earth at its base. It is the abode of the deities *(devas)* and powers *(shaktis)*. Everything gets absorbed into it, and it supports all. Described as luminous, imperishable, perfect, and omnipresent, revealed by true knowledge and deep meditation, it bestows bliss and all good. Beautiful as molten gold, it shines like 10 million suns and radiates cool rays like the full moon. The face of *svayambhu linga* is said to lie downward, and its color is described as black, green, red, or gold.

Svayambhu linga has kundalini coiled around him, and he roams in constant motion, because he is born of *kama bija* (seed mantra of desire) — *kling,* which is desire continually seeking fulfillment.

Kundalini Shakti

Kundalini shakti (curled-up power) is described as subtle as a lotus filament, akin to fire or an unsteady flame, splendorous as the luster of young lightning. Her face shines like 10 million suns and is bright and cool as 10 million moons. She has been pictured as black, red, or white.

Like a serpent, she makes three and a half coils from right to left around svayambhu linga. Three of these coils represent the three *gunas: sattva, rajas,* and *tamas,* and the half-coil symbolizes transcendental consciousness, *turiya* (fourth state).

The mouth of this serpent covers and blocks the *brahmadvara* (mouth of brahma) at the entrance to svayambu linga, the lower end of *brahma nadi.* Brahmadvara is called "sweet mouth" because the nectar of immortality (amrita) flows through it. The serpent's head is usually turned downward, which suggests kundalini is asleep. In Figure 9a (page 123), it is turned upward, showing kundalini beginning to rise with spiritual awakening.

The entrance to the void in svayambhu linga (the hollow brahma nadi) is guarded by kundalini, which maintains the flow of *ida* and *pingala* in respiration in all beings. When respiration is suspended in deep meditation, the entrance opens and kundalini rises up through brahma nadi (see Figure 5c on page 46).

Kundalini is in continuous flux, making a constant indistinct humming sound, like the buzzing of bees. This is the OM sound, precursor of all sounds in the cosmos. Thus, all the mantras of the Sanskrit alphabet, from *a:* अ to *ksha:* क्ष are embedded within her. Kundalini is asleep, in latency, until she is somehow awakened, usually through spiritual practices. As the coiled power of *maya* (delusion), she is called *mahashakti,* which causes forgetfulness, ignorance, and bewilderment — the underlying basis of cosmic creation and of human incarnation.

Muladhara Attainments

"The wise man who always contemplates on this Muladhar obtains darduri-siddhi (frog-jump power); and by degrees he can altogether leave the ground (i.e., rise in the air). The brilliancy of the body is increased, the gastric fire becomes powerful, and freedom from disease, cleverness, and omniscience ensue." —Siva Samhita[2]

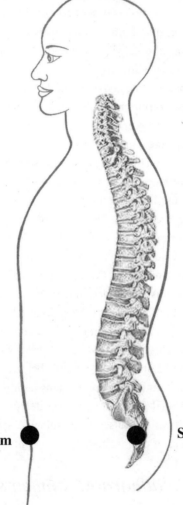

Svadhishthana Kshetram   **Svadhishthana Chakra**

Pelvic Chakra

Chapter Ten

CHAKRA 2: SVADHISHTHANA

*"May Hari, who is within it [the bindu of Vam], who is in the pride of early
youth, whose body is of a luminous blue, beautiful to behold, who is
dressed in yellow raiment, is four armed, and wears the Srivatsa,
and the Kaustubha, protect us." —Purnananda[1]*

The word *svadhishthana* (abode of the self) derives from the Sanskrit roots *sva* (one's own) and *adisthana* (dwelling place, residence). Commonly called pelvic or sex chakra, it is the seat of subconscious mind, ruled by the Moon, sphere of emotion and procreation. Its esoteric color is orange and its day of the week is Monday. Its astrological house is the fourth house of fecundity, nourishment, and motherhood, ruled by the sign Cancer.

Location of Svadhishthana

Svadhishthana, the second chakra, the sacral point, lies inside the *chitrini nadi* in the vertebral column, in the area of sacral vertebra IV, within the *filum terminale*. The chakra *kshetram* (frontal trigger point) of svadhishthana is near the pubic bone at the root of the penis in the male and the clitoris in the female. This chakra corresponds to the genital region and prostatic plexus. Therefore, it is the seat of procreation.

Opening Svadhishthana

To locate and awaken *svadhishthana kshetram*, repeatedly contract and release the muscle that stops and starts the flow of urination. To stimulate the chakra point in the sacrum, practice *ashvini mudra* (page 221) with great force, but without undue strain. Also, the following *yoga asanas* in my book *Exploring Meditation* can open this chakra: *Ustrasana,* page 113; *Matsyasana,* page 116; *Bhujangasana,* page 117.

After these exercises, close your eyes and feel the fire of kundalini highly concentrated in your genitals. Allow this sensation to become increasingly intense. Feel your genitals glowing with sexual arousal. Then say the following affirmation aloud:

"I AM the fire of kundalini, which awakens my sexual energy.
This energy grows into an all-consuming flame, filling my entire body with
Shakti. I am a vibrant being of radiant light, charisma, and magnetism.
I AM at peace. Thank you God, and SO IT IS."

Water Element

Inside svadhishthana is a bright crescent moon-shaped region of water element *(apas mahabhuta).* This is said to be white in color. This chakra is associated with the gonads, and it represents the sense object of flavor *(rasa tanmatra),* which is white color.

Six Lotus Petals

Six petals form the lotus of svadhishthana chakra. These petals are described as vermilion or whitish-red. The letters on its petals are labials: *bam, bham, mam:* बं भं मं and *semivowels: yam, ram, lam:* यं रं लं.

Or mantras: *bang, bhang, mang, yang, rang, lang:* बँ भँ मँ यँ रँ लँ. These letters are said to be diamond-white. The *vrittis* (special qualities) on its petals are affection or indulgence, pitilessness, all-destructiveness, delusion, disdain, and suspicion. The petals of svadhishthana radiate energies from the chakra's center into *ida* and *pingala nadis* with six main radiations. Because the color of these petals is considered vermilion, the red radiations of the vital air *apana vayu* are mixed with golden vibrations of *vyana vayu.*

Figure 10a. Svadhishthana Chakra.

Bija Mantra Vam (Vang)

The *bija mantra* of svadhishthana is *vam:* वं or *vang:* वँ. This mantra is moon white in color and rides a white alligator *(makara)*. The immense power symbolized by makara maintains bodily circulation while the body is active, inactive, or relaxed. Makara also represents sexual vitality, because it develops the gonads and also induces penile erection. Makara regulates all bodily muscular movements, including voluntary muscular relaxation and inactivity, blood purification, and mental control of erection.

Figure 10b. Varuna.

Varuna, the four-armed deity of water, is the form that arises from bija mantra *vam* or *vang.* He radiates yellow lightning and carries a noose *(pasha).* The five *pranas* bring health and vitality to your bodily organs (see page 22). Circulation is increased by *vyana,* and sexual function is improved by *apana.* Water is the key to physical energy, because it is the medium through which the five vital airs *(vayus)* function. The subtlest form of water is *amrita,* also known as *soma,* nectar of immortality. The gross forms are blood, lymph, semen, and other liquid bodily substances.

The life substances with the greatest creative power are the eggs and sperm in the gonads. When these substances are conserved, they are transmuted into *ojas,* a sweet-smelling substance that coats the skin with charismatic personal magnetism. Those who waste these substances are caught in the net of Varuna's noose, which fetters their mind with *pasha* (noose) qualities: disgust, bashfulness, fear, sleepiness, sorrow, anger, slander, family traits, and prejudice. It is said that meditating on Varuna overcomes these negative emotions.

Lord Vishnu in Bindu

Sitting in the lap of the water bija mantra *vam:* वं, in its bindu point, above the letter *va:* व, is the presiding deity of the second chakra, Lord Vishnu, also named Hari, with four arms and bright eyes. His skin color changes in different *yugas* (ages). In *satya yuga,* he is white. In *treta yuga,* he is red. In *dvapara yuga* he is yellow, and in *kali yuga,* he is dark-blue or black (*shyama*).

Figure 10c. Vishnu.

Lord Vishnu is graceful, youthful, serene, pleasing, kindly, and he frees his devotees from fear. He is dressed in yellow and wears a curly mark called *shrivatsa* on the left side of his chest. This mark symbolizes *Prakriti* (see page 85). The renowned *kaustubha* gem adorns his neck. This gem is *atman,* the higher self. Vishnu wears a large multicolored garland of flowers of all seasons *(vanamala),* which represents *maya* (illusion), progenitor of the diversified universe. Although maya controls all beings, Vishnu controls maya, which is held around his neck as a garland.

He is ornamented with a crown, armlets, and alligator-shaped earrings. On his feet are the marks of the divine ensign and umbrella. The accouterments in his hands signify that he supports the universe, via nature's elements: His conch shell (*shankha*) represents ether (*akasha*), wheel (*chakra*) symbolizes air (*vayu*), mace (*gada*) connotes fire (*vahni or agni*), and lotus (*padma*) indicates water. The earth (*bhumi*) element is in his feet.

The conch (*shankha*) of Vishnu is called *panchajanya* (five parents) because it expresses five elements as their bija mantras: *hang* for fire, *yang* for air, *rang* for fire, *vang* for water, and *lang* for earth. The conch also symbolizes joy.

Vishnu's wheel *(chakra),* called *sudarshana* (supreme vision), symbolizes consciousness. The spokes, radiating in all directions, represent the ever-fluctuating mind. The hub is consciousness in a one-pointed, concentrated state. When consciousness is focused during deep meditation, the supreme vision of God arises. This is the vision worthy to be seen, thus *sudarshana.*

The mace *(gada)* of Vishnu, called *koumodi* or *koumodaki*, is the source of happiness. This weapon destroys ignorance by imparting spiritual knowledge inherent in the 50 mantras of the Sanskrit alphabet that arise from kundalini.

Vishnu's lotus *(padma)* is your heart lotus in full bloom, where the supreme Being lives in divine form. The lotus also symbolizes the cosmos, supported by Vishnu.

Vishnu holds a bow *(sharnga dhanu),* which represents deep meditation, because drawing back the bow is similar to experiencing the transcendent, where senses are withdrawn from their objects and the body deeply relaxes. When the arrow flies, you are thrust from meditation into dynamic action.

Vishnu is seated on Garuda, king of birds, Vishnu's customary vehicle. Garuda is the most concentrated form of prana that can be developed through the yogic breathing method called *kumbhaka* (breath suspension—see page 236). *Garuda pranayama* develops kumbhaka to such a degree that bodily levitation can occur.

Lord Vishnu absorbs the entire universe during *mahapralaya,* "the big crunch" of dissolution, an enormous cyclical period when the cosmos collapses into the unmanifest bindu point before the "big bang" recurs.

During the manifested phase of the universe, Vishnu is the all-pervading preserver of the cosmos. In fact, his name derives from *visha* (ubiquitous). He is the source of all power—spiritual and otherwise.

Doorkeeper Rakini

Lord Vishnu's *shakti* (power) is the two-headed, four-armed Rakini, who is said to be either dark blue lotus or vermilion red. Seated on a red double lotus, she is dressed in splendid white raiment, adorned with various ornaments, beautiful and delightful. She has three red eyes, gracefully painted with collyrium, and prominent teeth. Her red eyes symbolize the sun, by which all outer objects are known. Her beautiful moonlike face represents meditation, where worldly knowledge is absorbed.

In one hand Rakini holds a trident *(trishula)*. The trident's three prongs represents three spiritual disciplines:

Figure 10d. Rakini.

1. Discipline of prana through breathing exercises *(pranayama)*.

2. Discipline of the senses through reversing their outward direction and turning inward *(pratyahara)*.

3. Discipline of the mind through one-pointed meditation *(dharana)*.

In another hand Rakini holds a lotus, which is the heart chakra *(hrit padma)*, opened by deep meditation.

Her third hand holds a drum *(damaru)*, representing the highest silent spiritual sound *(para nada)*, through which *shabdabrahman* (transcendental sound) manifests.

Her fourth hand holds a sharp chisel *(tanka)*, which removes deep-seated ignorance and unspiritual qualities.

Svadhishthana Attainments

"He who daily contemplates on this Swadhisthan lotus, becomes an object of love and adoration to all beautiful goddesses. He fearlessly recites the various Sastras [scriptures] and sciences unknown to him before; becomes free from all diseases, and moves throughout the universe fearlessly. Death is eaten by him, he is eaten by none; he obtains the highest psychic powers like anima [body becoming size of an atom], laghima [levitating], etc. The vayu moves equably throughout his body; the humors of his body also are increased; the ambrosia exuding from the etherial lotus also increase in him." —Siva Samhita[2]

Chapter Eleven

CHAKRA 3: MANIPURA

"I worship the blue, cloud-hued One who has sought refuge in your Manipura-Cakra and adorned by lightning through the effulgence of the darkness-destroying Power, shines with the bow of the Indra, studded with various lustrous gems and rains mercy on the three worlds burnt by the destroyer in the great dissolution." —Adi Shankaracharya[1]

Manipura is the solar plexus lotus: center of power. The Sanskrit word *manipura* (city of lustrous jewels) derives from the roots *mani* (gem, jewel) and *pur* (city). This chakra has the greatest concentration of intense pranic energy, because so many *nadis* (conduits of pranic energy) radiate from it.

Often compared to the dazzling power of the Sun, which gives life to the planets, manipura gives you life by distributing pranic energy throughout your body. It is also vital for directing prana from the base of the spine upward through sushumna into higher chakras. It is often associated with transmuting pranic energy into more subtle pranic energy called *ojas*, the substance that imparts luster and charisma to your body.

This is the third chakra, known as navel or solar plexus, center of willpower. Its esoteric color is red and its day of the week is Sunday. Its nature is primarily *rajasic* (see page 85). Ruled by the Sun, commander of the solar system, its astrological house is the fifth house, and sign Leo, associated with authority, resolution, dominion, royalty, leadership, and meritorious deeds.

Location of Manipura

Manipura chakra is seated at the lumbar point, in the vertebral column near lumbar vertebra IV, within the *filum terminale internum,* in the *chitrini nadi* on the same horizontal plane as your navel. You can locate its chakra point and *kshetram*

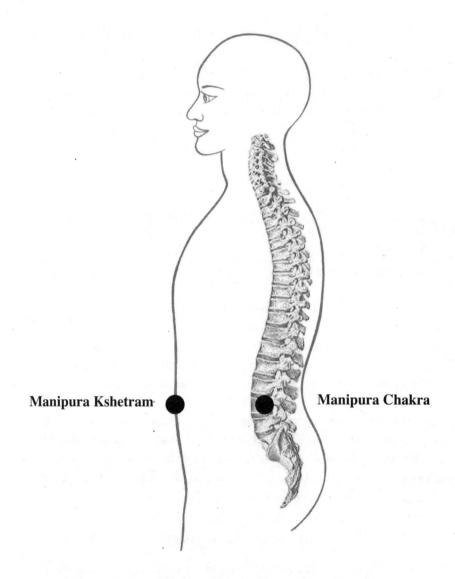

Manipura Kshetram   **Manipura Chakra**

Solar Plexus Lotus: Center of Power

trigger points by pressing a left finger on your belly button on your abdomen. Then press a right finger on your spine at the same horizontal level.

Opening Manipura

Practice *uddiyana bandha*, page 220, and *kapalbhati*, page 233, to locate and awaken the navel trigger points. Also practice the following yoga asanas in the book *Exploring Meditation: Paschimottanasana*, page 111; *Ustrasana*, page 113; *Yoga Mudra*, page 116; *Bhujangasana*, page 117; *Salabhasana*, page 118; *Mayurasana*, page 119; *Padahastasana*, page 121; *Konasana*, page 122.

Close your eyes and feel a huge glowing sun in the area of your navel. Imagine this sun growing increasingly brighter with more and more radiance. Feel this radiant light consuming your entire body with warmth and heat. Feel vital energy vibrating throughout your being. Then say the following affirmation aloud:

"I AM filled with the radiant light of the sun.
My entire body is filled with vibrant energy and divine light.
I AM a beauteous being of radiance, power, health, and vitality.
I AM at peace. Thank you God, and SO IT IS."

Fire Element

The fire element region *(tejas mahabhuta)* inside manipura is triangular in shape and its color is blood red. This chakra is associated with the pancreas, the abdominal organs, and the sense object of form *(rupa tanmatra),* which is red in color. This is the seat of willpower and ego.

Ten Lotus Petals

The manipura chakra is like a lotus with 10 petals, described as the color of dense rain-clouds or black. This chakra has 10 radiations from its petals, designated by 10 mantras.

The black letters on the petals are cerebrals: *dam, dham, nam:* ड दं णं; dentals: *tam, tham, dam, dham, nam:* तं थं दं धं नं; and labials: *pam, pham:* पं फं. Or the mantras: *dang, dhang, nang, tang, thang, dang, dhang, nang, pang, phang:* डँ दँ णँ तँ थँ दँ धँ नँ पँ फँ. These letters are like lightning. The black petals as well as black mantras on this

Figure 11a. Manipura Chakra.

chakra indicate a predominance of prana vital air *(prana vayu).*

The *vrittis* (special qualities) on the petals of manipura are spiritual ignorance, thirst, jealousy, treachery, shame, fear, disgust, foolishness, and sadness.

Bija Mantra Ram (Rang)

The *bija mantra* of manipura is the fire seed mantra *(vahni-bija* or *agni-bija):* *ram:* र or *rang:* रं. The mantra is red and lightning-like. Vahni, four-armed, shining red, is the form of the deity in this bija mantra. He embodies all forms of heat and light energy concentrated as prana, increased by yogic breathing *(pranayama),* and transformed into *satchitananda* (absolute bliss consciousness). The red color symbolizes *rajas guna* (activity mode) in great concentration, by virtue of both *prana* and *apana.*

Vahni rides his vehicle, a male sheep *(mesha),* which embodies several energies:

1. The solar plexus energy.

2. The divine energy of Lord Shiva.

3. The creative Brahma energy.

4. Vishnu consciousness energy.

5. The energy of prana.

6. Sexual vitality and ejaculatory control, which can be harnessed to energize the body and increase mental concentration.

In one hand, Vahni holds a *rudraksha* rosary (*aksha sutra*), which represents the thread (*sutra*) kundalini, from which the first mantra of the Sankrit alphabet "*a*": अ arises and into which the last mantra of the alphabet "*ksha*":क्ष absorbs all creative principles. Rudraksha also symbolizes Rudra, the presiding deity of this chakra.

In his second hand, Vahni holds a spear (*shakti*), representing all forms of energy highly concentrated and transformed into wholeness. It also signifies spiritual powers that develop God consciousness. Vahni's other two hands dispel fear and grant boons.

Figure 11b. Vahni.

Lord Rudra in Bindu

The deity Rudra sits in the lap of the vahni bija, which is the bindu point above the letter *ram:* रं. The name Rudra derives from *ruda* (crying), because of his destructive power, which makes humans weep. Also called Shambu, he is the fierce form of Lord Shiva. His color is vermilion, but appears white because his body is smeared with holy ash. He has three eyes, two arms, and is dressed in a tiger skin. On his forehead is a crescent moon.

Rudra is seated on a bull *(vrisha),* which represents virility and vitality, emits power, and bestows knowledge. The bull embodies *Veda* (supreme knowledge) and *dharma* (the path of truth). Lord Shiva is the guru of knowledge, and the bull, symbol of knowledge, upholds Shiva, acting as his vehicle.

As supreme Brahman, Rudra is the absolute oneness of Being. As *Ishvara* (God), he manifests his supreme power as creator, maintainer,

Figure 11c. Rudra.

and destroyer of the cosmos. He also brings about *laya* (absorption) of all *tattvas* (cosmic principles), which have bound you to worldliness and ignorance. His destructive power absorbs all that causes diversity of consciousness by merging everything into one-pointed awareness of supreme Brahman.

Rudra holds a trident *(trishula)* and a drum *(damaru),* Lord Shiva's two main traditional accouterments. At the beginning of creation, Shiva's drum played the sound of all the letters of the Sanskrit alphabet. Therefore his drum connotes *nada* (primal sound) and mantra.

According to some ancient scriptures, Rudra appears in manipura as a black *shiva linga* called *rudra linga.* This linga has six faces and is endowed with perfection and supernormal powers.

Doorkeeper Lakini

The power (shakti) of Rudra is Lakini, doorkeeper of manipura, also called Bhadrikali. The three-headed powerful Goddess Lakini, beautiful as the moon,

Figure 11d. Lakini.

has three eyes in each face, four arms, and large teeth. Her brilliant eyes are beautifully painted with collyrium.

She is described as black, vermilion, or red. Dressed in yellow or white, she is adorned with various ornaments and a garland of skulls. She sits in deep meditation on a red lotus.

Lakini is often pictured black, the color of *tamas guna,* the destructive force. The Sanskrit root *la* means "that which takes." So she removes all ignorance, freeing her devotees from bondage. She also brings about *laya* (absorption) of the *tattvas* (creative principles).

Her three heads represent the three gunas. *Tamas guna* makes the body inert and dulls the senses. *Rajas guna* develops one-pointed concentration. *Sattva guna* maintains divine awareness.

In one of her right hands Lakini holds a thunderbolt *(vajra),* which symbolizes adamantine discipline. In her other right hand she holds a spear *(shakti),* which transforms diverse energy into concentrated one-pointedness. Her left hands dispel fear and grant boons.

Manipura Attainments

"When the Yogi contemplates on the Manipur lotus, he . . . becomes lord of desires, destroys sorrows and diseases, cheats death, and can enter the body of another. He can make gold, etc., see the adepts (clairvoyantly), discover medicines for diseases, and see hidden treasures." —Siva Samhita[2]

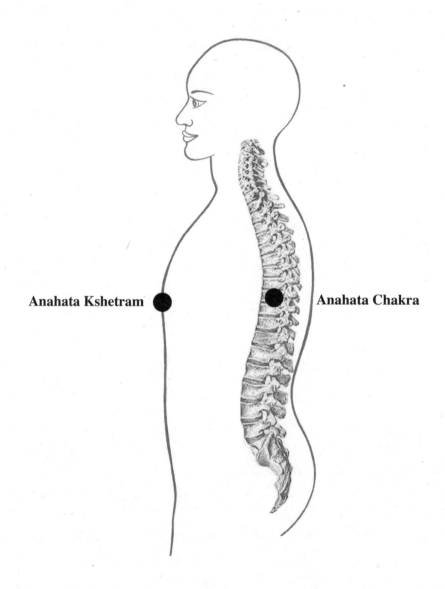

Anahata Kshetram

Anahata Chakra

Heart Lotus: Center of Consciousness

Chapter Twelve

CHAKRA 4: ANAHATA

"The Person not larger than a thumb, the inner Self, is always settled in the heart of men. Let a man draw that Self forth from his body with steadiness, as one draws the pith from a reed. Let him know that Self as the Bright, as the Immortal; yes, as the Bright, as the Immortal." —The Upanishads[1]

In the next two chapters, you will discover the heart lotus. This unique center contains two parts: *hrit* chakra and *anahata* chakra. Let us first consider the anahata chakra. The term *anahata* (unstruck sound) is the sound of oneness, made without contact of two objects. The heart center is the soundless sound of silence, the cosmic sound known as *shabda brahman*.

Anahata is the fourth chakra, seat of consciousness, sense of "I-ness," and point of contact between soul and body. It is the center of direct revelation and inner quietude. In many scriptures, anahata is described as the chakra from which all 72,000 *nadis* originate.

The esoteric color of anahata is violet, and its day of the week is Saturday. It is ruled by Saturn, planet of contraction, which governs the pumping action of heart and lungs. It is also the planet of austerity and introversion, whereby *moksha* (liberation from bondage) is attained. Its astrological house is the 10th house, and the sign Capricorn, on the midheaven, the highest point in the zodiac. Thus anahata is the gateway to the infinite.

Location of Anahata

Anahata, at the thoracic point, lies in the vertebral column within *chitrini nadi,* near the heart and cardiac plexus, in the area of thoracic vertebra IX, within the central canal of the spinal column. To find your anahata chakra trigger point and anahata *kshetram,* press your left finger in the center of your chest between your nipples and press your right finger on the spinal column directly behind that point on the same horizontal plane.

Opening Anahata

To locate and awaken these trigger points, practice the "middle breathing" exercise (see page 230) with awareness on the trigger points. Also, the following practices in *Exploring Meditation* will help you open this chakra: "Developing the arms" and "Developing the chest," page 106; *Matsyasana*, page 116; *Chakrasanas*, pages 118 and 119; *Mayurasana*, page 119; *Konasana*, page 122.

Close your eyes and imagine your heart is a gateway or large double doors. As the doors open, imagine the shining radiance of divine love pouring over your being, showering you with the light of consciousness. Bathe in the golden light of divine love. Then say the following affirmation aloud:

> "I AM a radiant being of divine love.
> God's light fills and surrounds me now with peace.
> I AM bathed in an ocean of divine grace, joy, and beauty.
> I AM the love that God is. I AM at peace in the heart of God.
> Thank you God, and SO IT IS."

Air Element

The form of anahata is a six-pointed star with 12 petals. This hexagonal shape is the region of air (*vayu mandala*) that is said to be smoke-colored. Here lies *vayu mahabhuta* (air element) and the sense object of touch *(sparsa tanmatra),* which is ash colored. This chakra is associated with thymus and lungs.

The air region is symbolized by the hexagonal star, where the upward-pointing triangle represents higher understanding and spiritual awareness, Shiva (*Purusha*: unmanifest consciousness). The downward-pointing triangle indicates earthly, material pursuits, Shakti (*Prakriti*: manifest creation).

The upward path of the upper triangle is *nivritti* (return to the divine source). The downward path of the lower triangle is *pavritti* (entanglement in worldly illusion). Anahata is the perfect balance between the upper and lower regions, gateway to both spiritual and material worlds.

Twelve Lotus Petals

Twelve petals surround the lotus of anahata chakra. The petals glow with shining deep red color. Twelve energies radiate from the center of this chakra. The shining deep red color of the radiations in this chakra indicates the predominance of the vital air *prana* along with *udana*.

The letters on the petals are the gutturals: *kam, kham, gam, gham, nam:* कं खं गं घं ङं; palatals: *cham, chcham, jam, jham, nam:* चं छं जं झं ञं; and cerebrals: *tam, tham:* टं ठं. Or *kang, khang, gang, ghang, nang, chang, chchang, jang, jhang, nang, tang, thang:* कँ खँ गँ घँ ङँ चँ छँ जँ झँ ञँ टँ ठँ.

These letters are of various reddish hues.

The *vrittis* (special qualities) on the lotus petals of anahata are lustfulness, fraudulence, indecision, repentance, hope, anxiety, longing, impartiality, arrogance, incompetence, discrimination, and defiance.

Figure 12a. Anahata Chakra.

Bija Mantra Yam (Yang)

Within the air region of anahata chakra is *pavana akshara* (the mantra embodying the air element): *yam:* यं or *yang:* यँ, the air seed (*bija mantra*). This mantra is described as smoke-colored, with four arms, wearing a crown, and seated on an antelope. Vayu, Lord of air, is the form of this bija mantra. The ancient scriptures describe him as very subtle, and life itself.

Vayu's vehicle, the antelope (*krishnasara*), a swift deer (*mriga*), symbolizes the force of pranic energy that speeds through your muscles, expressing life through your body, causing all motion, physical and mental.

Vayu is the power field that operates with pranic forces. The five main *vayus* are *prana, apana, samana, udana,* and *vyana.* (See pages 22–24.) Another aspect of prana is *deva prana* (supernormal life force energy), the most efficient, rarified pranic power. Free from all disturbances, it is responsible for stillness of body and suspension of breath (*samadhi*) during deep meditation, as well as muscular movement without dissipation of energy. Therefore deva prana

Figure 12b. Vayu.

supports the highest level of consciousness—supernormal mind *(deva manas),* in which samadhi is maintained as normal everyday functioning.

Vayu is the presiding deity of deva prana and of yogic breathing *(pranayama),* whereby pranic forces are refined. A practice called *"mriga* (deer) process," which invigorates and purifies the cardiopulmonary system, consists of swift running, slow running, long walks, and swimming. In addition, various methods of pranayama are used. (See Chapter 22 to learn pranayama.)

Through spiritual discipline, ordinary prana is refined into deva prana. This process is symbolized by the *ankusha* (goad) held by the deity Vayu. Because Vayu is very kind, with three of his hands he grants boons to the three worlds: the earth realm (*bhu*), astral world (*bhuvah*), and subtle realm (*svah*).

Lord Isha in Bindhu

Seated on the lap of the mantra yam is Lord Isha, one of the six Shivas. He resides in the bindu point of *yam:* य or *yang:* यँ. Said to be like a swan, he is all-merciful, bright, magnificent, shining white like 10 million moons, pure and unsullied—the embodiment of *sattva guna.*

His hands are held in gestures of dispelling fear *(abhaya mudra)* and granting boons *(vara mudra),* showering benevolence on the three worlds. Isha has no vehicle to ride. Therefore he dwells in the air in lotus posture, seated on a tiger skin in a state of levitation.

Isha, also named *Ishvara* (God), is the form of Brahman as the source of supreme yoga power. According to ancient Upanishads, Isha is omniscient, omnipresent, infinite, beyond the universe, as well as within it, and hidden within all beings. The power emanating from Isha dispels all fear and strengthens concentration and absorption during meditation. His third eye is the eye of *samadhi* knowledge. His other two eyes watch his devotees both during meditation and activity.

Lord Isha, with a beautiful lotus-like face, is adorned with a crown, earrings, armlets, bracelets, *rudraksha* beads, string of pearls, anklets, red garland, and is dressed in tiger skin and silk raiment. His hair is matted and twisted.

Figure 12c. Isha.

Pitha Shakti

Within the lotus of anahata, below the *vayu bija mantra (yam),* lies Shakti power in the form of *yoni* (female genitalia), a triangle with its base upward and apex downward (see Figure 12a on page 145). This triangle is said to have a delicate body, red in color, shining like 10 million lightning flashes, and adorned with varied ornaments.

The purpose of the triangle is to hold or support the deity *(devata)* in her center. By her power, Shakti maintains the deity (Shiva linga) in its seat.

This is termed holding power *(pitha shakti)* or power of concentration. Therefore this triangle represents consciousness that maintains internal focus rather than being swayed by external sensory stimuli.

Bana Linga

Seated within the triangle is a *Shiva linga* (phallus of Lord Shiva) called *bana linga,* brilliant as a thousand suns, radiating either luminous gold or shining red light (see Figure 12a on page 145). At the head of the linga is a subtle void region *(bindu)* like a gem. This void is within a bindu point over a half moon *(ardha chandra).* Thus, Lord Shiva is usually depicted with a half moon on his forehead. In the void dwells the roused supernormal yogic power, Goddess Lakshmi, adorned with golden ornaments. The bindu point represents the concentrated form of the supreme Being (Brahman), absolute pure awareness—without name, form, or qualities.

Jivatman

In the lotus of anahata, the spark of your human soul *(hangsahkala)* shines. Here is also the region of the sun, by which the filaments of the lotus are illumined.

The soul of your higher self *(jivatman),* seated in anahata chakra, is golden, resplendent, luminous, and motionless, in the form of a still flame of a lamp or candle in a windless place, tapering upward. He is seated below bana linga within the Shakti triangle (see Figure 12a on page 145). Jivatman is your spiritually purified, enlightened, illumined Being in embodiment.

The flame of jivatman (divine light in humanity) is represented by *akhanda jyoti* (eternal flame), kept burning night and day in many ashrams, temples, and also in all Jewish synagogues. This light of consciousness spreads in all directions, so it is unlimited and all-pervading.

Doorkeeper Kakini

The doorkeeper of anahata chakra is known as Kakini, also called Bhuvaneshvari. She is described as many colors. Her yellow color represents divine consciousness. Her shining red color symbolizes the power that controls the *prana vayus* (vital airs). Her white color is Isha consciousness.

She is said to be like new lightning and clad in white garments. Graceful and pure, her three eyes are painted splendidly with collyrium. With face beautiful as millions of moons, she has four arms and large breasts. She dons a necklace of bones like the rays of the sun, along with other gold- and gem-encrusted ornaments.

Kakini is said to be auspicious, joyous, the benefactor of all. Fully absorbed in meditation, in supreme bliss and death-conquering union with Brahman, she drinks the nectar of immortality. Her grandeur is like the celestial trees, and she appears agitated with power. Kakini stabilizes the discipline that allows prana vayus to be maintained in a motionless state.

Figure 12d. Kakini.

She holds a noose *(pasha)* in one of her four hands. Pasha (desire to attain the knowledge of atman) is derived from the Sanskrit roots *pang* (knowledge of atman) and *asha* (desire).

In another hand she holds a human skull *(kapala)*, which preserves *kang* (excellent knowledge) and *sukhang* (spiritual knowledge).

In her third hand, Kakini holds a trident *(trishula)*, and her forth hand holds a drum *(damaru)*.

Anahata Attainments

"He who always contemplates on this lotus of the heart is eagerly desired by celestial maidens. He gets immeasurable knowledge, knows the past, present, and future time; has clairaudience, clairvoyance, and can walk in the air whenever he likes. He who contemplates daily the hidden Banalinga undoubtedly obtains the psychic powers called Khechari (moving in the air) and Bhuchari (going at will all over the world)." —Siva Samhita[2]

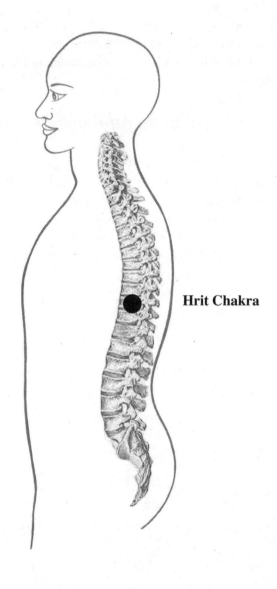

Hrit Chakra

Heart Lotus: Center of Devotion

Chapter Thirteen

HRIT CHAKRA

"He is the gem that lies embedded in the cubit of the heart. Until they see Him, they think not of Him; Into them who cherish and muse on Him over and over, As a gem-set Jewel He shines." —Thirumoolar[1]

H*rit* (heart) chakra or *hridaya* (he who dwells in the heart) is also known as *ananda kanda* (root or bulb of bliss). In this chakra, devotees visualize an image of their *ishta devata* (personal deity). Thus, all deities are seated in hrit chakra, where devotion and unconditional love are intensified. Hrit is depicted as stainless, subtle, and untouched by any physical impurities.

Location of Hrit Chakra

Hrit chakra is located in the vertebral column in the *chitrini nadi* near the heart and cardiac plexus, in the area of thoracic vertebra IX, within the central canal of the spinal column. Hrit chakra faces downward and is seated just below the 12-petaled anahata chakra, discussed in the previous chapter. In fact, hrit is the lower part of anahata (the fourth chakra).

Opening Hrit

Close your eyes and imagine a thumb-sized blue divine being, such as Vishnu, in the cave of your heart. Or visualize any other deity for whom you have affection. See or feel this deity within yourself and realize that you are one with that being of light. Then say aloud:

"The light of God surrounds me. The love of God enfolds me.
The power of God protects me. The presence of God watches over me
Wherever I AM, God is, and all is well. Thank you God, and SO IT IS."

Eight Lotus Petals

Hrit chakra is described as a delicate, beautiful lotus, red as the morning sun. The petals are characterized as golden or white. These petals radiate eight particular superpowers used to command the five elements of nature *(mahabhutas)*. The super-

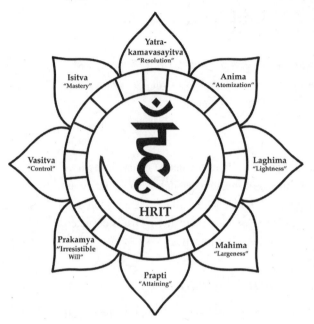

Figure 13a. Hrit Chakra.

powers in hrit chakra are embodied by deities called *Vasus* (literally *dwellers),* which are attendants of Indra (king of the Gods). All supernormal abilities are called *siddhis* (perfections). These eight particular siddhis *(ashta siddhi),* described by the ancient sage Patanjali in the *Yoga Sutras,*[2] and their eight presiding deities, are known by the following names:

1. *Anima* (atomization): The ability to transform your body size to that of an atom. Presiding deity: Agni or Anala (fire God).

2. *Laghima* (lightness): The power to decrease your physical weight or levitate. Presiding deity: Vayu or Anila (wind God).

3. *Mahima* (immensity): The power to increase your bodily size or stature or become mighty. Presiding deity: Prthivi or Dhara (earth God).

4. *Prapti* (attaining): The capacity to fulfill desires and go anywhere at will, described by the ancients as "touching the moon with your fingertips." Presiding deity: Nakshatrani or Dhruva (God of the stars or polestar).

5. *Prakamya* (irresistible will): The ability to pass through solid earth, walk through walls, or not be immersed in water, and to assume any desired form. Presiding deity: Antariksha or Aha (ether or space God).

6. *Vashitva* (control): The greatest power and dominion over the five elements *(mahabhutas):* earth, water, fire, air, and ether, and the subtle sense objects

(tanmatras), of which these elements are made: odor, flavor, form, touch, sound. This is also the power to attract and enslave others by enchantment. Presiding deity: Dyaus or Prabhasa (sky God).

7. *Isitva* (king): Mastery over the appearance, disappearance, and aggregation of the five elements and objects in the material world. With this siddhi, you can transcend all human limits. Presiding deity: Aditya or Pratyusha (sun God).

8. *Yatrakamavasayitva* (none could defy his desires; resolution): The ability to determine the five elements and their nature and to transform them at will. It is also the power to conquer or subordinate others. Presiding deity: Chandrama or Soma (moon God).

Region of Brahman

In hrit chakra are seated Indra, king of the Gods, and his attendants, the Vasus. Inside hrit chakra is the vermilion sun region, which encompasses the white moon region. Within the moon region is a deep red fire region. Inside the fire is a realm of radiant light, called superlight (Brahman light).

> *"Harih, Om. There is this city of Brahman (the body), and in it the palace, the small lotus (of the heart), and in it that small ether. Now what exists within that small ether, that is to be sought for, that is to be understood . . . As large as this ether (all space) is, so large is that ether within the heart. Both heaven and earth are contained within it, both fire and air, both sun and moon, both lightning and stars; and whatever there is of him (the Self) here in the world, and whatever is not (that is, whatever has been or will be), all that is contained within it."*
> —The Upanishads[3]

Wish-Fulfilling Tree

Within this fire region grows the wish-fulfilling tree (*kalpataru, kalpa vriksha,* or *kalpaka*), shining red. In some Tantric texts, the wish-fulfilling tree is called *chintamani,* derived from the Sanskrit roots *chinta* (thoughts) and *mani* (jewels). Chintamani is a tree growing in the center of a divine lake, which is in the midst of a beautiful garden. This garden is the abode of divine beings.

Figure 13b. Narayana Seated under Wish-Fulfilling Tree.

The tree is said to be Indra's heaven, where all wishes are granted. This means those who live at the level of hrit chakra have divine awareness, with all desires fulfilled.

At the base of this tree is a dazzling seat ornamented with jewels. Here sits Lord Narayana, the first full incarnation (*avatar*) of the deity Vishnu into human form. He is also called *Purusha* (person), the supreme Being as the male principle, the precursor to and silent witness of all creation.

The scriptures say that *hridaya* (hrit chakra) with its face downward should be raised upward by a yogic breathing (pranayama) method called *sitkara*, in which the tip of the tongue is placed inside the upper teeth and breathing is done through the mouth. When hrit chakra is raised, then the flame of kundalini is seen, radiating the light of Brahman (superlight). Eventually, Purusha is revealed within this kundalini. It has also been stated that *atman* (the "I AM" self) dwells within hrit chakra.

> *"Out of compassion for them I, who dwell within their heart, destroy the darkness born of ignorance by the shining lamp of knowledge. O Arjuna, I am the Atma abiding in the heart of all beings. I am also the beginning, the middle, and the end of all beings."* —Lord Krishna[4]

At the boundary of hrit chakra is a subtle hole or aperture (*sushumna* energy tube) within which lies the entire chakra system. This is said by ancient yogis to be the body's "solar entrance." Out of the innumerable rays in the heart, one ray of effulgent light (*sushumna* ray) goes right through the solar region. After passing *Brahma loka* (divine realm), the departed soul attains the highest point via this ray.

The three *nadis*—ida, pingala, and sushumna—intersect in hrit chakra. Also, the *prana vayus* are said to be situated there. The *astra bija* (weapon seed mantra), located in hrit chakra, is *hung:* हूं.

Hrit chakra is the abode of the indwelling Spirit, atman (the "I AM") Brahman (absolute), and deities of all religions. Therefore, it is the ideal place to contact your own personal deity *(ishtadevata),* the God of your understanding, whether that be Jesus, Buddha, Allah, Vishnu, Ganesh, Krishna, Kali, Durga, Saraswati, Lakshmi, Mother Mary, Hashem, or any other form of God or Goddess.

"The shining Self dwells hidden in the heart. Everything in the cosmos, great and small, lives in the self. He is the source of life, truth beyond the transience of this world. He is the goal of life. Attain this goal!" —The Upanishads[5]

Hrit Attainments

"The shrine which consists of the ether in the heart, the blissful, the highest retreat, that is our own, that is our goal, and that is the heat and brightness of the fire and the sun.[6] He who knows Brahman, which is (cause, not effect), which is conscious, which is without end, as hidden in the depth (of the heart), in the highest ether, he enjoys all blessings, at one with the omniscient Brahman."
—The Upanishads[7]

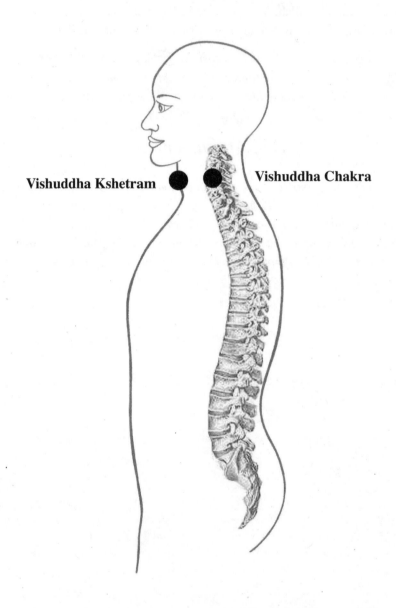

Vishuddha Kshetram   **Vishuddha Chakra**

Throat Lotus: Center of Purification

Chapter Fourteen

CHAKRA 5: VISHUDDHA

*"I worship the Auspicious One residing in your Visuddhi-Cakra, shining like a
pure crystal, the Creator of ether and you the Goddess of identical disposition;
by the radiance—resembling moonlight—emanating from them, the world
enveloped in the darkness of ignorance rejoices, like the Cakori bird bathing in
the rays of the moon." —Adi Shankaracharya[1]*

Vishuddha (purity) chakra, referred to as throat chakra, is the seat of purification, which harmonizes all diversity. Also called *bharati sthana* (place
of Bharati, Goddess of speech), it is responsible for creative expression
and communication.

This chakra is ruled by the planet Venus, planet of creativity, wealth, and artistic expression, and the sign Taurus and second astrological house, which denotes
speech, art, and real estate. Its day of the week is Friday, and its esoteric color is
indigo.

Location of Vishuddha

Vishuddha chakra, at the cervical point, is situated in the area of cervical vertebra
IV of the spine, in *chitrini nadi* within the central canal of the vertebral column
in the neck region. It is associated with the cervical plexus and thyroid gland. Vishuddha *kshetram* is located on the front surface of the neck in the region of the
Adam's apple.

To locate vishuddha trigger points, press the protrusion at your throat with a
left finger and feel the back of the neck on your spine with your right finger on the
same horizontal plane.

Opening Vishuddha

To awaken vishuddha, practice *ujjayi pranayama* (page 224) while paying attention to these trigger points. Also, do the following practices in *Exploring Meditation:* "Clearing the pharynx," page 103; "Strengthening the neck," page 104; "Strengthening shoulder blades and joints," page 105; *Urdhvasarvangasana,* page 112; *Halasana,* page 113; *Matsyasana,* page 116.

Close your eyes and imagine that your throat is filled with an empty void. Feel this void growing larger, like the size of an orange, then the size of a grapefruit. Then notice this void consuming your entire body. Your whole being is inside a vacuum, the golden egg of creation *(hiranyagarbha).* Enjoy the sensation of being suspended in emptiness. Then say the following affirmation aloud:

"I AM one with oneness. I AM one with peace. I AM free from all ties that bind me to the earthly existence. I AM free to be whole, complete, self-sufficient, and content within myself. I AM in control of my life now and always.
Thank you God, and SO IT IS."

Ether Element

Within the center of vishuddha, a pure white, void, circular region *(nabhomandala)* blazes like the full moon. This void principle *(shunyatattva)* embodies the deity Sadashiva (ever-beneficent), one of the six Shivas.

The void is also known as ether element *(akasha mahabhuta),* associated with the sense object of sound *(shabda tanmatra),* which is white in color.

Five aspects of akasha are as follows: attributeless ether *(gunarahita akasha),* highest ether *(parakasha),* bright ether *(tattvakasha),* sun ether *(suryakasha),* and great ether *(mahakasha).* These are all aspects of the supreme void; the ultimate reality; the nameless, formless absolute; the emptiness of fullness; and the fullness of emptiness.

The lotus filaments of vishuddha are said to be red. Within the circular void of vishuddha lies a smoke-colored triangle where Sadashiva sits.

Sixteen Lotus Petals

The petals of vishuddha chakra are described as shining smoke-color. Its letters, radiating deep red light, are all 16 vowels of the Sanskrit alphabet: *a, aa, e, ee, u, uu,*

Figure 14a. Vishuddha Chakra.

kr, kree, lre, lree, ye, yai, o, ow, am, ah: अ आ इ ई उ ऊ ऋ ॠ ल़ ॡ ए ऐ ओ औ आं अ.
Or the mantra forms *ang, aang, ing, iing, ung, uung, ring, rring, lring, lrring, eng, aing, ong*, and *oung*: अँ आँ इँ ईँ उँ ऊँ ऋँ ॠँ ल़ँ ॡँ एँ ऐँ आँ आँ .

Sixteen special qualities (*vrittis*) are seated on the petals of vishuddha chakra. Because this chakra governs speech and expression, the petals hold various mantras and musical notes. The first nine vrittis are the mantras: Pranava (mantra *OM*: ॐ); *udgitha* (hymns of Sama Veda); mantras *hung, phat, vashat, svadha, svaha, namah;* and the nectar of immportality, *amrita*. The remaining vrittis are seven musical notes: *nishada, rishabha, gandhara, shadja, madhyaman, dhaivata*, and *panchama*.

This chakra is considered the center of *udana* vital air *(udana vayu)*. From its petals, 16 radiations vibrate *akasha* (ether*)* energy and *udana vayu* into *ida* and *pingala*.

Bija Mantra Ham (Hang)

Within the circular region at the center of vishuddha lotus is the Sanskrit *kha bija* or *akasha bija* (ether seed mantra), *ham:* हं or *hang:* हँ. The mantra *ham* is white

Figure 14b. Ambara.

and sits on its vehicle, a snow white elephant *(hasti)*. The elephant represents physical prowess, which arises from bodily purity. The deity Ambara embodies this mantra and the element of ether, the void.

In his first hand, the four-armed Ambara holds a goad *(ankusha)*, representing physical strength arising from mental and physical discipline. In another hand he holds a noose *(pasha)*, indicating freedom from bondage, which also arises from mental and physical discipline.

His third and forth hands are in the gestures of granting boons *(vara mudra)*, which imparts spiritual knowledge, and dispelling fear *(abhaya mudra)*, which removes all obstacles from the spiritual path.

Sadashiva as Ardhanarishvara in Bindu

Sadashiva (ever-auspicious) is seated in the lap of the bija mantra *ham:* हं in the bindu point above the mantra *ha:* ह. He is white in color and has five faces, three eyes in each face, 10 arms, and crescent moon on his forehead. His five faces are smoke, yellow, vermilion, white, and deep red. He is dressed in a tiger skin, and his body is smeared with ashes and adorned with snakes. The River Ganges flows from his matted locks.

The fivefold expression of divine activity in the cosmos is depicted by Shiva's five faces:

1. Looking upward is Ishana (ruler), the revealer, also known as Sadashiva. He appears in temples in the *shiva linga* (phallus of Shiva) form. He is on top of Shiva's head and is the embodiment of all forms of learning.

2. Facing east is Tatpurusha (supreme soul), the concealer, the power of obscuration, also known as Maheshvara.

3. Looking to the west is Sadyojata (sudden-born), the creator, also called Brahma.

4. Facing north is Vamadeva (lovely, pleasing), the sustainer, also called Vishnu.

5. Southward is Aghora (non-terrifying) or Bhairava, the power of absorption and destruction, also known as Rudra.

The white color of Sadashiva's body represents the purity of sattva guna, expressing divine knowledge. His five faces symbolize knowledge of the five elements (*bhutas*) and subtle sense objects (*tanmatras*) that arise from the mantras *lang*, *vang*, *rang*, *yang*, and *hang*.

Although he possesses three eyes in each face, Sadashiva sees only with his third eye, because his other two eyes are closed in deep meditation. His third eye sees only true knowledge (*samadhi prajna*) of absolute bliss consciousness (*satchitananda*). His tiger skin symbolizes discipline and spirituality for the purpose of attaining liberation.

Figure 14c. Sadashiva as Ardhanarishvara.

In vishuddha chakra, Sadashiva's body is merged with his power (*shakti*) or consort, called Girija, Gauri, or Uma. This form is called Ardhanarishvara or Hara-Gauri: The right half of his body is the white God Sadashiva and the left half is the Goddess Shakti. Her golden color indicates the multidirectional *vyana* vital air, which effects stillness of *prana vayus*.

The vehicle of Shiva is the bull (*vrisha*), and vehicle of Shakti is the great lion (*mahasingha*). Therefore, the vehicle of Ardhanarishvara is half-bull and half-lion. The lion represents Shakti's full control over her power.

Ardhanarishvara represents complete union of the two aspects of divinity: supreme consciousness (Shiva) and power (Shakti). When oneness becomes duality, then pranic forces that create life split into two energies: red bindu (*rajas*)—female genital fluids, which unite with white bindu (*shukra*)—male genital fluids. The red energy creates femininity in the female, while the white energy produces masculinity in the male.

Because of the natural affinity of the red and white energies, male and female long to unite. But there is a physical limit to their ability to do so. That is why secret sexual practices called *maithuna* help male and female to absorb the essence of the fluids of their partner. These practices include multilevel contacts with semen retention along with masterful motions during copulation. Ardhanarishvara is the form where male and female energies are so unified that they manifest full power in total union of Shiva with Shakti. Sadashiva holds nine implements in his hands:

1. The trident (*shula*) represents the power of absorption of *Prakriti*, consisting of three basic attributes: *sattva, rajas,* and *tamas gunas*.

2. The axe (*tanka*) is spiritual strength, which removes all that is unspiritual.

3. The sword (*kripana*) destroys all forms that seem to limit the infinite formless Being *(Brahman).*

4. The thunderbolt (*vajra*) represents adamantine control of *apana* function (sexual energy).

5. The fire (*dahana*) symbolizes the *kundalini* fire of all cosmic principles.

6. The great serpent (*nagendra*) is kundalini in its roused state.

7. The bell (*ghanta*) represents the silent sound of mantra.

8. The goad (*ankusha*) stimulates the silent void to create sound.

9. The noose (*pasha*) keeps spiritual pride in check.

His 10th hand is in the gesture of dispelling fear (*abhaya mudra*).

Doorkeeper Shakini

The splendorous power (*shakti*) named Shakini, doorkeeper of vishuddha chakra, abides in a shining lunar region within vishuddha. Her luminous form has five exquisite faces, with three eyes in each face, painted with collyrium, and four beautiful arms. White like the ocean of nectar, she is clad in yellow garments and splendid ornaments. Amiable, charming, and delightful, her sweet smile shows beautiful teeth. She has large breasts, matted hair, and is adorned with varied ornaments.

Shakini is beyond the *Veda,* as well as source of the Veda. She embodies the knowledge of mantra. Her

Figure 14d. Shakini.

THE BIG BOOK OF CHAKRAS AND CHAKRA HEALING

body is moist with flowing streams of pure nectar *(amrita)*. Her yellow garments indicate full control of *vyana vayu*.

In one of her lotus hands, Shakini holds the goad *(srini)*. In another, she holds the noose *(pasha)*. Her third hand holds a book of the Veda, of which she is the source. Her forth hand is in the gesture of wisdom *(jnanamudra)*, with tip of her index finger touching the tip of her thumb.

Vishuddha Attainments

"This (region) is the gateway of great Liberation for him who desires the wealth of Yoga and whose senses are pure and controlled. He who has attained complete knowledge of the Atma (Brahman) becomes, by constantly concentrating his mind (Citta) on this Lotus, a great Sage, eloquent and wise, and enjoys uninterrupted peace of mind. He sees the three periods [past, present, and future], and becomes the benefactor of all, free from disease and sorrows and long-lived, and, like Hamsa, the destroyer of endless dangers." —Purnananda[2]

Chapter Fifteen

TALU CHAKRA

"Having successively fixed the breath, after it had been restrained, in the palate, thence having crossed the limit (the life), let him join himself afterwards to the limitless (Brahman) in the crown of the head." —The Upanishads[1]

T*alu* (uvula) chakra, which is not part of the seven-chakra system, is also called *lalana* chakra or *taluka*. This is depicted in the ancient scriptures as a secret chakra taught by gurus to their disciples. Is it believed that by using the mantra *hangsah,* the yoga disciple makes kundalini pass through this chakra while traversing *sushumna nadi.*

Location of Talu Chakra

The talu chakra lies near the junction between the front end of the central spinal canal in the medulla oblongata and the lower part of the brain's fourth ventricle, within *chitrini nadi,* behind the uvula. Its *kshetram* trigger point is in the root of the palate at the back of the mouth.

Opening Talu

To locate and open this chakra, notice the trigger point while practicing *khechari mudra* (see page 223). After this practice, say the following affirmation:

"Flow, soma, in a sweet and exhilarating stream. Flow, amrita, in abundance.
Flow into my being with streams of vitality and energy.
Flow, sweet nectar, and fill my being with fluidity, peace, and serenity.
Thank you God, and SO IT IS."

Palate Lotus: Center of Nectar

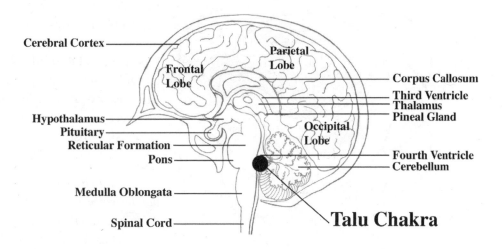

The following yoga asanas in *Exploring Meditation* will also help you open this chakra: *Matsyasana*, page 116; *Bhujangasana*, page 117; *Chakrasanas*, pages 118 and 119.

Twelve Lotus Petals

According to the ancient Indian scriptures, the color of the petals of talu chakra is said to be either shining white or red. Twelve specific qualities *(vrittis)* are on the petals of this chakra. They are respect, contentment, offense, self-control, pride, affection, sorrow, depression, purity, dissatisfaction, honor, and anxiety.

Moon Region

In the center of talu lotus is a red circular region associated with the uvula. Inside this circle is a region where the moon's nectar-oozing power *(chandra kala)* resides. This lunar region, which shines like a million moons, is the reservoir of nectar *(amrita* or *soma)*. When stimulated, the ambrosia of immortality issues copiously from it.

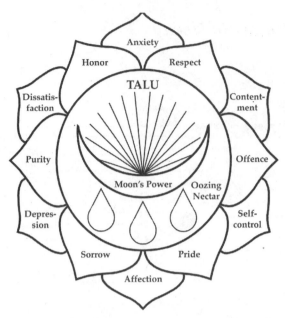

Figure 15a. Talu Chakra.

The key to attaining physical immortality, talu chakra is the pot of nectar *(amrita kalash),* and the soma oozing from it drips with rejuvenating power. This amrita fluid is called ambrosia, food of the Gods, elixir of life, nectar of immortality. The Tantrics call it *madya* (wine), Sufi poets call it "sweet wine," and Christians call it "blood of Christ."

"But whosoever drinketh of the water that I shall give him shall never thirst; but the water that I shall give him shall be in him a well of water springing up into everlasting life."
—*Jesus of Nazareth*[2]

The source of this nectar is a divine fluid that cascades downward from the highest chakra, sahasrara. This fluid represents satchitananda (absolute bliss consciousness), which originates in upper sahasrara at bindu, the gateway between the infinite and finite.

A point named the "10th," also called uvular point (*ghantika lingamula randhra* or *ghantika linga vivara*), is the pathway to the nectar reservoir in talu chakra. The nectar is retrieved by "10th point process" (*dashama dwara marga*), which consists of a yogic practice called tongue lock (*khechari mudra*).

This is accomplished by elongating the tongue through an involved process accomplished under the care of a fully enlightened master. Once the tongue is sufficiently lengthened, then it is curled back and pressed against the "10th point" in the uvula. This practice deepens meditation, strengthens the power of concentration, and brings tremendous energy and well-being. (See page 223 to practice a modified version.)

"But God clave a hollow place that was in the jaw, and there came water thereout; and when he had drunk, his spirit came again, and he revived."
—*Judeo Christian Bible*[3]

The talu or lalana chakra is sometimes called *kala chakra* (center of division) because it is the center where sushumna nadi bifurcates into an anterior branch, which passes through ajna on its way to *brahmarandhra*, and a posterior branch, which travels around the back of the skull before reaching brahmarandhra.

> *"The artery, called Sushumna, going upwards (from the heart to the Brahmarandhra), serving as the passage of the Prana, is divided within the palate. Through that artery, when it has been joined by the breath (held in subjection), by the sacred syllable Om, and by the mind (absorbed in the contemplation of Brahman), let him proceed upwards, and after turning the tip of the tongue to the palate, without using any of the organs of sense, let greatness perceive greatness. From thence he goes to selflessness, and through selflessness he ceases to be an enjoyer of pleasure and pain, he obtains aloneness (kevalatva, final deliverance)." —The Upanishads[4]*

Talu is seated at the hub of four pathways of breath. Two are of ordinary breath: the first to the lungs and second to the trachea. The other two are forms of *pranakundalini*: *adhahkundalini* and *urdhvakundalini*.

When breath is suspended and collected at talu chakra, *adhahkundalini* (lower kundalini) energy spirals down through sushumna, vibrating all the chakras.

When the inhaled and exhaled breaths become more rarified, they unite as *samana prana* (even breath), awakening the dormant energy in muladhara (root chakra). Then, transformed into udana prana (vertical breath) or *urdhvakundalini* (raised or ascendant kundalini), this energy pierces and dilates sushumna nadi (median channel). As it rises to the crown chakra, urdhvakundalini becomes purified and converts into vyana prana (all-permeating energy).

Talu Attainments

> *"Between the two palates there hangs the uvula, like a nipple—that is the starting-point of Indra (the lord) . . . He there obtains lordship, he reaches the lord of the mind. He becomes lord of speech, lord of sight, lord of hearing, lord of knowledge. Nay, more than this. There is the Brahman whose body is ether, whose nature is true, rejoicing in the senses (prana), delighted in the mind, perfect in peace, and immortal. Worship thus, O Prakinayogya!"*
> *—The Upanishads[5]*

Chapter Sixteen

CHAKRA 6: AJNA

"The light of the body is the eye: if therefore thine eye be single, thy whole body shall be full of light." —Jesus of Nazareth[1]

The *ajna* (command, order) chakra is so named for several reasons: As the distribution center for transmitting prana to various areas of the body, it commands prana. It is the key to the yoga technique *prana vidya* (psychic control and healing). When this chakra is awake, *sankalpa shakti* (willpower) is intensified and desires are fulfilled almost immediately. The transference of guru's *ajna* (order) occurs in this chakra.

The word *ajna* is pronounced phonetically as follows: "aagnya." It is not pronounced "aajnah."

This is the third eye (*tisra til*) of higher mind, the eye that looks inward rather than outward, the eye of Shiva (higher consciousness), center of divine sight, clairvoyance, wisdom, divine experiences, insight, spiritual discernment, revelation, and higher voice. Ajna is the seat of *sukshma prakriti* (primordial power of everything) and *atman* (higher self).

Whereas the five lower chakras are associated with the five elements, ajna chakra is the seat of the mind. The planetary ruler of ajna chakra is Jupiter. The Sanskrit name for this planet is *Guru* (the light that dispels darkness). In the ancient Vedas, ajna is symbolized by *Brihaspati, guru* (preceptor) of the *devas* (deities). Its day of the week is Thursday, and its esoteric color is blue. The astrological house ruled by ajna is the ninth house of wisdom, higher education, spiritual teaching, and learning, ruled by Sagittarius.

Location of Ajna

Ajna chakra is located in the center of the skull, within *chitrini nadi*, in the region of the pineal gland in the back portion of the brain's third ventricle. Directly in front of

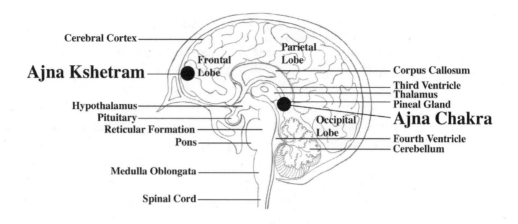

ajna on the same horizontal plane is the *ajna kshetram* trigger point—between the two eyebrows in the forehead at the center called *bhrumadhya* (brow center). The ajna chakra is directly connected to *bhrumadhya* through a *nadi* called *mahanadi* (great nadi). By placing a drop of tiger balm or camphor between your two eyebrows, you can increase sensitivity and intensify perception of bhrumadhya.

Awakening Ajna

You can awaken ajna by practicing *shambhavi mudra* (see page 224), as well as the following yoga asanas in my book *Exploring Meditation: Urdvasarvangasana,* page 112; *Halasana,* page 113; *Siddhasana,* page 114; *Padmasana,* page 115. In addition, you can learn and practice many powerful exercises to help you open ajna chakra in my book *Awaken Your Third Eye.*

Also, practice *pranayama* (breathing exercises, see Chapter 22) as follows: While practicing the inhalation and retention phases, place your attention on the muladhara chakra at the base of your spine. During the exhalation phase, place your attention on bhrumadhya in the forehead.

After practicing these techniques, say the following affirmation:

"I AM filled with God's peace and grace.
I AM a radiant being of beauty, power, and glory. I AM God's philanthropist,
God's messenger, and God's ambassador on earth.
My power is now used in God's service. Not my will but thy will be done.
Thank you God, and SO IT IS."

Pineal Gland

Ajna chakra corresponds to the cavernous plexus and is associated with the pineal gland—an endocrine gland in the middle of the brain responsible for receiving light, a biological clock that regulates your activities.

Light entering your eyes is directly sent to the hypothalamus and pineal gland, regulating the entire sympathetic nervous system. The pineal gland produces melatonin and other hormones in response to cosmic rhythms and cycles. These control sexual behavior, menstrual cycles, nervous energy, and other biological rhythms.

For example, in northern climates, such as Norway and Finland, the decreased sunlight causes higher incidences of irritability, fatigue, illness, insomnia, depression, alcoholism, and suicide.

The pineal gland is a gateway between the physical and subtler realms, a portal that opens or restricts psychic awareness. Hence, direct stimulation of your pineal gland via yogic practices can awaken ajna chakra.

Hexagonal Region

An "excellent" fluid, namely the *soma* nectar *(amrita),* is said to abide in the hollow of *ajna kshetram.* There the nadis of *ida, pingala,* and *sushumna* meet together at the junction of these three power conduits *(tripatha sthana* or *trikuti),* which forms a red hexagonal region. In fact, ida and pingala nadi end in ajna at the point where they conjoin with sushumna.

Therefore, bhrumadhya is termed *mukta triveni* (three strands where liberation is attained). It is also called Prayag, the ancient name for Allahabad city, India, where the three rivers Ganges, Yamuna, and mythical underground river Saraswati meet. The Ganges represents ida, Yamuna symbolizes pingala, and Saraswati indicates sushumna. In Allahabad, a special festival called *Kumbh Mela* (festival of the pot of nectar of immortality) celebrates bathing in the nectar of this chakra at the juncture of these three rivers. In 2001, 2007, and 2013, I took tour groups to this event, which 100 million people attended (the largest spiritual gathering in history).

Another symbol for the meeting of these three nadis is the Christian cross, where ida is balanced with pingala. The left side of the cross is ida, the right side is pingala, and the vertical line is sushumna, which continues upward to sahasrara. The three lines meet in ajna chakra, the egoless state, where you die (are crucified) to your old self.

Triangular Region

Within the hexagon is a triangle called *trirasra,* which is a *yoni* (female geni-talia)—the seat (*pada*) of the *linga* form (phallus) of Lord Shiva called *itara* (another, different from) *linga,* so named because it is different from, but leads directly to, the *para linga* in sahasrara (see Figure 16a).

Itara Shiva is the power of Shiva, representing full control over his desires in meditation. This linga, described as red, golden, or shining white, is more pre-cisely denoted as a *bindu* point in the center of the triangle, rather than a linga.

The triangular yoni, seat of Lord Shiva, is the supreme *shakti kundalini* (*para-makula*). Her energy, like streaks of lightning flashes, radiates from guru chakra to ajna as the mantra *aing,* which causes *brahma nadi* to arouse, manifesting the first *bija* (seed sound), primary source of the Vedas, the *pranava* in the ajna triangle, where kundalini is in its *pashyanti* (radiant sound) form OM.

Two Lotus Petals

The two petals of the ajna chakra are described by the ancients as vibrating with nectarous cool rays and intensely white color *(sushubhra)* or lightning-like color. The two petals of ajna represent the sun nadi (pingala) and moon nadi (ida), which merge in ajna.

The Sanskrit letters on these petals are the shining bright white letters *ham:* हं and *ksham:* क्षं. Or the mantras of Shiva *(hang:* हं *)* and Shakti *(kshang:* क्षं *).*

Figure 16a. Ajna Chakra.

The two petals of ajna are two radiations of power. One of these radiates down-ward through the five lower chakras. The other moves toward the upper chakras.

These radiations of *hang* and *kshang* are white, pure *(sattvic),* and powerful. In the radiations are the five *vayus* (vital airs), five divine powers, and kundalini power.

The white color indicates a preponderance of *udana vayu.* This vayu arouses the five *mahabhutas* (elements) and five *tanmatras* (sense objects) in the five lower chakras and the *antahkarana* (threefold mental capacity) in the manas and indu chakras.

When *hang* and *kshang* merge during meditation, the lower radiation stops and power gets concentrated in the upper radiation. Then the forceful upper radiation does not stop at manas or indu chakras, but instead passes directly to nirvana chakra, which causes *samadhi* (transcendence).

Bija Mantra OM (Ong)

Within the triangle is the moon-white, shining, splendorous, imperishable seed *(akshara bija)* mantra *OM*: ॐ. *OM* is believed to be the primary source of the Veda, and Veda is the precursor of the entire universe. Therefore, the first seed *(adi bija)* mantra is *OM*.

Ajna is the seat of kundalini as splendorous, pure, aroused inner consciousness. She emerges from her subtle form through the first sounds *(varna)* that form the *pranava (OM)*. The coils of kundalini are described as a luminous circle of light.

Lord Parashiva in Bindu

The sixth Shiva, known as Parashiva, dwells in the *bindu* point above the mantra *OM*: ॐ. He represents the subtle form of Brahman as *hiranyagarbha* (golden egg of creation), characterized by the bija mantra *OM*, which is the seed of the entire universe.

"I venerate the Supreme Creator of bliss situated in your Ajna-Chakra—between
the eye brows—resplendent like millions of suns and moons, adorned on his
side by the Supreme Power, meditating on whom with devotion, one lives in the
effulgent world which needs no light and is beyond the reach of the sun, moon,
and fire." —Adi Shankaracharya[2]

Doorkeeper Hakini

The power *(shakti)* and doorkeeper of ajna is Goddess Hakini, who is white like the moon. With six beautiful moon-like faces, curly hair, six arms, and three eyes in each face, her awareness is in supreme consciousness. Her eyes, beautifully

⊠ THE BIG BOOK OF CHAKRAS AND CHAKRA HEALING

painted with collyrium, are said to roll like a moving black bee. Her upper garment is white and her lower garment is red. She sits on a white lotus, and her white body symbolizes her rarified, pure form *(sattva guna).*

The third eye of Hakini is the light of deep meditation, while the other two eyes represent knowledge gleaned through sensory input and thought. The six faces of Hakini represent the five elements (mahabhutas) centered in the five lower chakras, and the mind (manas) located in ajna chakra.

Figure 16b. Hakini.

In one of Hakini's hands is a book *(vidya),* which is the highest supreme wisdom translated into understandable words. In another hand, she holds a skull *(kapala),* which is the perpetuation of spiritual consciousness (developed through meditation) even after death. In her third hand is held a drum *(damaru),* which symbolizes the silent mantra sounds transformed into *vaikhari* (audible sound). The fourth hand of Hakini holds a *rudraksha* rosary *(japavati),* indicating the spiritual practice *(sadhana)* of mantra repetition *(japa),* which awakens the mantra vibrations. Her fifth hand is in the gesture of granting boons *(vara mudra),* which imparts spiritual knowledge. The sixth hand is in the gesture of dispelling fear *(abhaya mudra),* which removes all obstacles to meditation.

Ajna Attainments

"He who always contemplates on the hidden Ajna lotus, at once destroys all the karmas of his past life, without any opposition. . . . All the fruits which have been described above as resulting from the contemplation of the other five lotuses, are obtained through the knowledge of this one Ajna lotus alone. . . . The wise one, who continually [contemplates] this Ajna lotus, becomes free from the mighty chain of desires, and enjoys happiness. When, at the time of death, the Yogi contemplates on this lotus, leaving this life, that holy one is absorbed in the Paramatma [supreme soul]." —Siva Samhita[3]

Chapter Seventeen

AJNA SUBCENTERS

*"Draw the breath up to the Brahmarandhra at the top of
the head. Kindle the fire, purify the subtle channels, burn
up the impurities. This is the yoga-fire of deliberation . . .
The pure energy of the Supreme."*
—*Swami Nityananda*[1]

In addition to the two-petaled *ajna chakra* (third eye wheel), three other chakras exist within the brain: *manas chakra, indu chakra,* and *nirvana chakra,* which you will explore in this chapter. According to ancient scriptures of India, there are three seats *(pithas)* in the forehead region. They are called *bindu, nada,* and *shakti.* The bindu lotus is the dot above the mantra *OM:* ॐ in ajna. The nada is manas chakra, and the shakti is indu chakra.

Manas Chakra: Sensory Mind

Manas (mind) chakra, your mental vehicle, consists of three parts: conscious mind or lower, instinctive mind *(manas chitta);* subconscious, emotional, or impression mind *(sanskara chitta);* and habitual, patterned mind *(vasana chitta).* This chakra is ruled by the planet Mercury, which governs mental activity, the sign Gemini, ruler of lower mind, and the third house of the astrology chart.

Also known as sensory or lower mind, manas is responsible for perceiving sensory impressions. More powerful and rarified than your physical senses, it makes your senses operate by transporting sensations to your higher chakras in the brain.

Sense operations such as seeing or hearing are dependent on bodily eyes or ears, but manas can operate independently of these sense organs, even after death. Subtle manas *(sukshmarupa manas)* is not only responsible for outer sensory per-

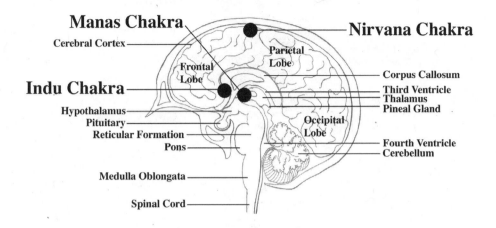

Manas Chakra
Cerebral Cortex
Nirvana Chakra
Parietal Lobe
Frontal Lobe
Indu Chakra
Corpus Callosum
Third Ventricle
Thalamus
Pineal Gland
Hypothalamus
Pituitary
Reticular Formation
Pons
Occipital Lobe
Fourth Ventricle
Cerebellum
Medulla Oblongata
Spinal Cord

ception, but also awareness of subtle sense perception, such as clairvoyant sight, not dependent on physical eyes.

Location of Manas

The location of manas chakra is a sub-center within ajna. It is found in chittrini nadi, above ajna chakra, above the bindu of *OM*: ॐ in a second *nada* (crescent moon shape). This corresponds to the front part of the brain's third ventricle.

Six Lotus Petals

Manas chakra, said to be white color, has six petals, which are connected to the five sense objects *(tanmatras)* of odor, flavor, form, touch, and sound. The sixth petal is connected to sleep. The colors of the petals are associated with the senses: Smell is yellow, taste is white, form is red, touch is ash, sound is white, and sleep is black.

Chitta: Center of Sense Impressions

The part of your mind called *chitta* (awareness) is located in manas chakra. There are two aspects of consciousness: the relative, dualistic nature and the absolute nature. Your individuality (I-ness) experiences external and internal sensory objects—things, people, thoughts, and impressions. This "I" awareness is called *chitta*—sense consciousness.

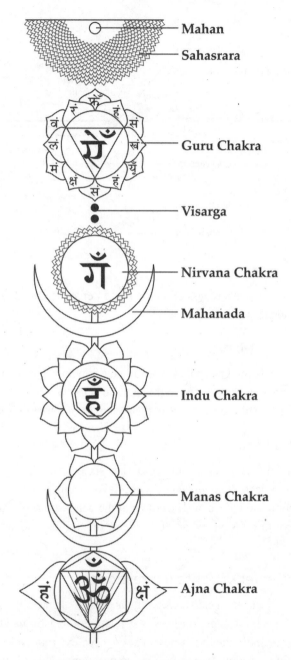

Figure 17a. Ajna and Sahasrara System.

THE BIG BOOK OF CHAKRAS AND CHAKRA HEALING

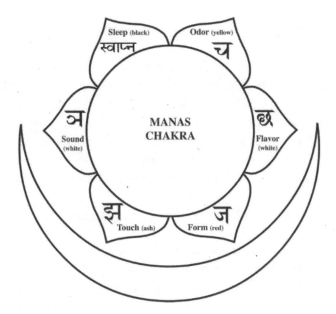

Figure 17b. Manas Chakra.

When your mind settles to quietude in deep meditation, then objects of perception become subtle images, ideas, and feelings. To perceive these subtle objects, your chitta transforms into superconsciousness (*dhi*), which uses subtle senses, such as clairvoyance, clairaudience, and clairsentience.

Once you transcend the relative dual nature of your mind and unify with the absolute, your "I" awareness of chitta and dhi are absorbed. At this stage, your awareness is no longer dual. You are in the state of *samadhi*—evenness of intellect.

In waking life, you are continually receiving impressions through your sensory organs: nose, tongue, skin, eyes, and ears. The sensory impulses reach the brain and are then transformed into subtle *vayu* (vital air) impulses, which pass through *ida nadi* to the chakras.

The vayu form of smell is conveyed to muladhara, taste goes to svadhishthana, form and color go to manipura, touch passes to anahata, and sound goes to vishuddha. After these sense impulses are processed in the chakras, they radiate through the chakra petals to ida nadi and then travel to manas chakra through ida nadi.

Manas then sends these impulses to chitta, where they are transformed into senses of smelling, tasting, seeing, feeling, and hearing. When these mental/sensory impulses are blocked by *tamas guna* (destructive force) in the chitta, you become unconscious and fall asleep.

Chitta permanently stores every sensory impression passing through it, although most of the impressions are not consciously recognized or remembered. These indelible impressions are called *samskaras*.

Perceptions and thoughts that create impressions of pleasure travel to chitta as notion (*bodha*), which becomes feeling (*bhava*). Feeling then becomes love (*raga*), mixed with desire (*kama*). Desire, mixed with will (*manasyana*), becomes volition (*chikirsha*) and then conation (*kriti*). Conation becomes the conative impulse (*kratu*), which is then conveyed to one of the five lower chakras, where it then emerges as a pre-motor impulse, carried to the brain by *pingala nadi*.

Indu Chakra: Intellect

The Sanskrit term *indu* (drop, moon) refers to drops of nectar *(soma)* that drip from the moon region in your subtle body. Indu chakra is also called *brahma chakra* (wheel of brahma), *chandra mandala* (moon circle), and *soma chakra* (nectar wheel). This chakra is ruled by the planet Uranus, which governs the intellect and higher mind, the sign Aquarius, and the 11th house in astrology.

Figure 17c. Indu Chakra.

Location of Indu

Indu chakra is located in the brain within the *chitrini nadi*, just above ajna chakra, in the front part of the brain's third ventricle, in the region of the *lamina terminalis* and *commissura anterior*. See page 175 for a diagram.

Opening Indu

The following practices in my book *Exploring Meditation* will help you open this chakra: "Developing Intellect," page 104; and *Urdhvasarvangasana,* page 112.

Indu chakra, moon-white in color, has 16 lotus petals. On the petals of this chakra are the following special qualities *(vrittis):* mercy, gentleness, patience, non-attachment, control, excellent qualities, joyous mood, deep spiritual love, humility, reflection, restfulness, seriousness, effort, controlled emotion, magnanimity, and concentration.

Bija Mantra Hamsah (Hangsah)

In the moon lotus or indu chakra is a nine-cornered region within which is an isle of gems *(manidvipa)*. Within this isle of gems is the seed mantra of Shiva *(shambu bija)*, hang: हँः.

Because the mantra of Shiva is *hang* and mantra of Shakti is *sah,* the mantra denoting Shiva-Shakti is *hangsah:* हँसः, otherwise known as *hamsah:* हंसः. This mantra, in its power as consciousness, is supreme Being (Brahman). In its power as sound, it is Shiva in divine form. Hangsah is in the form of a swan, which sits on a golden lotus.

The beak of the swan is the *pranava (OM)*. The wings are two forms of Tantra called *agama* and *nigama.* The feet are the power of consciousness. The swan's three eyes are the three *bindus* (see pages 81-82 and 106).

Paramashiva in Bindu

In the lap of hangsah, which is the bindu above the crescent moon of hangsah हँसः, sits the deity Paramashiva, also called Mahadeva, seated to the right of his consort (shakti), called Siddhakali. The crystal white Paramashiva is eternal bliss, the immutable, supreme being Bhagavan (God), endowed with supreme yoga power.

With braided hair and adorned with the crescent moon in his forehead, Paramashiva is dressed in a tiger skin. His shakti Siddhakali is four-armed, yellow in

Figure 17d. Paramashiva-Siddhakali.

color, beautiful, and decorated with various ornaments. She holds a drum, trident, and noose, and makes the gesture of dispelling fear.

Buddhi Tattva

Indu chakra is the seat of *buddhi* (intellect). This aspect of mind gains higher knowledge than chitta: the sense mind located in manas chakra. Chitta, responsible for sensory perception, can only derive sensory knowledge *(sangjnana)*. In contrast, the knowledge obtained by buddhi is intellectual knowledge *(vijnana)*. The primary functions of buddhi are higher intellection *(manisha)*, thought *(mati)*, intellection *(manana)*, insight *(drishti)*, and retention *(medha)*.

Nirvana Chakra: Concentrated Mind

Nirvana (extinguishing or dowsing a flame) chakra is where your ego, along with its cravings and defects, gets annihilated when kundalini passes through it. This chakra is ruled by Neptune, planet of ego dissolution, the sign Pisces, and the 12th house in astrology, which connotes absorption and loss.

Nirvana chakra is also known as *parabrahma chakra* (highest brahma wheel), *shatapatra* (hundred-petaled lotus), *shantipada* (lotus of peace), *kala chakra* (wheel of time), and *brahmarandhra* (hollow of brahma).

Location of Nirvana

Nirvana chakra is the highest center in *chitrini nadi*. Inside chitrini lies *brahma nadi,* otherwise known as *brahmarandhra,* so subtle that it does not manifest until kundalini passes through it.

Three nested energy tubes (*nadis*) called *sushumna*, *vajrini* or *vajra*, and *chitrini* arise from the center of the bulb root (*kanda mula*) just below the first chakra (muladhara). These three nadis then ascend through the middle of the vertebral column into the brain. (See Figure 5c on page 46.)

At the innermost core of these three nadis is *brahma nadi*. Brahma nadi does not start from kanda mula, however. It originates from the mouth of *svayambhu linga* in muladhara. From that point the four nadis travel up the spine to the top of the brain, where they all terminate at a point called *brahmarandhra*—that is, the point where brahma nadi (also known as brahmarandhra) ends.

Brahma nadi is described as hollow, a subtle vacuum deep within sushumna. Normally it is closed at the lower end. When kundalini is roused, she unlocks this closure and travels up to the brain. Brahma nadi is called path of brahma (*brahma marga*), because kundalini passes through it to reach sahasrara and unify with Lord Shiva. All the cosmic principles (*tattvas*) are absorbed by kundalini on her way up the spine. Therefore, it is said that brahma nadi devours all tattvas.

Brahmarandhra, also called nirvana chakra, is located in the upper portion of the cerebral cortex, about five fingers back from the hairline, at the soft spot where the skull bones come together in infancy: *anterior fontanelle*. (See the figure on page 175.)

Opening Nirvana

The following practices in my book *Exploring Meditation* can help you open this chakra: "Developing mind and will power" and "Developing memory" on page 103.

Close your eyes and imagine that the subtle yet powerful kundalini is slowly rising up your spine, piercing every chakra and absorbing each of the tattvas within the chakras. Finally, see kundalini arriving at nirvana chakra at the top of the skull. Then say the following affirmation aloud:

"I AM absorbed in kundalini's all-consuming power.
I surrender to the will of God. My being expands to touch the infinite
as I disappear into wholeness. I AM filled with the bliss of nirvana,
and I AM at peace. Thank you God, and SO IT IS."

One Hundred Lotus Petals

The nirvana chakra has 100 lustrous white petals surrounding its center. Within the chakra is *jalandhara pitha* (seat of a large network of nadis), which leads to liberation. This is consciousness, shining with blue light. The chakra is the seat of kundalini's supreme consciousness power. It is also said that Shiva dwells in nirvana chakra in shining smoke color.

Figure 17e. Nirvana Chakra.

Bija Mantra Gam (Gang)

The mantra of jalandhara is the bija mantra *gang*: गं. This mantra embodies the spiritual knowledge developed in meditation *(prajnana)*, which is higher than knowledge acquired through the sense mind *(sangjnana)*, or knowledge discovered through the intellect *(vijnana)*.

Dhi Tattva

Nirvana chakra is the seat of the focused mind *(dhi)*, as well as the center of the ego or "I-ness" *(aham)*. Dhi is the part of your mind that sifts through innumerable sensory objects and focuses on a particular object. By concentrating on one object, your mind develops clearer thought, greater intellection, and better retentive power. Thus dhi is responsible for arousing deeper thought intellection *(manisha)*.

The main function of dhi is the ability to concentrate. The bindu point is the symbol of the highest form of concentration, in which consciousness is centralized in oneness. The practice of *samyama*, according to the sage Patanjali's *Yoga Sutras*, develops oneness in three stages:

Dharana (concentration) is holding the attention of the mind (chitta) fixed on a particular object or point of space.

Dhyana (meditation) is the continuous, unbroken flow of the same knowledge. Here the mind lets go of the object and allows it to be absorbed or disappear into wholeness.

Samadhi (evenness of intellect) is the transcendental state of pure awareness, the experience of oneness and wholeness in *satchitananda*, absolute bliss consciousness. Here even "I-ness" gets absorbed into oneness.

"When the object of meditation only shines forth in the mind, as if devoid of the thought of self even, then it is called samadhi or concentration." —Patanjali[2]

The perfections *(siddhis)* of supernormal powers described in *Yoga Sutras*, such as levitation, omniscience, disappearing, walking through walls, and so forth, are accomplished through this process of samyama. The state of *samaprajnata samadhi* is accomplished by practicing samyama on material objects, subtle objects, the forms of deities *(devatas)*, and the formless absolute.

Higher Mind Attainments

"As a lamp does not flicker in a windless place, so is the yogi of subdued thought, absorbed in the union (yoga) with the Self. That state in which the mind finds rest, quieted by the practice of yoga, in which, seeing the Self by the Self alone, he finds contentment in the Self. Knowing that infinite joy gained only by the intellect, beyond the senses, established in that, he does not waver from reality." —Lord Krishna[3]

Chapter Eighteen

GURU CHAKRA

"There in the lotus within the moon, High in the top of the head of man. The Guru dwells in the Sahasrar, Enclosed by a figure whose sides are three. Supreme Hamsa is also there; Remember the Guru with love each day." —Shree Guru Gita[1]

The *sahasrara* chakra, otherwise known as the thousand-petaled lotus or crown chakra, consists of three aspects:

Guru chakra, the lower part of sahasrara.

Sahasrara, the thousand-petaled lotus.

The higher aspect, consisting of Shankhini and supreme *bindu*.

In chapters 18 and 19, you will discover all three aspects of sahasrara.

Guru Chakra

The lower part of Sahasrara is the lotus named *guru* chakra, from the Sanskrit roots *gu* (darkness, ignorance) and *ru* (removing). Thus guru dispels spiritual darkness by restoring sight to those blind to their true nature.

The Sanskrit word for the planet Jupiter is *Guru*. Therefore, Jupiter is the planetary ruler of this chakra. The astrological seat of Jupiter is the ninth house, which represents the spiritual preceptor.

Location of Guru

The ancient scriptures say that Guru is seated in a circular, lustrous, white, nectarous moon region just below the thousand-petaled lotus. Guru chakra is an upward-facing 12-petaled lotus, located in the lower part of the downward-facing, thousand-petaled lotus. Therefore the energy within guru is always directed upward.

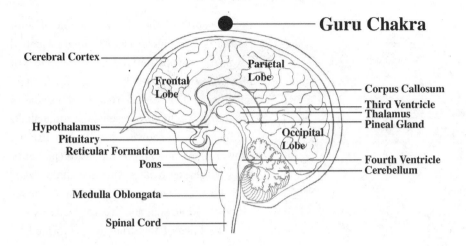

The guru chakra is described as a head ornament of the stalk *(chitrini nadi)* that supports the passage of kundalini, running from muladhara chakra to sahasrara chakra. Above the top endpoint of *chitrini nadi,* guru chakra is situated in the lower deep hollow part of sahasrara.

Opening Guru Chakra

To awaken guru chakra, first thing upon arising in the morning, sit up on your bed and imagine a white divine form in the white 12-petaled lotus just above your head. Then imagine that *amrita,* the nectar of immortality, is flowing from the divine form. After you have completely bathed in amrita, say aloud:

> "I AM energized and immortalized by the nectar of ambrosia, amrita.
> I AM filled with vitality, youthfulness, immortality, and happiness.
> Thank you, God, and SO IT IS."

Twelve Lotus Petals

Guru chakra is 12-petaled. The white mantras on the petals of guru chakra are *ham, sam, kham, freng, ham, sam, ksham, mam, lam, vam, ram, yung:* हं सं खं फ्रें हं सं क्षं मं लं वं रं यूँ. These 12 letters comprise the guru mantra: *ha, sa, kha, freng, ha, sa, ksha, ma, la, va, ra, yung:* ह स ख फ्रें ह स क्ष म ल व र यूँ.

A-ka-tha Triangle

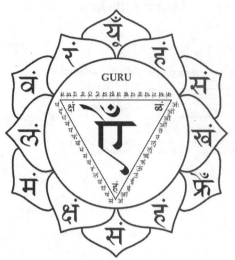

Figure 18a. Guru Chakra.

In the center of the circular region of guru chakra is a triangular shaped diagram called a *yantra,* a word derived from the Sanskrit root *yam* (to support the energy inherent in an object). This is the triangle of kundalini (*abalalaya*), which represents the three shaktis: *iccha shakti* (power of will), *kriya shakti* (power of action), and *jnana shakti* (power of knowledge), associated with the three *gunas* of Prakriti: *sattva, rajas,* and *tamas,* in the regions of moon, sun, and fire, respectively.

The lines of this triangle are formed by the letters of the Sanskrit alphabet, and its apex is pointed downward. These three lines begin with the letters *a, ka,* and *tha.* In the corners of the triangle are letters *ha, la,* and *ksha.*

The line of 16 vowels from *a* to *ah,* beginning with the letter *a,* starts at the apex of the triangle, pointed downward. This line of letters moves up the left side of the triangle. This *"a"* line of letters is called *vama,* the rajas guna line.

The line of letters *ka* to *ta,* beginning with *ka,* starts from the top of the left side and forms the base of the triangle. This *"ka"* line of letters is called *jyeshtha,* the sattva guna line.

The line of letters from *tha* to *sa,* beginning with *tha,* starts from the right end of the base and moves downward toward the apex. This *"tha"* line of letters is called *roudri,* the tamas guna line.

It is said that within this triangle the splendorous kundalini, in the form of three-and-a-half coils, is seated.

Bija Mantra Aim (Aug)

Within the triangle is the mantra known as *vagbhava bija* (guru seed mantra) *aing:* This mantra embodies as aspect of supreme consciousness.

Between the white half-moon (*nada*) and the red dot (*bindu*) above the Sanskrit mantra aing: ऐं is a jeweled altar (*manipitha mandala*), encrusted with gems of pink luster. This altar is said to shine with more radiance than a brilliant lightning flash. It is also called a bright throne (*singhasana*), between nada and bindu of the mantra *aing*: ऐं, on which the lustrous white Guru is seated.

Hangsah in Bindu

The ancients tell us that primordial *hangsah* sits in the red dot or points (bindu) above the bija mantra *aing:* ऐं. The magnificent hangsah is Lord Shiva and Shakti (kundalini) in union. Hangsah is described as growing like a flame and destroyer of the universe. Thus the power of kundalini absorbs all cosmic principles and hence devours them. The form of hangsah is a swan.

> *"'Ham' and 'Sah' are the symbols of the Guru's eyes; He is the source of the universe. By His will He appears in living form on earth, Lifting up the hearts of men. Free of bonds, He is everywhere eternally, Deathless Spirit, God Divine. Everywhere He is manifesting as the world." —Shree Guru Gita[2]*

Guru in Bindu

Within the seat of hangsah, the lotus feet of Guru are resting on a footstool (*paduka*). He is seated on a jeweled throne in the red bindu (dot or point) above the mantra: *aing:* ऐं. The feet of Guru are described as red, like young leaves, glistening with nectar, beautiful as lotuses in a lake, with nails bright as the moon. From the lotus feet of Guru, the saffron red life substance (*amrita*) continually flows. Guru is moon white in color, with a motionless, calm, quiescent body anointed with white sandal paste, emanating the fragrance of purity. He is described as seated in one of the following yoga postures: lotus posture (*padmasana*), hero posture (*virasana*), or auspicious pose (*svastikasana*). Contented, delighted, and tranquil, he is dazzling as the autumn moon.

Figure 18b. Guru-Shakti.

Wearing a sweet-smelling white flower garland, clad in divine white silk clothing, and decorated with white ornaments, Guru has a smiling, beautiful, moonlike face, two arms, and two ruddy eyes that are bright and full of supreme bliss. He holds a lotus and makes gestures of granting boons (*vara mudra*) and dispelling fear (*abhaya mudra*). He is seated under an umbrella-like lotus with 1,000 petals, facing downward.

His look is kind, he is full of knowledge and bliss, and he embodies all the deities *(devatas)*. Because he is supreme Brahman, he is, therefore, greeted with respect. Guru is a manifestation of both Paramashiva and Ishvara. Paramashiva is the highest, most abstract form of Brahman, its formless and attributeless nature, infinite and supreme, without limitations of mind, time, or space. This is the state of consciousness known as *asamprajnata samadhi*. When Guru as consciousness appears in a form, he manifests as God *(Ishvara)*, the omnipotent and omniscient deity.

"The Guru is Brahma, He is Vishnu; There is no doubt He is Shiva, too. God and Guru in fact are one; Salutations I offer Him. He is the Cause of the universe; He is the Bridge to cross over change. He is the Source from which knowledge comes. To Shiva, the Guru, I bow my head." —Shree Guru Gita[3]

Shakti in Bindu

The consort of Guru, his Shakti (power), is seated on his left thigh. She holds Guru's body with her right hand, and her left hand holds a blue lotus. Self-luminous, glowing with a divine lotus face, with red lips and a red body, she is arrayed with various red ornaments.

She is kundalini in form and also *unmani,* the power by which awareness severs itself from all objects and is established in the highest state of *samadhi*. This power arises from kundalini.

When the form of Guru and his Shakti are absorbed into kundalini, then she appears as magnificent, splendorous light.

Guru Attainments

"The mire of sin will be washed away, And the knowledge of Truth will shine; With the water of Guru's feet, Cross the ocean of ignorance. Ignorance can be rooted out; Put an end to the round of births. Non-attachment and wisdom gain; Drink the wine of the Guru's feet." —Shree Guru Gita[4]

Chapter Nineteen

CHAKRA 7: SAHASRARA

"The Saivas call it [Sahasrara] the abode of Siva; the Vaisnavas call it Parama Purusa; others again, call it the place of Hari-Hara. Those who are filled with a passion for the Lotus feet of the Devi call it the excellent abode of the Devi; and other great sages (Munis) call it the pure place of Prakrti-Purusa."
—Purnananda[1]

O ften termed crown chakra, *sahasrara* (thousandfold), the thousand-petaled lotus, is the center of godliness, illumination, and spiritual enlightenment. Sahasrara is a shining sheath-like hemispherical formation resembling an umbrella over your skull. In its center is supreme spirit *(antaratman)*.

The esoteric color of sahasrara is green, its day of the week is Wednesday, and its planet is Mercury, the planet that represents a network of infinite interrelated connections. Sahasrara is ruled by the astrological sign Virgo and the sixth house, which governs the *nadi* system. The *bindu* point in upper sahasrara is associated with the eighth house, connoting annihilation, and Pluto, planet of death and transmutation.

Location of Sahasrara

Sahasrara is situated above *brahmarandhra*, which means beyond the point where the four internally nested *nadis (sushumna, vajra, chitrini,* and *brahma)* terminate at nirvana chakra. Thus it is located outside the physical body, above your head.

Kundalini travels from nirvana chakra to sahasrara by piercing the skull, passing through a subtle power bridge called *visarga*, and reaching guru chakra and sahasrara. (See figure on page 190 and Figure 19b on page 194.)

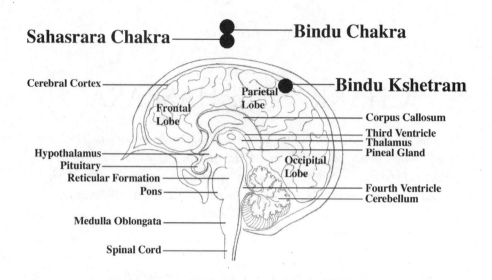

Sahasrara Chakra — **Bindu Chakra**

Cerebral Cortex — — **Bindu Kshetram**

Parietal Lobe

Frontal Lobe

Corpus Callosum

Third Ventricle
Thalamus

Hypothalamus — Pineal Gland

Pituitary

Reticular Formation — Occipital Lobe

Pons

Fourth Ventricle
Cerebellum

Medulla Oblongata —

Spinal Cord —

Opening Sahasrara

To awaken sahasrara, close your eyes and imagine an umbrella of 1,000 radiances of light above your head. See or feel these radiances *(rashmi)* pouring divine light into your being. Imagine they are filling every pore of your body with beauteous white light. Then say the following affirmation aloud:

"I AM a radiant being of light. I AM filled with God's light.
I AM the light that God is. I AM a beautiful being of light.
My being is filled with the light of divinity.
God's infinite rays of light are pouring upon me now with
beauteous streams of nectar, ecstasy, and bliss.
I AM at peace. Thank you God, and SO IT IS."

Moon Region

In the center of sahasrara is a circular full-moon region, shining with countless brilliant rays of light. Nectarous and delightful, the abode of immortality, its nature is consciousness. The center of the lotus is golden and endowed with various pow-

THE BIG BOOK OF CHAKRAS AND CHAKRA HEALING

ers. Inside the moon region is a brilliant triangle (*trikona* or *trikuta*), the abode of Shiva (Mount Kailasa).

Supreme Bindu

Within the triangle is a circular void *(shunya)* called supreme bindu *(parabindu)*, seat of Shiva-Shakti. In the center of this circle is supreme void *(paramashunya)*, dwelling place of Paramashiva, the seventh Shiva, subtle, infinite, formless, changeless, beyond mind and matter. Paramashiva is beyond *samprajnata samadhi* and realizable only through *asamprajnata samadhi*.

This subtle void, the main source of never-ending supreme bliss, bestower of immortality and liberation, is kept secret and worshipped by the yogis. Through long, regular practice of meditation, this pure form of supreme *bindu* is realized.

When kundalini reaches supreme bindu, then all principles *(tattvas)*, as well as their source, Prakriti, are absorbed in supreme bindu, beyond *maya,* nameless, formless, and absolute. What remains is Shiva in eternal union with Shakti. Their infinite power condenses into supreme bindu, a highly concentrated point of contraction, potential, and creative energy.

The reality of supreme bindu is ultimate illumination, where awareness becomes superconsciousness, and there is neither experiencer nor experience. There is only wholeness, oneness, and absolute bliss consciousness *(satchitananda)*, permanently established in everyday life.

One Thousand Lotus Petals

Sahasrara is said to face downward, with its arrangement of petals appearing bell-shaped, like an umbrella. The petals of this lotus shine white like the moon. Its lightning-like splendorous filaments are red. It is described as mixture of white and red, because the bindu of Shiva is white and bindu of Shakti is red. Their combination is called *kamala,* from the Sanskrit roots *ka* (sun) and *mala* (emitting both light and sound). The petals of sahasrara are the abode of all powers, all Sanskrit letters, and all mantras.

According to legend, upon reaching sahasrara chakra and encountering Lord Shiva, kundalini encircles the Shiva linga (bindu or void) as a garland strung with all 50 letters of the Sanskrit alphabet from *a* to *la*, with *ksha* in the mouth, meaning the central letter. This is the garland of 50 letters *(panchashika mala)* on the string

Figure 19a. Sahasrara Chakra.

of Shiva-Shakti. It is said that the splendorous, supreme kundalini encircles the circumference of the void with three-and-one-half coils, like a snake.

In the Upanishads, Lord Shiva (as consciousness) is described as Surya (Sun), possessing 1,000 light radiances (*rashmi*). He is in union with supreme kundalini in supreme bindu, where she is *shabdabrahman,* the source of sound vibration as supreme sound *(para nada).*

When the *prana* of supreme kundalini becomes intensely concentrated in bindu, she becomes potential sound power: *para nada* in the latent triangular form of A-U-M in equilibrium—Prakriti embodying the three gunas in balance (see pages 85–86).

THE BIG BOOK OF CHAKRAS AND CHAKRA HEALING

When fully infused with prana, *nada* becomes the principal of sound (*para-shabda*), which emits as radiant sound (*pashyanti*) in the form of *pranava: aum:* ૐ, the seed sound and source of all possible mantras. This is the first manifestation of light, with 1,000 light powers. When radiant sound (*pashyanti*) is transformed into subtle sound (*madhyama*), the thousand light powers become distinct petals (radiations), resonating mantra sounds (see pages 107–109).

Then *aum* splits into 50 distinct mantra sound units in 20 different strengths: kundalini power, three bindus, three attributes of creation (gunas), three specific powers, five deities (devatas), and five vital airs (pranas), totaling 20. Thus the petals of sahasrara are arranged in 20 layers, with 50 petals per layer. Each of the 20 layers has all 50 letters on its petals.

The 50 mantras in sahasrara radiate as light beams (*rashmi*) to the petals in the first six chakras (from muladhara to ajna). Therefore, the letters on the petals of these six chakras total 50—all the letters of the Sanskrit alphabet.

The *japa* (recitation) of the 50 mantras is performed in two ways: from *a* to *la,* which is called *anuloma,* and from *la* to *a,* which is called *viloma.* When taken together, these anuloma and viloma mantras constitute 100 mantras.

The Sun God Surya, in the form of light (*jyotirupa*), radiates 1,000 light beams *(sahasrarashmi)* in 100 forms. Thus, from sahasrara arises the hundred-petaled nirvana chakra.

The Kalas in Bindu

Let us now understand the *kalas* (from *kal*—count, reckon) in the mysterious bindu by exploring the *kalachakra* (wheel of time) for a moment. The *nityas* (eternities) of the Divine Mother represent the 15 lunar days *(tithis)* of the waxing moon. The full circle of nityas equals 21,600 *shvasas*—the average number of human breaths taken in one day and night. The arms or rays of the 15 nityas total 108, and each nitya has 1,440 breaths—1/15th part of 21,600 breaths.

The Goddess appears in phases, just like the moon. Her 15 nityas are three gunas in five elements of ether, air, fire, water, and earth. The 16th kala (full moon day) is the supreme Goddess herself.

The 16 nityas equate to the 16 vowels in the Sanskrit alphabet. The 36 tattvas equal 36 consonants in the alphabet. When these 36 tattvas are multiplied by 16 nityas, the total is 576. Multiples of this number can be used to calculate the number of years in various *yugas*—cycles of time. (See pages 72–78.)

Human life has the same structure of 16 kalas as the cosmos. The nityas are identified with various stages of deep sleep, dreaming, waking, and full consciousness or *turiya* (fourth state). The nityas are 16 parts of the continuum of consciousness, and the 17th kala is transcendental awareness.

Kundalini's Path to Supreme Bindu

In order to express her powers of absorption, *kundalini shakti* manifests a triangle within sahasrara and displays herself in four aspects: *ama kala, nirvana kala, nirodhika vahni,* and *nirvana shakti*. Finally she is absorbed into the void within the triangle.

In the triangle, kundalini appears as the 16th phase (kala) of the moon, called *shashi* or *ama* (moon) *kala,* shining red as the morning sun. Pure, lustrous, and soft, like 10 million lightning flashes, her form is as subtle as the 100th part of a delicate lotus filament. Her face is downward, in one-half coil (crescent moon shape). *Ama*

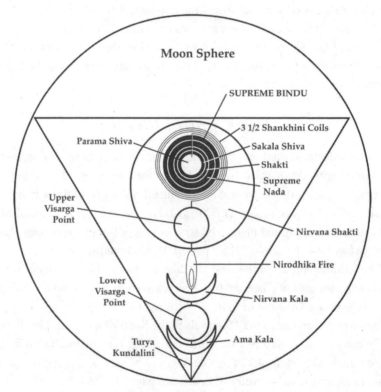

Figure 19b. Kundalini Absorption in Supreme Bindu.

THE BIG BOOK OF CHAKRAS AND CHAKRA HEALING

kala is always aroused, immutable, and immortal. She is the source of an abundantly flowing stream of nectar from the blissful union of Shiva and Shakti in bindu.

Nirvana kala, which lies within ama kala, is kundalini's manifested power of absorption, said to be most excellent and subtle, like the 1,000th part of the end of a hair. The supreme Goddess (Bhagavati), she abides within the personal God *(ishtadevata).* In crescent moon shape, bright as the luster of 10 million suns and cool as 10 million moons, she is the 17th *niranjana kala* (unstained crescent moon), from the Sanskrit roots *nir* (without, nil) and *anjana* (form, stained).

Within nirvana kala is supreme control power *(nirodhika)* in the form of fire *(vahni),* where sound is unmanifest *(para nada).* There lies the supreme, primordial *nirvana shakti* (all-absorbing kundalini power). She is red and lustrous like 10 million morning suns, mother of the three worlds, source of the universe as mantra, subtle and hidden, like the 10 millionth part of the end of a hair. She is pure and ever aware of Lord Shiva. Her love and gladness flow in a constant stream. The life of all beings, she graciously imparts the knowledge of Brahman to the mind of the sages. She is consciousness itself and is without support; that is, in herself.

"Within Her [Nirvana Shakti] is the everlasting place called the abode of Shiva, which is free from Maya, attainable only by Yogis, and known by the name of Nityananda. It is replete with every form of bliss, and is pure knowledge itself. Some call it the Brahman; others call it Hamsa. Wise men describe it as the abode of Vishnu, and righteous men speak of it as the ineffable place of knowledge of the Atma, or the place of Liberation." —Purnananda[2]

Visarga Power Bridge

Above the circular moon region in sahasrara is a power bridge *(visarga),* consisting of the two dots to the right in the Sanskrit letter *ah,* written thus: अः. Visarga is described as kundalini, shining red, like red lightning. Within visarga lies the essence of the five vital airs *(pranas),* the five deities *(devatas),* and all knowledge.

The letter *a:* अ, first in the string of letters in the kundalini coil, is the starting point of kundalini's upward-thrusting motion. The end point—the dual nature of *aham* and *idam*—is visarga.

In sahasrara chakra, the first dot of visarga is located just above ama kala, and the second dot is just below supreme bindu. These two dots form a bridge of duality through which kundalini travels from sahasrara to the oneness of supreme bindu.

Power Shankhini

After passing through sahasrara, kundalini becomes supreme kundalini in spiral form, known as Shankhini. She is located above sahasrara and above the second dot of visarga. Shankhini, as supreme knowledge, is united with Sakalashiva, and then finally absorbed into *dhruva mandala* (polestar region), the infinity of Paramashiva.

Shiva Shakti

In the center of sahasrara lies a nectarous ocean. Within it, on an isle of gems, the wish-fulfilling tree grows. On that isle, inside a radiant temple with four doors,

is an altar with the 50 mantra letters of the Sanskrit alphabet. On the altar is a jeweled throne, where Shakti (Mahakali) and Paramashiva (Maha Rudra) are seated in union. As individualized beings, they are in sexual union (called *rasa*). However, because they are formless, non-dual, and not individualized, they are one and the same (*virasa*).

Here Shiva, like the sun, destroys the darkness of unspirituality, delusion, and ignorance. At the same time, Shakti gives rise to the mirage of duality—the origin of this finite, phenomenal, ephemeral world that veils the infinite imperishable absolute. Therefore, she is called *maya* (that which does not exist—illusion).

In the state of asamprajnata samadhi, the supreme power Shakti is one and the same as Paramashiva. Because they are unified in a seamless oneness, without distinction, the Ardhanarishvara form is fitting to depict this wholeness. In this form of the merged Shiva-Shakti, the right half of the body is Shiva and left half is Shakti. According to the ancients, Para-

Figure 19c. Ardhanarishvara

mashiva is like pure crystal, joyful and smiling, with three lotus eyes, eight beautiful arms, a garland of 1,000 lotuses, adorned with earrings, a pearl necklace, and handsome anklets.

Kundalini's Forms and Powers

The ancients say that when kundalini travels into the void region (sahasrara), she remains only momentarily, then returns to muladhara (root chakra). Only by consistent practice does divine union become permanent. When Shakti unites with Paramashiva in sahasrara, the perfected *siddha* (adept) becomes *jivan mukti* (liberated soul), dwelling in eternal bliss, possessing all powers.

As kundalini travels through the chakras, she exhibits various forms:

1. In root chakra (muladhara), she is Kula (root, lineage, dynasty) Kundalini. Here she rests in *samadhi* (transcendence) as *svayambhu linga*. She is a nonentity, as if asleep.

2. When awakened, she is termed Vahni (fire) Kundalini, deep red in color as she moves from muladhara to the heart chakra (anahata).

3. In anahata, she becomes Surya (Sun) Kundalini of brilliant vermilion color as she moves to the bottom of third eye chakra (ajna).

4. In ajna, she is called Chandra (Moon) Kundalini, white and nectarous as she travels to nirvana chakra.

5. In sahasrara, she becomes Turya (fourth state) Kundalini—samadhi, beyond the three states of waking, dreaming, and sleeping. Here she is the nature of pure consciousness, experienced in samprajnata samadhi.

As kundalini pierces each of the chakras in turn, she absorbs the principle (*tattva*), element (*mahabhuta*), and sense object (*tanmatra*) associated with each chakra. In the root muladhara, she absorbs the earth element and odor. In pelvic svadhishthana, she absorbs water and flavor. In solar plexus manipura, she absorbs fire and form. In heart anahata, she absorbs air and touch. In throat vishuddha, she absorbs ether and sound. In third eye ajna, she absorbs *manas* (lower mind). In manas chakra, she absorbs *chitta* (sensory mind). In indu she absorbs *buddhi* (intellect). In nirvana chakra, she absorbs *dhi* (higher mind) and *ahamkara* (ego).

After nirvana chakra, Chandra (moon) Kundalini passes through the visarga power-bridge to the triangle lying in the nectarous moon region of guru chakra. From there she travels into the luminous triangle within the moon region in the center of sahasrara chakra. Here Chandra Kundalini becomes Turya Kundalini, only realizable in samadhi.

While in the luminous triangle of sahasrara, kundalini exhibits three aspects:

1. Her *ama kala* form, the experience of *samprajnata samadhi*.

2. Her *nirvana kala* form, beyond samprajnata samadhi, into which she absorbs even samadhi consciousness by virtue of her power of supreme control (*nirodhika vahni*).

3. Her *nirvana shakti* form, the all-absorbing kundalini power. Here she absorbs Prakriti, Purusha, and Maya, and passes into supreme void, the circular region within the luminous triangle. The center of the void is Shiva. Kundalini coils around the circular void, forming the circumference. The void, experienced only in *asamprajnata samadhi,* contains four aspects: supreme bindu, supreme nada, Shakti, and Shiva.

- Kundalini first coils around supreme bindu, absorbing supreme bindu.

- Kundalini then coils around supreme nada, absorbing supreme nada.

- Kundalini's third coil is around Shakti, which she then absorbs.

- Kundalini coils halfway around Shiva, whom she unites with and absorbs.

- Kundalini is then without coils and is absorbed into Paramashiva. This is the final stage of asamprajnata samadhi—the supreme absorption.

Sahasrara Attainments

"Men, as soon as they discover this most secret place, become free from rebirths in this universe. By the practice of this Yoga, he gets the power of creating or destroying the creation, this aggregate of elements. When the mind is steadily fixed at this place, which is the residence of the Great Swan and is called Kailas, then that Yogi, devoid of diseases and subduing all accidents, lives for a great age, free from death." —Siva Samhita[3]

Part Three

AWAKENING
KUNDALINI

Chapter Twenty

THE POWER OF HEALING

"After the awakening, the devotee lives always at the
mercy of Kundalini, wafted to a new state of existance and
introduced to a new world as far removed from this one
of rapid change and decay as reality is from a dream."
—Gopi Krishna[1]

Many books about kundalini and the chakras describe their wonders and benefits. Few warn of the dangers of opening these channels of energy when unprepared. If kundalini awakens prematurely, before the nadi system has been sufficiently developed to receive the powerful blast of current, dangerous results can occur, ending in psychosis or suicide. When recreational drugs are involved, the outcome is particularly devastating. That is why the yogis admonish such "experiments." Also, without a well-rounded, balanced life, including work, play, love, compassion, and interest in the welfare of others, awakening of kundalini could prove disastrous.

An anonymous guru once said, "They all want spiritual experiences—until they get them." This saying has great wisdom. Before embarking on any spiritual path, it is wise to examine your motive for such an adventure. Is it to develop "supernormal" powers? Is it to be more "evolved" than others? It is to feel superior and "special"? Or is it to know God, love God, and serve God? In my opinion, if your heartfelt focus is on God above all else, and if you seek guidance in sincerity from a qualified teacher, then you will not encounter the kundalini casualties that some people have reported.

Bizarre Kundalini Experiences

Here are just a few of the many strange experiences that have been reported by those who have experienced kundalini:

- Involuntary astral travel and out-of-body experiences.

- Involuntary unconsciousness or trance states.

- Twitches, muscle spasms, or cramps.

- Involuntary movements, such as jerks, tremors, or shakes.

- Body being forced into strange postures or positions.

- Strange itches, vibrations, prickles, or tingles.

- Hypersensitivity and raw nerves.

- Intense pain in the chakra regions.

- Feelings of energy or electrical currents rushing through the body.

- Crawling sensations, especially up the spine.

- Intense cold shivers or waves of heat.

- Sleep interruptions or sleep patterns disturbed.

- Chronic hyperactivity or chronic fatigue.

- Sex drive greatly diminished or highly intensified.

- Diminished sensory sensations or numbness.

- Headaches and other pressures in the skull.

- Racing heartbeat and pains in the chest.

- Nausea, digestive problems, loss of appetite, or constipation.

- Sudden weight loss or gain.

- Numbness or pain in limbs, especially left foot and leg.

- Back and neck pain.

- Diminished sweating, mucous secretions, and semen production.

- Frequent yawning.

- Emotional outbursts, rapid mood shifts, loss of emotional control.

- Spontaneous vocalizations, including laughing or weeping.

- Mental confusion and lack of concentration.

- Panic attacks.

- Disassociation and loss of connection to the world.

- Intense fear of losing one's mind.

- Psychosis.

Medical doctors invariably misdiagnose these symptoms. Their unfortunate patients are given drugs and sent home, but, because there is no cure for higher consciousness, the patients do not improve. Therefore, knowledge of these kundalini symptoms and how to handle them would be an excellent adjunct to medical knowledge today.

In this chapter, you will read some reports of kundalini experiences and learn how to deal with strange encounters during your own exploration. However, remember that kundalini experiments should be undertaken only under the personal care of an enlightened spiritual master and with permission from a qualified medical doctor.

Because the entire chakra and kundalini system is made of light and sound, the best way to effect changes in this system is through these two mediums. Thus yogis use mantras, visualization, thought intention, and other subtle techniques to raise kundalini through the chakras.

Here you will employ the power of the Word, the sound *(nada)* in speech, to awaken kundalini, heal your aura and chakras, and overcome unusual experiences. Vishuddha chakra is the center of speech as well as purification. Thus speech can be used powerfully to purify your awareness and lift your consciousness.

This chapter is divided into two sections. The first section deals with purifying your auric field, and the second helps you heal your chakras and thereby raise kundalini.

Let us begin our exploration of spiritual healing now.

Part 1: Healing Your Aura

Your aura, otherwise known as *sukshma sharira* (subtle body), is a repository of deep, unconscious thoughts, beliefs, habits, and patterns amassed from all your experiences. A compendium of past emotional traumas as well as ordinary memories, these old thought-forms build a crusty subtle armor around your body.

When kundalini rises through your chakras, this armor begins to crumble. Deep-seated memories might rise to the surface, along with confusing, unsettling, even terrifying experiences.

In addition to these internal memories, environmental influences can impinge upon your auric field, adding to a dingy cloud that obscures your true nature of radiant light. These influences may cloud your aura, causing physical, mental, and spiritual problems. No blame is placed either internally or externally. What is needed is healing.

Therefore, you will learn a few powerful healing affirmations for cleansing and healing your auric field now. All these affirmations have the most powerful effect when spoken aloud in a clear, audible voice. It is not necessary to use the exact words printed here, as long as you convey the same general idea.

Closing Your Aura

Probably the most common difficulty of those who walk a spiritual path is hypersensitivity. Opening new levels of awareness can be confusing without understanding both the spiritual realms and lower planes of existence. With your aura wide open, you may be inadvertently exposed to lower energies. You might even leave your physical body unintentionally, as did this man from Omaha, Nebraska:

> I was losing control. People and things around me were closing in on me. I hated crowded places. Anything and everything penetrated me: sounds, light, vibrations, visions. I could feel everything, especially other people's pain or negative emotions. Everyday encounters became draining, like people were psychic vampires, sucking my energy dry. They often became hostile towards me, attacking me verbally and sometimes even physically, with no apparent cause. When I was in public, I became panic-stricken. All I wanted to do was rush home and lock the door . . . The scariest experience was when I actually left my body and found it difficult to reenter.

This first affirmation will keep your energy field open to the spiritual realm but closed to the lower planes of existence. Speaking this affirmation can effectively prevent external influences from entering your auric field. It also provides greater self-command, so you do not become subject to uninvited experiences.

Use this affirmation many times daily. It is an excellent precursor to spiritual practices, meditation, or prayer. It is essential for overly sensitive people or "psychic sponges," who absorb vibrations around them as a sponge absorbs water, and who find external influences draining, invasive, or coercive. This affirmation immediately clears your auric field of negative influences. It can be used anytime you feel intimidated, under pressure, frightened, or out of control. Let us speak it aloud now:

"I AM in control. I AM the only authority in my life.
I AM divinely protected by the light of my being.
I close off my aura and body of light to the lower astral levels of mind,
and I open to the spiritual world, now and forevermore.
Thank you God, and SO IT IS."

Column of Light

After speaking the words in the previous affirmation, you may also visualize a brilliant white or golden light above your head, in your sahasrara (crown chakra), streaming a beautiful ray of light down through the midline of your body. Then imagine this ray of light and the chakra centers in the core of your body growing larger until the light fills and surrounds your entire body with a beautiful column of light. Figure 20a on page 206 may help you visualize this light column.

Spiritual Self-Authority

Sometimes kundalini seems to take control of people, rather than being controlled by people. Many sincere aspirants succumb to bizarre experiences that seem completely out of control, like the experience of this woman from Austin, Texas:

Typically, kundalini woke me up in the middle of the night with heat and intense feelings at the base of my spine. Then small balls of energy shot around my body haphazardly like pinballs. All sense of reality disappeared as I entered a world of strange visions and loud sounds. Horrible demonic beings surrounded me. Sometimes I felt ferocious pains in my chakras. One time the energy was pushing forcefully against something

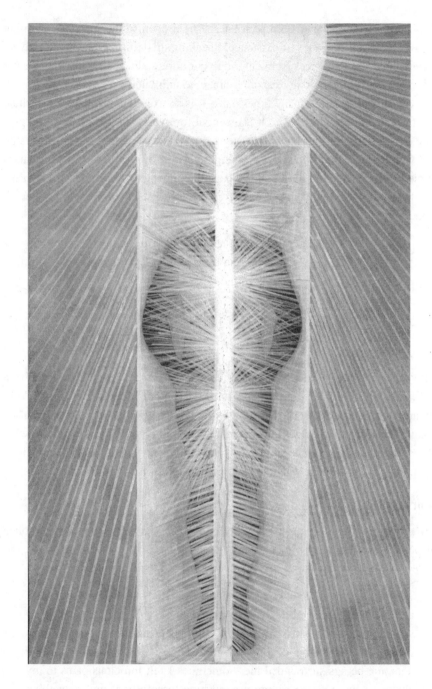

Figure 20a. Column of Light.

THE BIG BOOK OF CHAKRAS AND CHAKRA HEALING

inside my head, causing great pain. Finally it broke through violently and exploded in my brain. Then the energy sped around my body and exploded in my brain several times again. My nostrils opened wide and remained so dilated that my nose bled for several days. After this the world became a strange, weird, foreign, dreamlike place. I no longer inhabited my body, but seemed to live above it. My body became numb. Whenever someone touched me, I felt strange electric sensations rather than normal sensations or bodily feelings. Sexual feelings disappeared. My mind raced with anxiety and fear that my brain and nervous system were permanently damaged.

Because this woman's kundalini energy moved haphazardly rather than rising up through sushumna, her experience was perhaps the equivalent of seizures (chaotic electrical activity in the brain). Gopi Krishna, in his book *Living With Kundalini,* said, "If by mistake kundalini were aroused through any other nadi (nerve) except sushumna, there was every danger of serious psychic and physical disturbances, ending in permanent disability, insanity, or death."

No spiritual experience should be so uncontrollable and disruptive. With proper guidance, you can be captain of your ship rather than tossed about on stormy seas, under peril of drowning. Your spiritual experiences can be gentle and easy. Anytime you feel kundalini is getting out of control, the following affirmation can help you take command of your spiritual awakening:

"I call upon God [or Holy Spirit, Goddess,
or whatever deity you wish to invoke] to intervene in my life now.
I give over to God, knowing that my life is in God's hands.
I humbly ask for the gentle hand of God to bring healing balm, comfort, and
peace to my inner being. My nadis are balanced, harmonized, and at peace.
My body is preparing the way slowly and gradually for my kundalini awakening,
which takes place gently, comfortably, gradually, and slowly.
The God in me is in control. The God in me is the only authority in my life.
I close off my aura and body of light to all but God's loving grace
and infinite power, which is at work in my life now and always.
Thank you God, and SO IT IS."

Integrating New Experiences

When you have passed your entire life in a daze and then, through spiritual practices, the fog begins to lift, the blinding light can be overwhelming. Suddenly, you are aware of subtle dimensions that were heretofore hidden from view. Imagine encountering nonphysical, other-dimensional beings, and bizarre energies running rampant through your body, like this experience of a man from Lancaster, Massachusetts:

> Late at night I lay sleepless in bed, the fierce energy sweeping throughout my body. I wondered whether I could live through the agonizing pain. A hectic burning sensation seized my genitals, anus, and buttocks so violently that I thought my blood vessels would burst or that I would spontaneously combust. Then a tornado spun through my navel and heart, making a blasting noise. Suddenly, a forceful stream of liquid light rocketed up my spine and exploded in my brain. It roared like a waterfall. The light intensified and became a halo of brilliant sunlight. My awareness expanded, no longer confined to my body. I became one with that immense light, as waves of light filled my being. My body became completely numb, as though it never existed. Then I floated free in a sea of magnificent radiance, a crystalline light of every hue and texture. The exaltation of this experience is beyond words.

As your old reality dissolves, new perceptions awaken. Higher states of awareness may feel like your old life has died, as it did for this woman from Cincinnati, Ohio:

> My spiritual experiences have culminated in an experience of being in a kind of no-man's land. I want nothing, except to help other people. Past, present, and future have merged into nothingness. I have no interest in anything that happens. I feel like a zombie, dead to the physical world, as though all this is going on like a puppet show and I am the audience.

Strange experiences of religious traditions other than your own might spontaneously occur, as it did for this woman from Arlington, Virginia:

> The sound of buzzing in my forehead woke me up. Suddenly, I received what felt like a gunshot of light pierce my skull and enter my forehead. Amazingly, a lump on my forehead still exists today. In my inner vision, I saw a woman with a black face dressed in a white sari standing in front of a tall doorway. She said, "My husband always comes with ringing bells." Soon I heard the bells reverberating like thunderclaps inside my head. Then suddenly supreme bliss swept through my body, which filled with light. I heard the words, "I AM Shiva."

Bizarre sexually related experiences might occur, as this man from Spokane, Washington discovered:

> During meditation, I suddenly got a strange, throbbing, painful erection. My penis felt hard and large as a totem pole. An intense sexual sensation grabbed the head of my penis, which traveled down the shaft. My penis seemed to suddenly turn upside down and inside out, with the head deep inside the shaft and pumping sensations traveling inward rather than outward . . . My whole body vibrated. My being expanded as the energy and light slowly pushed up my spine to the back of my neck. A bluish-white beam of light pierced my head from above with a sound of deafening pitch. Then an orgasm exploded in my head while I was pulled through a hole in the top of my head. I became one with God as my inner male and female merged into oneness. I remained in that state of immeasurable, unspeakable bliss of awe and wonderment for weeks afterward.

This next affirmation will help you integrate your new spiritual experiences. Use it repeatedly whenever you feel worried or frightened that your new perceptions and experiences are overwhelming. Speak it aloud now in a clear voice.

> "I AM filled with the light of God. God's grace pours upon me now with joy,
> wisdom, and truth. I AM filled with God's love, power, and energy.
> I AM free from fear and open to receive my good.
> God is my protector and savior. I AM held in the arms of God,
> and there is nothing to be afraid of. God's light protects me from all harm.
> I AM free to experience my true nature of being, without fear.
> I AM safe and secure in the comfort of God's love, and all is well.
> Thank you God, and SO IT IS."

Cutting Psychic Ties

Psychic ties are undue attachments or repulsions to internal or external influences. With clairvoyant sight, you can see cords, ties, or bonds between your chakras and certain people, places, things, organizations, situations, circumstances, memories, experiences, or addictions. These influences seem to control you when a psychic tie binds you to them. Psychic ties are made of subtle matter: thought-stuff crystallized into form.

Psychic ties arise from repetitious habit patterns, emotional or negative encounters, or shameful memories. Nearly everyone has many psychic ties to coworkers or to loved ones. Psychic ties are never beneficial. They need to be healed and released. Speak this affirmation audibly to cut psychic ties between yourself and people in your environment. I guarantee that if you do this daily, you will have better, more intimate relationships, starting now. Read my book *The Power of Auras* for more information.

"I now call upon the Holy Spirit to cut, release, loosen,
and let go of all psychic ties and karmic bonds between myself and _____.
These psychic ties are now lovingly cut, blessed, loved, lifted, healed, dissolved,
released, and completely let go, layer by layer, group by group by group.
Thank you God, and SO IT IS."

Astral Entity Healing

During your explorations of inner space, if you do not keep your aura closed off to the lower realms, you might encounter some astral beings along the way. These are either earthbound spirits that passed over but did not enter the divine light after death, or beings that inhabit the netherworlds.

These entities may appear in various disguises. That is why it is essential to learn to distinguish between such lower astral beings and divine beings of light, such as angels and deities.

Out of the many kundalini casualties that I have read about, nearly every resulting psychosis was due to the direct influence of astral possession or oppression, such as this experience of a man from Rochester, New York:

My kundalini awakening was horrible. It started unintentionally, soon after I read the book [of a famous Indian guru]. I began hearing vicious, cruel voices in my head—so loud that I was constantly distracted. I couldn't concentrate on a conversation or follow a movie. I mistakenly believed my inner guru was speaking. Instead the voices drove me mad. I tried to commit suicide once and landed in a mental hospital three times. The drugs did nothing for me. When I brought my dilemma to the ashram officials, I was basically told to get lost. They only wanted to hear "uplifting" experiences. My mind was smashed to pieces and possessed by many spirits. I saw visions of demons and awful atrocities. This wreaked havoc, both physically and mentally. After 10 years, I am still trying to put my life back together.

I recommend reading some of my other books for more information about astral entities, as well as healing affirmations that are not included in this book:

Divine Revelation, Exploring Meditation, Instant Healing, Miracle Prayer, and *The Power of Auras.* Meanwhile, let us learn a simple healing prayer to clear your aura of any astral influence, possession, or oppression. Say this affirmation audibly anytime you feel a creepy, scary, draining, or highly negative influence impinging upon your auric field. This healing prayer is addressed directly to the entities needing healing:

> "Beloved ones, you are unified with the truth of your being.
> You are lifted in divine love. You are forgiven of all guilt and shame.
> You are healed and released from loss, pain, confusion, and fear.
> Divine love and light fills and surrounds you now.
> Attachment to the earth no longer binds you.
> You are free to go into the divine light now. Go now in peace and love."

Thought-Form Healing

The awakened kundalini is the supreme healer of deep-seated psychological traumas and other energies stored in your mental body. Unfortunately, sometimes her method of freeing these obsessions is a kind of psychic surgery, whereby these subterranean, embedded energies are unearthed and brought to the surface. When this happens, your mind might resemble wreckage for a while, as it did for this woman from Australia:

> Great depression, pain and misery took over. I felt I had fallen into a dark pit, with no means of escape. There was no longer any purpose or meaning to life. Sometimes fits of agony lasted months at a time, so hard to bear that all I could imagine was escape. Terrifying thoughts of suicide plagued me. I was alone, lost, and utterly abandoned. I couldn't tell anyone about my bizarre experiences. I knew if I told my doctor, he would pump me with drugs. Instead I suffered in silence.

Such disheartening experiences can be prevented or healed. The next affirmation can clear your auric field of negative thoughts and emotions. At any given moment, your aura is radiating either harmonious, serene, positive vibrations, or negative, discordant, dissonant energies.

Your every thought, word, and deed affect not only your own mental and physical health but also people around you; indeed, the entire cosmos. Your personal vibrations and emanations can either cultivate or counteract world peace and harmony. Figures 20b and 20c are illustrations of this.

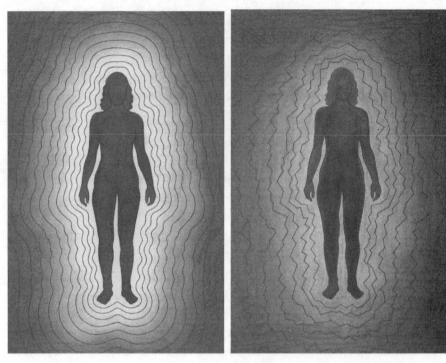

Left: Figure 20b. Mental Harmony. Right: Figure 20c. Mental Discord.

Let us now learn how to transform disharmony into harmony by transmuting negative emotions and energies into positive ones. This affirmation can transmute and heal anything that needs healing. Therefore, it has wide application for use in self-healing as well as healing others.

When you come to the first blank space below, close your eyes and speak whatever negative thoughts and feelings are coming up for you at this moment. In the second blank space, place their positive correlates. For example, if you said "doubt" in the first space, say "faith" in the second. If you said "confusion," in the first space, then insert "clarity" in the second space.

"I invoke the divine presence to eliminate all negations and limitations that no longer serve me. I now dispel all negations of _____ and any other thoughts and emotions that do not reflect the truth of my being. They are now lovingly lifted, transmuted, and transformed through the power of the Holy Spirit.
I am now open and free to embrace positive, life-supporting, energizing thoughts and emotions. I now welcome thoughts of _____.
I AM in balance. I AM in control. Thank you God, and SO IT IS."

Part 2: Healing Your Chakras

In this section, you will learn seven special healing affirmations. These seven powerful prayers can cleanse and awaken your chakras. By speaking these aloud in sequence, you can transform your awareness, increase pranic energy flowing through your subtle body, and awaken higher consciousness. As you use each of these affirmations, place your attention on the corresponding chakra trigger point. Let us speak these powerful affirmations now!

Cleansing Muladhara: Root Chakra

"I AM no longer chained to the material world. I call upon the Holy Spirit to release and let go of all limiting patterns that bind me to the earthly vibration. All thoughts of fear, doubt, unworthiness, guilt, blame, confusion, and shame are dissolved from my mental body now. They are lifted into the light of God's love. I AM free and open to receive my good. God's bounty flows into my life now. God is my provider and protector, and my life is in God's hands. I AM safe and secure in the arms of God's love. Thank you God, and SO IT IS."

Cleansing Svadhishthana: Pelvic Chakra

"I AM free to be myself. I call upon the Holy Spirit to release and let go of all limiting patterns and beliefs that bind me to sexual addiction, shame, fear, and inhibition. These thoughts are lifted into the healing light of God's love. I AM free to express and enjoy my sexuality in healthy channels of love expression with my consenting adult partner. God's love expresses through me now. I AM the love that God is. Thank you God, and SO IT IS."

Cleansing Manipura: Navel Chakra

"I AM a brilliant being of light, blazing life force energy all around me. I call upon the Holy Spirit to release from my mind all beliefs, patterns, and ideas of fear, anger, frustration, and resentment now. I release the need to control and manipulate my environment. I accept and welcome peace, love, contentment, inner strength, and forgiveness. I AM free to radiate the power that is my true nature of being. God's divine power, cosmic energy, and radiant glory express through me now. I AM the strength and power that God is. Thank you God, and SO IT IS."

Cleansing Anahata: Heart Chakra

"My heart is filled with love and peace. I AM the love that God is. God's grace and serenity radiate and vibrate through my heart now. I AM God's grace. I AM the blessing that God is. I AM perfect peace. I AM God's instrument of peace. I AM the serenity that God is. I AM perfection. I AM God's vehicle of perfection now. Thank you God, and SO IT IS."

Cleansing Vishuddha: Throat Chakra

"I AM a perfect vessel of God's expression. The purity and beauty of God flow through me now. I AM God's messenger of purity. I AM perfect creativity. God's wisdom flows through all of my creative expressions now. My voice is an instrument of God's holy presence. I live in God's light. I express God's love. Thank you God, and SO IT IS."

Cleansing Ajna: Third Eye Chakra

"God's grace and wisdom radiate and vibrate through me now. I AM the eye of all-seeing, all-knowing wisdom. I AM the wisdom that God is. God's loving presence fills my being with light. I AM now free from the bondage of ego-attachment. I let go of all need for psychic powers and spiritual superiority. I surrender to God's grace, and I AM God's instrument of light. Let God's will be done in all matters, now and always. Thank you God, and SO IT IS."

Awakening Sahasrara: Crown Chakra

"I AM the source of light. God's light pours through me now with a thousand radiances of glory. God's grace pours through me now with supreme joy. God's ambrosial nectar flows through my being now, bathing every pore of my being with unlimited vibrancy and energy. I AM filled with God's radiant glory. I AM immersed in the ocean of God's love. I AM blessed with God's infinite peace. Thank you God, and SO IT IS."

Chapter Twenty-One

THE POWER OF
SECRET YOGIC PRACTICES

"Those who wish to swim across the ocean of samsara (world of delusion)
should practice this bandha in a lonely place. Practice brings about control of
the prana residing in the body. Do it in silence, with care and determination.
All lethargy will vanish."
—Gherand Samhita[1]

In this chapter, you will learn secret yoga practices that have been, until recently, hidden in caves and forests of India. The Sanskrit word *yoga* (integration) derives from the root *yuj* (to yoke). From the standpoint of kundalini, yoga means unifying individuality with universality, which occurs when your inner Shakti unites with your inner Shiva at sahasrara chakra (crown chakra).

Pathways of Yoga

All paths of yoga seek to attain integration by various means:

1. *Raja* (royal) *Yoga* uses meditation and repetition of mantras to develop one-pointed steadiness of mind.

2. *Karma* (action) *Yoga* attains union through alternating meditation with dynamic daily activity, while living in accord with natural law.

3. *Jynana* (knowledge) *Yoga* uses the intellect to discern reality from illusion, thereby eliminating the veil of ignorance and attaining supreme knowledge.

4. *Bhakti* (devotion) *Yoga* opens the heart of the seeker, bringing direct divine contact through surrender to God.

5. *Integrated Yoga* seeks to unite heart, mind, and will in an ecumenical and universal way, while honoring all paths and traditions.

6. *Tantra* (expansion, liberation) *Yoga* seeks to see, feel, and know the infinite in and through the finite. It aims at achieving higher awareness by experiencing everyday life to the fullest. The Goddess energy, also known as kundalini or Shakti, is worshipped by *Tantrics*.

7. *Kundalini Yoga, Laya Yoga,* or *Kriya Yoga* awakens pranic energy in the body through raising kundalini power upward through the chakras.

8. *Hatha* (solar-lunar) *Yoga* is concerned with physiological culture and raising kundalini through *asanas* (body postures), *pranayama* (breathing exercises), disciplined lifestyle, special diet, and vigorous elimination program.

Because this book is mostly concerned with increasing pranic energy and raising kundalini, its teachings and techniques stem from ancient wisdom traditions of India: Tantra, Kriya, Kundalini, and Hatha Yoga. Yoga *asanas* (postures) will not be covered in this book. However, asanas are essential for awakening kundalini. Therefore, I highly recommend reading my book *Exploring Meditation,* where you can learn to practice yoga asanas.

The ancient yogis of India kept their mysterious practices secret. However, many of these techniques are available to anyone today. In this chapter, you will learn some of these arcane methods, called *bandhas* (to hold, lock, or tighten) and *mudras* (gestures), as well as cleansing methods specifically designed to harmonize *ida* and *pingala* prana flows. These practices profoundly affect your subtle body. They markedly increase the flow of pranic energy, awaken kundalini energy, and provide direct experience of the chakras.

Let us learn some of these powerful methods now!

Jala Neti

If nasal passages or sinuses are obstructed, then the natural alternation of breath through ida and pingala is disturbed. *Jala* (water) *neti* (nose) is a yogic method for cleansing these passages with salt water.

You have a powerful internal purification system that conditions the air before it enters your lungs: your nasal passages. If your nose is blocked, then you are forced to breathe through your mouth. This is a dangerous alternative, because your mouth and throat do not possess the filtration system of your nose. That is why jala neti is essential. (The only exception would be specialized mouth-breathing pranayama practices such as *sitkara*.)

Practicing jala neti removes impurities, stimulates various nerve endings, and clears your brain and other organs. Jala neti also stimulates the ajna chakra (brow center).

Let us learn to practice it now.

Practicing Jala Neti

Take a *neti lota* (pot designed for jala neti) or small teapot with a spout that fits comfortably into your nostril. Mix about a pint of pure boiled or distilled luke-warm water with one teaspoon of pure sea salt, or ½ teaspoon of pure sea salt and ½ teaspoon of baking soda. Dissolve the solution completely. Fill the neti pot with the saline solution.

Bend over a sink and tilt your head toward the right. Gently insert the end of the spout into left nostril with a tight fit. Continue to tilt head to the right while raising neti pot until saline solution flows into left nostril, up through nasal passages, and out right nostril. While doing this, open your mouth so you can breathe. Remember to consult your doctor before practicing!

If you tilt your head too much, water will enter your throat instead of the other nostril. If you tilt the pot too much, water will overflow from the pot. Adjust your head and the pot until the water flows correctly.

If jala neti is performed right, water will not enter your mouth or throat. However, if it does, just spit it out. Allow solution to flow through nostrils 10 to 20 seconds. Remove neti pot and blow your nose.

Then repeat entire process, placing spout of the neti pot in right nostril, tilting head toward left, and allowing solution to flow out left nostril. After completing jala neti, dry nostrils by blowing your nose to expel moisture.

This entire procedure takes less than five minutes. Once a day is enough, unless you have a cold or nasal blockage.

Alternate Method without Neti Pot

Make saline solution as previously described. Cup left palm and pour some solution into palm. Close right nostril with right thumb, place left nostril close to your left palm, and sniff the liquid up into your nose, through nasal passage, and spit it out. Do the same with other nostril.

Do not try either of these methods without the salt or with water too cold or too hot. Otherwise you will be sorry! With proper temperature and correct amount of salt, there is little or no discomfort. If you suffer from chronic nosebleeds, do not practice jala neti. No matter what your state of health, get your doctor's permission before practicing jala neti.

Jala neti is excellent for preventing or healing colds; sinusitis; ailments of eyes, nose, or throat; tonsillitis; cataract; asthma; pneumonia; bronchitis; tuberculosis; and inflammation of the adenoids and mucus membranes. It can remove headaches, insomnia, migraine, epilepsy, tension, depression, and tiredness. It has a subtle effect on various nerves that end in the nasal passages, such as the olfactory bulb and nerves associated with eyes and ears.

Padadirasana

A yoga asana (posture) called *padadirasana* (breath-balancing pose) controls or balances the flow of ida and pingala. By applying pressure under your armpits, you can directly influence the flow of breath. Steady pressure under right armpit tends to make left nostril flow, and pressure under left armpit makes right nostril flow. In padadirasana, press under both armpits as follows:

Sit in any comfortable pose, such as *vajra asana* (see Figure 21c on page 219). Cross arms in front of chest. Place right hand under left armpit with thumb upward in front of right shoulder. Similarly, place left hand under right armpit. Close eyes and breathe slowly and deeply. Continue to press until your breath equalizes. This takes at least one minute.

Yogic Muscular Locks

The *granthis* (psychic knots) are located in the pelvis center (svadhishthana), heart center (anahata), and brow center (ajna chakra). These three knots disallow prana from flowing freely through *sushumna nadi*, your main pranic passage, through which kundalini flows. Therefore, to experience full kundalini awakening, the granthis must be removed.

Practicing bandhas can effectively open these blockages. Prana can then flow through sushumna nadi, which leads to greater mental receptivity and higher consciousness. The bandhas are therefore among the most powerful practices for awakening kundalini through the chakras.

Now let us practice them. (Be sure to ask your physician before attempting any of the exercises in this book.)

Jalandhara Bandha: Throat Lock

The Sanskrit word *jalandhara* derives from roots *jalan* (net) and *dhara* (stream, flowing fluid). The word *adhara* (base) refers to 16 specific body centers: toes, ankles, knees, thighs, perineum, coccyx, navel, heart, neck, tonsils, tongue, nose, brow center, eyes, back of head, and crown of head.

Figure 21a. Siddha Asana.

Jalandhara bandha is a physical lock that binds the network of nadis in your neck. This stops pranic flow to these 16 centers and thereby directs prana into sushumna nadi. Also the nectar or *amrit* flowing from talu chakra (see page 166) is blocked from flowing down the throat and getting burnt up by digestive fires in the stomach.

In addition, this bandha slows down heart rate due to compression of carotid sinuses. It also increases lung capacity, heals throat ailments, beneficially massages the thyroid, and brings mental balance, tranquility, and introversion. The ancient scriptures claim this bandha can prevent old age and death.

Figure 21b. Padma Asana.

Let us learn this simple bandha now.

Sit in a comfortable position. The best positions are *padma asana* (lotus pose), *siddha asana,* or *siddha yoni asana* (perfect pose). It can also be done in *vajra asana,* sitting in a chair, or in standing position, with feet close together. If seated, then place palms on your knees.

Close eyes and relax entire body. Inhale deeply through your nose and retain breath. Bend head forward and press chin tightly against sternal notch on chest. Place palms on knees. If seated, straighten arms and lock elbows while holding knees. Locking elbows intensifies pressure applied to neck. Simultaneously, hunch shoulders upward and forward. This keeps arms straight and elbows locked. Stay in position while holding breath as long as comfortable.

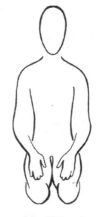

Figure 21c. Vajra Asana.

Meanwhile, maintain attention on throat area. Then, relax shoulders, bend arms, slowly raise head, and exhale slowly. Breathe normally. Repeat as many times as comfortable.

Practice jalandhara bandha after asanas and before meditation. If you have high blood pressure or heart ailments, do not practice this.

Uddiyana Bandha: Abdominal Lock

Uddiyana (raise up, fly upward) *bandha* causes your diaphragm to rise upward toward the chest. This practice directs prana into sushumna nadi and moves kundalini energy upward through the chakras to sahasrara. The ancient scriptures claim uddiyana bandha is useful for expanding awareness, reversing aging, and attaining immortality. It rouses intestinal activity, relieves constipation, stimulates the pancreas, relieves diabetes, balances the mind, brings ease and calm, and reverses depression. This bandha acts directly on your navel chakra (manipura), storehouse of prana. Therefore, it stimulates and redistributes prana throughout your body and strengthens your immune system.

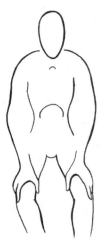

Uddiyana bandha can be practiced in padmasana, siddhasana, siddha yoni asana, vajra asana, or standing position. Let us do it standing, the easiest method.

Stand with feet about one and a half feet apart. Bend forward slightly at waist and bend legs slightly. Place palms on thighs near knees and place pressure on thighs. Exhale completely and empty lungs as much as possible by blowing out repeatedly. Bend head downward and press chin against chest in chin lock (jalandhara bandha).

Then make a false inhalation. That means expand chest as though breathing in, but without actually letting air into lungs. Straighten legs slightly. This automatically raises diaphragm, and abdomen takes a concave shape, inward and upward. Hold this position for as long as you can hold your breath.

Figure 21d.
Uddiyana Bandha.

Slowly relax chest and bend legs, thereby automatically allowing abdomen to resume its normal shape. Release jalandhara bandha, release arms, and gradually stand up straight. This is one round. Practice several rounds and gradually increase the number of rounds over several weeks. After practicing this in standing position for several months, practice it in a seated meditative posture.

THE BIG BOOK OF CHAKRAS AND CHAKRA HEALING

Practice uddiyana bandha early in the morning before breakfast, after asanas and pranayama, and before meditation. Your stomach must be empty, so wait four hours after your previous meal. Also, evacuate bowels first.

Pregnant women and those with heart problems, ulcers, colitis, or other serious abdominal problems should not practice uddiyana bandha. After childbirth, this practice helps new mothers reshape and strengthen the abdomen. This is an excellent exercise for anyone whose lower abdomen tends to be flabby.

Ashvini Mudra: Horse Attitude

In order to successfully practice the next bandha, called *moola bandha,* the practice of *ashvini mudra* (horse attitude) is invaluable preparation. In the Taoist system, this is called "deer exercise."

Method 1

Ashvini mudra can be done in any comfortable, seated posture, or even standing. Relax whole body and close eyes. Breathe normally while rapidly contracting and relaxing anus in rhythmical fashion. Although this practice is confined to the anal muscles, other pelvic muscles will also contract. Repeat the practice at least 20 times without straining.

Method 2

In an alternate practice, contract anus as you inhale. After inhaling, hold breath while holding the contraction. Contract muscles as tightly as possible without straining. Release contraction as you breathe out. This is one round. Repeat as many rounds as comfortable.

This mudra prevents constipation and hemorrhoids, stimulates intestinal peristalsis, heals prolapsed anus or rectum, heals incontinence, prevents prostate disease, and maintains male potency.

Moola Bandha: Root Lock

The Sanskrit word *moola bandha* (perineum contraction lock) derives from the term *moola* (base or root). Here it refers to muladhara chakra, seat of kundalini, and also the perineum. Let us learn to practice it.

In this bandha, the area to be contracted is the physical trigger point of muladhara chakra. In the male, it is in the perineum between the anus and genitals. In the female it is the G-Spot or Gräfenberg spot near the cervix, where the vagina meets the uterus. Most people practice moola bandha incorrectly by only contracting the anus.

The best positions for practicing this bandha are *siddhasana* for men and *siddha yoni asana* for women. Or sit in any comfortable seated position or practice it while standing.

Siddhasana for men: Sit with legs outstretched. Place sole of right foot against inside of left thigh. Press right heel firmly against perineum, between anus and genitals. Place left foot on top of right calf. If possible, press left heel into pelvis immediately above genitals. Push left toes between right calf and thigh. If possible, grasp right toes and pull them upward between left thigh and calf. Place heels on top of each other.

Siddha yoni asana for women: Same posture as for men, only press right heel firmly against labia at entrance to vagina.

Place palms on knees. Close eyes and relax entire body. Inhale deeply. Hold breath and practice jalandhara bandha (throat lock: see page 219). Apply firm pressure in region of perineum with one heel. This strengthens the physical contraction. Strongly contract muscles at muladhara chakra trigger point, without excessive strain. Hold attention at the point of contraction. Stay in bandha as long as possible while holding breath. Then let go of contraction, release jalandhara bandha, raise head, and exhale. This is one round. Practice several more rounds as comfortable.

If you find this bandha difficult, then practice ashvini mudra instead (see page 221) until you gain control over your pelvic muscles.

Moola bandha improves blood supply to pelvic region, stimulates nerves, and revitalizes genital organs. This supreme age-reversing bandha is essential for maintaining male potency, prostate health, and normalcy of bladder and colon. It also prevents sexual, bladder, and anal incontinence.

This bandha awakens muladhara chakra, arouses kundalini to enter brahma nadi in sushumna, and transmutes sexual energy. The ancients describe this practice as drawing apana upward to unite with prana. Apana is the downward vital air—the function of the body that exhales and expels bodily waste materials. Prana is the upward motion that inhales and supplies energy and bodily upkeep. Moola bandha balances prana and apana, providing equilibrium to incoming and outgoing energies. With this bandha, apana moves upward from muladhara and reaches the navel center (manipura chakra), which increases digestive fire. The flame then lengthens and reaches upward to heart center (anahata chakra).

"Due to the kindling of the fire, apana and prana, the sleeping kundalini is awakened; it becomes straight like a snake beaten by a stick."
—Hatha Yoga Pradipika[2]

Maha Bandha: Great Lock

Maha bandha (great lock) is a powerful bandha combining the three major locks. Here is how to practice it.

Exhale slowly with attention on muladhara (root chakra), imagining the luminous form of kundalini in awareness. At the same time, practice uddiyana bandha (abdominal lock) and contract perineum in moola bandha (root lock). Once you have exhaled completely, suspend breath with jalandhara bandha (throat lock).

Maintain these muscular contractions while continuing to imagine kundalini rising up your spine to the top of your head. Suspend breath as long as comfortable. Then release moola bandha, uddiyana bandha, and finally let go of jalandhara bandha.

This powerful practice is key for rousing kundalini. (Get permission from your doctor before practicing any method in this chapter.)

Khechari Mudra with Ujjayi

Many Tantric Yoga techniques use a yogic breathing practice called *ujjayi* along with a tongue lock called *khechari mudra* or *nabho mudra*. These are simple practices that produce profound results.

Khechari Mudra

Khechari mudra can be achieved through a long, complicated practice involving several surgical operations to the underside of the tongue. This procedure of gradually, painstakingly cutting away the *lingual frenulum* (membrane under the tongue) is described in the ancient scriptures of India, and should never be undertaken without the guidance of an enlightened master. However, the simple practice given here requires no preparation and is for everyone. Let us learn how to practice it now. (Be sure to get permission from your doctor first.)

Roll your tongue upward and backward, so the lower surface of tongue comes into contact with upper soft palate. Stretch tip of your tongue backward as far as possible, reaching toward the uvula, without straining. With regular practice, eventually your lingual frenulum will become more flexible and allow you to touch the uvula and even enter the nasal cavity above your soft palate.

Ujjayi Pranayama

Sit in any comfortable position. This can even be practiced in *savasana* (Figure 23a on page 257) to promote greater relaxation. Roll your tongue back into khechari mudra. Close eyes, relax, and breathe through your nose slowly and deeply. Partially close the glottis by slightly contracting throat muscles. Simultaneously, your abdominal muscles will slightly contract automatically. Keep facial muscles relaxed.

As you breathe in this position, you will notice a quiet rasping sound coming from your throat. This sound, caused by the air passing through the restricted glottis, is similar to the sound of a sleeping baby.

Because this breathing technique, combined with rolling back the tongue, places slight pressure on your carotid sinuses, it reduces your heartbeat and blood pressure. This produces mental and physical calm, and soothes and harmonizes your entire body, brain, and subtle body.

Shambhavi Mudra

Shambhavi (Shakti) is a name for the consort of Shambhu (Shiva). Supposedly taught to Shakti by Lord Shiva, this mudra, also called *bhrumadhya* (brow center) *drishti* (gazing), is often mentioned in the ancient scriptures. It stimulates and opens the ajna chakra and kshetram.

The fundamental experience of *shambhavi mudra* is that your eyes roll up and back into your head. When your third eye opens to genuine spiritual sight of divine light, this happens automatically.

Here is how to practice shambhavi mudra.

Version 1

Close eyes and relax entire body. Then open eyes and focus on a spot between your eyebrows. Direct eyes inward and upward as much as possible in that direction. If the practice is done correctly, you will see two curved images of the eyebrows merging with each other, making a V-shape. Do not strain your eyes. If you feel any strain, stop immediately and lie down. Begin again after a period of rest.

If you find this difficult, then place a fingertip on tip of nose and focus both eyes intently on it. Then slowly move finger up nose to center of eyebrows while keeping eyes firmly focused on fingertip.

Version 2

Keep your eyes half-open and focus all internal attention on the same spot, but without rolling your eyes upward. In this case, the focus is entirely mental.

Version 3

Once you have mastered this technique, you can then practice it with eyes closed. The inner light will dawn, and visions of celestial beings and divine lights will occur in your inner eye.

Yoni Mudra

Let us now learn a Nada Yoga method to hear the inner *nada,* the sound of sounds. The best time to practice this is late night or early morning when fewer external noises interfere with subtle sensory perception. This is often called *yoni mudra* (invocation of the source), which indicates merging with the source of nada. It is also called *shanmukhi mudra* (attitude of the seven gates), where the seven doors of outer perception are closed for awareness to turn within. Another name is *baddha yoni asana* (locked source pose), indicating closing the orifices of perception.

This profound practice can be done in any comfortable seated position or even standing. Relax entire body and hold spine and head upright. Raise hands in front of your face with elbows pointed sideways. Then plug your ears with your thumbs. Place index fingers lightly on eyelids. Do not press against eyelids. Close nostrils tightly with your middle fingers. Encircle mouth, pressing above upper lip with your ring fingers and below lower lip with your pinky fingers.

Then perform *kaki mudra* (crow's beak gesture). Here's how: First fully exhale the air from your lungs. Pout your lips in a small circle, as though ready to whistle. Relax your tongue. Suck in air vigorously through your mouth with sibilance and blow out your cheeks so they puff out. Retain your breath.

Now keep nostrils tightly closed, and at the same time, force pressure into your nose as though you were blowing your nose, just as you might do on an airplane to equalize air pressure in your ears. This will force air into the Eustachian tubes.

Then perform jalandhara bandha, lowering head to the sternal notch (see page 219). Hold breath as long as is comfortable without straining.

Meanwhile, notice any sounds you perceive at the top of your head, middle of head, right ear, or heart chakra. Keep attention on the inner nada. If you perceive a sound with a subtler sound in the background, then switch awareness to the fainter sound. Continue to move to subtler regions of sound as you travel deeper into your inner being. Do not dwell on any one sound but continue moving within.

When you can no longer hold breath without straining, then raise head, release fingers from nose, and exhale slowly through nose.

This is one round. Practice several rounds, as comfortable.

Here are some examples of sounds you might hear internally, enumerated in *Hamsa Upanishad: ghanta nada* (bells ringing), *shankha nada* (blowing of conch shell), *tantri nada* (Indian lute called *vina), tala nada* (cymbals), *bansuri nada* (flute), *bheri nada* (echoing drum), *mridanga nada* (double drum), *megha nada* (roaring thunder).

What you hear may be different from these sounds. Therefore, do not try to hear the sounds. By letting go, the sounds will come naturally. Practice yoni mudra several times before noticing any sounds whatsoever. This mudra reveals deep mysteries of your inner being. Practicing it even once is an unforgettable experience.

After practicing yoni mudra for at least one month, then add moola bandha, raising the pranic energy from your root chakra, during the practice. After another month, also add uddiyana bandha to raise pranic energy from your navel chakra.

Learning such powerful bandhas (muscular contraction techniques) and mudras (gestures) not only increases pranic energy, but these methods are also prerequisites for more advanced Kriya Yoga, Kundalini Yoga, and Laya Yoga practices. Such advanced practices can be learned from a qualified spiritual master.

Chapter Twenty-Two

THE POWER OF YOGIC BREATHING

*"Life is the period between one breath and the next; a person
who only half breathes, only half lives. He who breathes correctly
acquires control of the whole being."*
—*Hatha Yoga Pradipika*[1]

In this chapter, you will learn powerful *pranayama* (yogic breathing) methods to rouse kundalini and purify your chakras. The definition of pranayama is widely understood as "breath control." However, this concept is too limited. Although oxygen is a form of prana, yogic breathing engenders subtler forms of prana by cleansing the *nadis* (pathways of prana) throughout your system, increasing pranic flow, and awakening kundalini.

The Sanskrit word *pranayama* derives from the roots *prana* (moving or breathing forth) and *ayama* (stretching, extending, restraining, expanding in time and space). Thus pranayama overcomes limitations, expands energy, and increases sensitivity to higher vibrations and dimensions. By eliminating mental distractions and internal conflicts, pranayama allows consciousness to shine in pristine purity, without distortion.

*"When prana fluctuates then the chitta (mind) also fluctuates; when prana
becomes steady, then the chitta also becomes steady."*
—*Hatha Yoga Pradipika*[2]

If your pranic body is agitated and unbalanced, then your mind gets disturbed. When your pranic body is harmonized, then your mind attains equanimity. The practice of pranayama calms your mind by cleansing your subtle energy body, thus allowing prana to flow freely and harmoniously through your nadis (pranic passages).

> *"If pranayama is practiced correctly, then the entire pranic body will be well-integrated and the prana will flow easily through the sushumna (the most important nadi in the whole body), for pranayama will remove all blockages that tend to impede free flow of prana. This will give rise to steadiness of the mind."*
> —*Hatha Yoga Pradipika*[3]

In contrast to the previous statement, if pranayama is performed incorrectly, the same scripture states that it can cause illness. This is why pranayama should be practiced under close supervision of an enlightened master, and no pranayama practice should be undertaken without consulting a qualified physician.

In this chapter, you will learn several simple pranayama techniques. While practicing these techniques, if, at any time, you feel any headache or other bodily discomfort, stop the practice immediately and lie down to rest.

How Do You Breathe?

The power of breath is the key to awakening kundalini and experiencing the chakras. It is also primary in maintaining health and wellness. Breathing is an automatic, unconscious bodily function. Therefore, we rarely notice it, unless we are jogging or swimming. Most people do not take full advantage of the power of breath, and their respiratory muscles are not used to full capacity.

Your life is dependent on pranic energy received through various means, especially breathing. You can survive a few days without drinking water or a few months without eating. However, you will survive only a few minutes without breathing.

The ancient yogis say each person is born with a certain allocation of breaths. When those breaths expire, death occurs. Thus, yogis believe that slow breathing extends life, and rapid breathing shortens it. Tension, fear, anxiety, and worry speed your breathing rate. This leads to bad health, unhappiness, and short life span. Calmness, relaxation, and inner peace slow your breath rate, consequently extending your life.

Quick, shallow breathing allows only a small volume of air to enter your lungs. Shallow breathing breeds germs in the lower lungs and furnishes inadequate oxygen supply to your bloodstream. Quick breathing blocks optimum oxygen and carbon dioxide exchange, and leads to an array of diseases caused by oxygen-starved blood.

THE BIG BOOK OF CHAKRAS AND CHAKRA HEALING

In the rush of modern life, many people have adopted unhealthy lifestyles, completely out of touch with their true nature and alienated from their surroundings. Such disharmony causes the body to function at far less than prime capacity. It also arrests spiritual experiences and higher awareness.

Today we need to relearn how to breathe properly, reactivate normal respiratory reflexes, and maximize oxygen intake. Most relaxed individuals inhale about one pint of air per breath. However, this is less than one-eighth their full capacity. Through yogic breathing, you can greatly increase your potential to be nourished with the substance of life: prana.

This chapter will reveal several pranayama techniques, powerful ways to awaken kundalini energy by purifying your pranic pathways.

Slow and Steady Wins the Race

Your lungs are similar to two flexible, strong, inflatable and deflatable balloons, capable of immense expansion and contraction. They are surrounded at the top and sides by the thorax or ribcage and at the bottom by the diaphragm, a flat muscle separating your lungs from your abdomen.

When your ribs expand and diaphragm moves downward, a vacuum emerges in the space around the lungs. This vacuum causes your lungs to immediately expand to fill the vacuum. This is how inhalation occurs.

Conversely, when your ribs contract and diaphragm moves upward, then your lungs compress, pushing air out in exhalation.

The more your lungs expand and contract, the deeper you breathe. The ancient yogis of India recognize four basic styles of breathing:

1. Abdominal or diaphragmatic breathing.

2. Middle or intercostal breathing.

3. Clavicular or upper breathing.

4. Yogic breathing, which includes the previous three.

Because awakening of kundalini depends on free flow of prana through your nadis, pranayama is essential. Because yogic breathing is the foundation of pranayama, let us begin by practicing the four styles of breathing now.

Practicing Four Breathing Styles

Wearing loose, comfortable clothing, lie on a blanket or exercise mat on the floor in a well-ventilated, clean room with no breeze. All the following breathing practices are done through your nose, not your mouth.

Abdominal Breathing

Diaphragmatic, abdominal breathing draws in maximum air quantity for minimum effort. During inhalation, your diaphragm flattens and moves downward. This compresses abdominal muscles and expands your belly. As chest cavity enlarges, air rushes in. When diaphragm relaxes, it moves upward, reducing the volume in chest cavity, causing lungs to contract and exhale. As you lie on your back, relax completely and place one hand on navel. Breathe slowly and completely. While exhaling, feel your belly flatten. Your diaphragm will totally relax and bow upward into chest cavity. Hold breath a few seconds. Then inhale slowly and deeply. Do not distend chest or move shoulders. Feel belly expand as diaphragm moves downward, bowing toward abdomen. Hold breath a few seconds. Then exhale slowly and completely while feeling your navel collapse. Then hold breath a few seconds and repeat 10 to 20 times.

Middle Breathing

Middle breathing uses chest movements. During inhalation, intercostal (ribcage) muscles contract, moving ribs outward and upward. Your lungs automatically inhale and expand to fill the vacuum. When intercostal muscles relax, ribs move downward and inward. This compresses lungs, causing exhalation. Lie on your back and completely relax. Place hands on sides of chest. Now attempt to breathe using only ribcage muscles, not abdomen. Achieve this by slightly contracting abdominal muscles. Feel expansion and contraction of ribs with your hands.

Breathe in slowly by expanding ribcage outward and upward. This prevents deep breathing, because your chest is limited in its capacity to expand. After inhaling, hold breath a few seconds.

Then slowly exhale by contracting chest downward and inward without moving abdomen. After exhaling, hold breath a few seconds. Again inhale slowly and repeat process 10 or 20 times.

Upper Breathing

Upper breathing is achieved by moving your shoulders and collarbone. This requires great effort for little results, because only a tiny volume of air enters your lungs. Unfortunately, this stilted upper breathing method is commonplace in our tense, hectic world. Tight bras, belts, and other restrictive clothing necessitate it. Lie on back and relax completely. Now, breathe without expanding or contracting either abdomen or chest. This is not easy. Put one hand on chest and one on navel to make sure they do not move. Slightly contract abdominal muscles and try to inhale by drawing collarbone and shoulders up. To achieve this, you can inhale with a sniffing action, automatically inducing upper breathing. Exhale by letting shoulders and collarbone drop down. Do not continue this practice for long. You can easily see what effort it requires and how little air enters your lungs. Now that you have practiced three styles of breathing, let us learn full yogic breathing.

Yogic Breathing

Yogic breathing combines all three methods of breathing: abdominal, middle, and upper. Performed in one harmonious motion, yogic breathing results in maximum inhalation and exhalation. Lie comfortably on back and relax. Place one hand on navel and one on chest. Inhale so slowly that little or no sound is heard. Allow abdomen to expand. After belly has distended fully, begin to expand chest outward and upward. Once chest is fully expanded, draw collarbone and shoulders up. This process is completed in one smooth movement, like the swell of a sea, with no transitions between three breathing styles, and without jerking or straining. After inhaling, hold breath a few seconds. Now, exhale slowly by first relaxing collarbone and shoulders. Then let chest move downward and inward. Finally allow abdomen to contract, without straining. Achieve this by caving belly inward as far as possible. This entire exhalation occurs in one smooth, harmonious movement.

After exhaling, hold breath a few seconds. Then inhale again as before. Repeat this process for five rounds. Increase the number by two rounds per day. Eventually, practice 10 minutes per day. With enough practice, yogic breathing becomes completely effortless and natural.

Practicing this powerful method can work miracles. Imbibing more vital pranic energy into your lungs can increase inner strength, power, health, and happiness. Yogic breathing bestows immunity to disease, clarity of thought, energy, calm, and inner peace. Whenever you feel tired, weak, angry, or cranky, spend a few minutes practicing yogic breathing to completely revitalize your system.

Pranayama Practice

Various modes of activity are practiced during the breathing exercises called pranayama:

1. *Pooraka,* meaning inhalation.

2. *Rechaka,* meaning exhalation.

3. *Antar* or *antaranga kumbhaka,* meaning retention of breath after inhalation, with lungs full of air.

4. *Bahir* or *bahiranga kumbhaka,* meaning retention of breath after exhalation, with lungs emptied as much as possible.

5. *Kevala kumbhaka,* meaning suspension of breath during deep meditation, when pressure in the lungs corresponds to atmospheric pressure.

The goal of the first four modes of pranayama is to achieve the fifth—breath suspension. When your breath is suspended, you achieve the purpose of meditation: *samadhi* (stillness of body and mind).

"Those who are engaged in yogic practice, reach the breathless state by offering inhalation into exhalation and exhalation into inhalation as sacrifice."
—Lord Krishna[4]

The Power of Yogic Breathing

Pranayama is indispensable to successful meditation. It is the supercharger that makes successful deep meditation possible for average individuals. Here are a few tips for practicing pranayama successfully:

- Practice pranayama in any comfortable seated position with back upright.

- Dress in comfortable and loose clothing. No belts or bras.

- Practice in a clean, quiet, well-ventilated, insect-free, undrafty room.

- If possible, practice in the early morning before breakfast, after *yoga asanas* (postures), and before meditation.

- After practicing pranayama, wait at least half an hour before eating, and wait at least four hours after eating before practicing pranayama.

- Practice pranayama after emptying the bladder and bowels.

- If possible, do *jala neti* before pranayama (see pages 216–218 for instructions).

- Keep attention on the practice as much as possible, without straining.

- No force or violent respiration is advocated. Take it easy and do not strain.

- If any discomfort arises, stop your practice immediately, lie down, and rest.

Important Note: Never attempt the pranayama practices in this chapter without permission from your physician, especially if you have high blood pressure, hypertension, or neurosis. Do not attempt any pranayama practices without direct personal instruction from a qualified yoga teacher.

Kapalbhati

After practicing yogic breathing for a few weeks, you can begin *kapalbhati* (breathing like bellows), a powerful method for purifying your nadis and cleansing your lungs. Here is how to practice it.

Breathe deeply and quickly through your nose, exhaling and inhaling fully. While inhaling, distend abdomen. While exhaling, contract it. Place your hand on abdomen to make sure you are doing it correctly. Here is a hint: Placing attention on the exhale will allow the inhale to occur by itself. Contract abdominal muscles with a backward push while you quickly, forcefully exhale. Then abdomen will naturally distend during inhalation. Repeat at least 10 times.

Purifying Your Nadis

Continue to practice kapalbhati daily as you begin another practice, *nadi shodhana*, derived from the Sanskrit roots *nadi* (circuit, channel, or pathway) and *shodhana* (purification). Practicing *nadi shodhana* purifies and decongests your nadis (subtle pranic circuits), thereby increasing pranic flow. This calms your mind and prepares it for deep meditation.

Here you will learn several stages of nadi shodhana. Each stage must be mastered before advancing to the next. Proceed slowly, step by step, to gradually develop respiratory control over time. Attempting more advanced forms of nadi shodhana without adequate preparation can strain, injure, or permanently damage your respiratory and nervous system. (Be sure to consult your doctor before beginning any pranayama practice.)

Stage 1: Nadi Shodhana

To practice nadi shodhana, Stage 1, sit in comfortable meditative position with legs crossed or in *vajra asana* (see page 219). Or use a straight-back chair. Or sit on the floor or bed with legs outstretched and back supported against wall or headboard. Get comfortable, because you will not move for 10 minutes.

Close eyes and relax. Hold spine upright without arching or tensing back. Place left hand on left knee or in lap. Raise right hand in front of face, place right elbow in front of chest, and rest right lower arm against chest. Hold right forearm in vertical position.

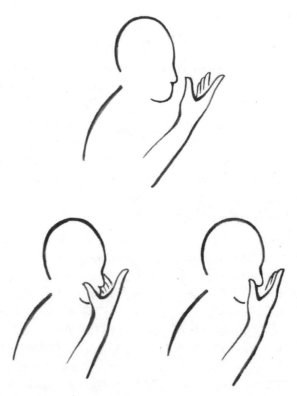

Figure 22a. Basic Nadi Shodhana Position.

THE BIG BOOK OF CHAKRAS AND CHAKRA HEALING

Nadi Shodhana, Stage 1, Part 1

Close right nostril with right thumb. Slowly practice yogic breathing (see page 231 for instructions) through left nostril, inhaling and exhaling silently and completely. Continue five minutes while fully aware of breath.

Then remove thumb from right nostril and close left nostril with middle and fourth fingers of right hand. Slowly practice yogic breathing through right nostril with full awareness on breath for five minutes. Practice this first part of nadi shodhana, Stage 1, for one week. Then move on to Part 2.

Nadi Shodhana, Stage 1, Part 2

Close right nostril with right thumb and practice yogic breathing through left nostril. As you inhale, mentally count the seconds: one, two, three, four.

During exhalation, mentally count the seconds again: one, two, three, four, five, six, seven, eight. In other words, exhale for twice the time as you inhale. If you inhale for three counts, then exhale six counts. If you inhale for five counts, then exhale for 10. Do not strain or make the duration longer than comfortable. Continue for 10 rounds through left nostril, with one round counted as one inward and outward breath.

Then take thumb off right nostril and close left nostril with third and fourth fingers. Breathe as above for 10 rounds through right nostril. If you have time, repeat another 10 rounds through each nostril. Practice this second part of nadi shodhana, Stage 1, Part 2, for two weeks. Then begin the next stage, called *sukha poorvaka*.

Stage 2: Sukha Poorvaka

Continue to practice nadi shodhana, Stage 1, and simply add the next process in the same sitting, right after completion. *Sukha poorvaka* (simple preliminary practice) is also called *bhal bhati* (forehead bellows) or alternate nostril pranayama. This practice equalizes the flow of air through the nostrils. Developing harmony and balance between solar (*pingala*) and lunar (*ida*) pranic poles, it brings deep relaxation—perfect meditation preparation.

Sit comfortably, with head and back upright, without straining. Close eyes and become aware of breath. Intend to become totally involved in the practice. Lift your right hand in front of your face and place right elbow in front of chest, and rest right lower arm against chest. Hold right forearm vertically.

Sukha Poorvaka, Part 1

Close right nostril with right thumb. Inhale through left nostril, slowly and noise-lessly, using yogic breathing. Fill the lungs completely, without straining. After inhaling, close left nostril with middle and fourth fingers of right hand. Open right nostril and exhale slowly. Empty lungs as much as possible. After exhaling, keep right nostril open and then inhale slowly. After inhaling, close right nostril. Open left nostril and exhale. This is one round. Repeat rounds for about 10 minutes. Practice this pranayama for one week and then begin Part 2.

Sukha Poorvaka, Part 2

Practice the same pranayama as Part 1, but now measure the time of inhalation and exhalation. Start to count, with each interval lasting about one second. At first, keep the time of inhalation and exhalation equal. For instance, if you count one, two, three, four, five to inhale, then count another five to exhale. Begin with whatever count is comfortable, without straining. Practice about 10 minutes.

Over a period of weeks, slowly increase the duration of exhalation, until exhalation is twice the time of inhalation. Practice this sukha poorvaka pranayama at least one month before advancing to the next stage.

To reap maximum benefits of pranayama, maintain full attention on breathing and counting. When your mind wanders, it does not matter. Just come back to the process whenever you notice it wandering.

Stage 3: Antar Kumbhaka

At least two months of practicing the first two stages of nadi shodhana are essential to prepare your lungs for the next stage: *kumbhaka* (breath retention). Without first developing slow, controlled breathing, pranayama with breath retention is impossible. It is easy to hold your breath once, but holding your breath after each inhalation requires acclimation to deep breathing, which is developed in the first two stages.

"A ringmaster tames a wild animal slowly and systematically. In the same way, one should gradually tame the prana in the body through the practice of kumbhaka. If one tries to break in and master a wild tiger or elephant too quickly without sufficient care, one can easily be injured. Similarly, if you try to control the prana in the body too rapidly and forcefully then this will also cause harm." —Hatha Yoga Pradipika [5]

Antar (inner) *kumbhaka* (breath retention) profoundly influences pranic flow through your subtle body and consequently strongly influences your mind. This practice slows down, harmonizes, and brings peace and unwavering mental concentration.

"During kumbhaka the mind becomes steady and one experiences timelessness.
One is able to concentrate intensely on the trikuti (the brow chakra)."
—*Hatha Yoga Pradipika* [6]

Now let us learn how.

First practice sukha poorvaka pranayama Part 2 for a few minutes. Once you attain a comfortable, relaxed breathing rate of exhalation twice the length of inhalation, then begin antar kumbhaka as follows.

Antar Kumbhaka, Part 1

Close right nostril with thumb and inhale through left nostril slowly, noiselessly, and completely, using yogic breathing. Count duration of inhale—identical to duration you may have been using for sukha poorvaka (Part 2). After inhaling, keep right nostril closed and also close left nostril with middle and ring fingers. At the same time, slightly contract the glottis (muscles in your throat) to prevent air escaping from lungs. Hold breath a short duration without strain or discomfort.

Then open right nostril and inhale a brief sniff. Then exhale through right nostril, slowly and completely. Count the duration of exhalation—twice the duration of inhalation. For instance, if you inhaled four counts, then exhale eight counts.

After completing exhale, then immediately inhale through right nostril, noiselessly and completely, for same number of counts that you inhaled through left nostril. Again, hold breath for short, comfortable duration and close glottis.

Then open left nostril and inhale briefly. Exhale through left nostril, slowly and completely. This completes one round of antar kumbhaka.

To begin the second round, immediately breathe in through your left nostril and continue in this manner for ten minutes. Continue to practice antar kumbhaka Part 1 for at least one month before advancing to Part 2.

Antar Kumbhaka, Part 2

Practice antar kumbhaka, Part 1, maintaining a ratio of two counts exhale to each one count inhale. Meanwhile, increase retention time (holding your breath) slowly—about one second per week. Eventually you will use the same duration for retention as exhalation. For instance, if your period of exhalation is eight seconds, then gradually build up to eight seconds for retention.

After achieving this goal, gradually increase duration for inhalation, exhalation, and retention. At the same time, maintain this same ratio of one count·inhalation per two counts exhalation per two counts retention. See the following chart for the proper ratios:

ANTAR KUMBHAKA, PART 2: RATIOS		
Right inhalation: 1 count	Retention: 2 counts	Left exhalation: 2 counts
Left inhalation: 1 count	Retention: 2 counts	Right exhalation: 2 counts

Take it easy with antar kumbhaka, and never strain. Some people find this easier to master than others, so be patient. If you find retention too difficult, then return to antar kumbhaka Part 1 until your lung capacity expands sufficiently.

Because antar kumbhaka is so powerful, your body might undergo deep cleansing. Eradication of impurities may cause skin rashes or other indications of purging. If this reaction becomes uncomfortable, then reduce or stop antar kumbhaka until your body acclimates to sustaining higher vibrations of pranic energy. Do not strain or try to achieve more than your capacity. Practice antar kumbhaka Part 2 daily for at least six months before advancing to Part 3.

Antar Kumbhaka, Part 3

Continue to practice antar kumbhaka as you have been doing, but gradually increase your period of retention, at the rate of about one second per week, until you achieve the ratio outlined in the following chart. Practice this for at least six months before attempting Part 4.

ANTAR KUMBHAKA, PART 3: RATIOS		
Right inhalation: 1 count	Retention: 4 counts	Left exhalation: 2 counts
Left inhalation: 1 count	Retention: 4 counts	Right exhalation: 2 counts

If you gasp for breath or become tired easily, then you are not ready to increase retention. In that case, just continue with antar kumbhaka Part 2 until you develop greater lung capacity.

Antar Kumbhaka, Part 4

Gradually increase your period of retention, at the rate of about one second per week, until you achieve the ration outlined on the following chart:

ANTAR KUMBHAKA, PART 4: RATIOS		
Right inhalation: 1 count	Retention: 6 counts	Left exhalation: 2 counts
Left inhalation: 1 count	Retention: 6 counts	Right exhalation: 2 counts

If you gasp for breath or become tired easily, then you are not ready to increase retention. In that case, just continue with antar kumbhaka Part 3 until you develop greater lung capacity. Absolutely do not strain to achieve retention. If the practice does not flow easily and comfortably, then you are trying something beyond your capacity. Slow down. Practice antar kumbhaka Part 4 at least six months before moving to nadi shodhana, Stage 4: bahir kumbhaka.

Stage 4: Bahir Kumbhaka

In the fourth stage of nadi shodhana, continue to practice antar kumbhaka (retention after inhaling), plus add bahir kumbhaka or bahiranga kumbhaka (retention after exhaling). The capacity to hold your breath externally, after exhaling, must be developed gradually and safely. Therefore, do not strain or try to achieve more than is comfortable. In the initial phase, be careful not to hold breath too long. Otherwise, you might get a headache or cause permanent damage to your respiratory or nervous system. Do not attempt bahir kumbhaka until you have practiced more elementary pranayama techniques daily for at least two years.

Let us practice bahir kumbhaka now.

Bahir Kumbhaka, Part 1

Continue the same ratio of breathing you have been using in antar kumbhaka, but now add bahir kumbhaka in the following ratio:

Begin by inhaling through left nostril for ratio of one count. Then retain breath internally for ratio of eight counts, while constricting glottis. Slightly inhale and then exhale through right nostril for ratio of six counts. Then retain breath externally for ratio of one count, while constricting glottis.

Slightly exhale through right nostril and then inhale through right nostril for ratio of one count. Then retain breath internally for ratio of eight counts, while constricting glottis. Then slightly inhale through left nostril and then exhale through left nostril for ratio of six counts. Then retain breath externally for ratio of one count, while constricting glottis. This counts as one round. See the following chart for proper ratios:

BAHIR KUMBHAKA: RATIOS			
Left inhale: 1 count	Retain: 8 counts	Right exhale: 6 counts	Retain: 1 count
Right inhale: 1 count	Retain: 8 counts	Left exhale: 6 counts	Retain: 1 count

Bahir Kumbhaka, Part 2

Continue to slowly and gradually build up your capacity for bahir kumbhaka until you can advance to ratio on the following chart:

BAHIR KUMBHAKA: RATIOS			
Left inhale: 1 count	Retain: 8 counts	Right exhale: 6 counts	Retain: 2 counts
Right inhale: 1 count	Retain: 8 counts	Left exhale: 6 counts	Retain: 2 counts

Continue to practice bahir kumbhaka at least six months before moving on to Stage 5. Do not advance until you have been practicing the previous pranayama practices for at least three years.

Stage 5: Bahir Kumbhaka with Jalandhara Bandha

Sit comfortably in any position with back erect. Breathe in through left nostril for ratio of one count. Then bend neck forward in *jalandhara bandha* (see page 219). Retain breath for ratio of eight counts. Then release the bandha and breathe out through right nostril for ratio of six counts. Retain breath in jalandhara bandha for ratio of two counts. Inhale through right nostril for ratio of one

BAHIR KUMBHAKA WITH JALANDHARA BANDHA: RATIOS			
Left inhale: 1 count	Jalandhara: 8 counts	Right exhale: 6 counts	Jalandhara: 2 counts
Right inhale: 1 count	Jalandhara: 8 counts	Left exhale: 6 counts	Jalandhara: 2 counts

count. Do jalandhara bhanda. Hold breath for ratio of eight counts. Then release the bandha. Exhale through left nostril for ratio of six counts. Retain breath in jalandhara for ratio of two counts. This is one round. Continue to do several rounds for 10 minutes.

When practicing this pranayama, take it easy and do not strain. If you feel any tendency toward suffocation, immediately stop. Lie down and rest. Practice this with jalandhara for at least one month before advancing to Stage 6.

Stage 6: Bahir Kumbhaka with Bandhas

Continue to practice bahir kumbhaka Stage 5, but add *uddiyana bandha* (see page 220) while you simultaneously perform jalandhara bandha during inward and outward retention.

BAHIR KUMBHAKA WITH BANDHAS: RATIOS			
Left inhale: 1 count	Bandhas: 8 counts	Right exhale: 6 counts	Bandhas: 2 counts
Right inhale: 1 count	Bandhas: 8 counts	Left exhale: 6 counts	Bandhas: 2 counts

If you find this combined practice too difficult, then continue bahir kumbhaka combined with jalandhara bandha and then separately practice bahir kumbhaka combined with uddiyama bandha.

After successfully practicing bahir kumbhaka combined with jalandhara bandha and uddiyana bandha at least six months, then practice bahir kumbhaka with *maha bandha* (see page 223).

To practice these powerful advanced stages of bahir kumbhaka, study with an authentic spiritual master who teaches traditional pranayama practices.

Be mindful of your teacher's credentials before embarking on such a journey. You are welcome to join one of our yoga journeys, cruises, or retreats to learn these practices from a yoga teacher. For more information, visit the Divine Travels website at *www.divinetravels.com*.

Chapter Twenty-Three

THE POWER OF
VISUALIZATION

*"The journey begins at the third eye. By putting our attention there, the soul
begins its voyage to the ultimate source of happiness."*
—Sant Rajinder Singh Ji Maharaj[1]

A powerful way to open your chakras and to awaken kundalini is through
the method known as "visualization." This technique has been practiced
for millennia in the Far East. But it has only become popular in the West
during the past decade. Today it still remains on the fringes and is not yet mainstream, because most Westerners have not accepted visualization as a creative process that in fact determines their destiny.

Brihadaranyaka Upanishad 4.4.5. says: "You are what your deep, driving desire is. As your desire is, so is your will. As your will is, so is your deed. As your
deed is, so is your destiny."[2] This pearl of wisdom means that you have the power
to influence the outcome of your intentions through thought, will, and action.

But this statement says something even deeper. It implies that you create your
own universe through your imagination. Because the chakras are located in your
subtle body, and because the subtlest aspects of creation are precursors and genera-
tors of gross physical creation, you can use subtle sight (visualization) and subtle
sound (mantras) to impact your life in positive, powerful ways.

According to the ancient Sanskrit scriptures, the primary purpose of the entire chakra system is to serve as a meditation tool for self-realization. There is
nothing in these scriptures that bestows upon chakras the kinds of properties
that modern-day authors do. According to the ancients, the chakras located at
specific bodily points form a template for *nyasa* (Sanskrit for "deposit, set down,
or place).

In the visualization practice of nyasa, you imagine placing mantras at specific points in your subtle body, based upon the template of the chakra or kshetram locations. This helps you to assign or locate divinity within you. During the practice, you envision specific Sanskrit letters in your energy body at the chakra locations while silently intoning their mantric sounds.

As I mentioned on page 112, mantras are sounds that embody the deities. So by visualizing and repeating mantras, you invoke the deities and install them on their designated seats or thrones, which are at your chakra points within your subtle body.

In this chapter are visualization methods that you may use to lift your awareness to higher consciousness. These are guided meditations, and I recommend that you record them onto your phone or computer, so you can listen and follow the instructions with eyes closed in a darkened room. Thus your visualizations will be more effective than trying to read them from a book. When you make your recording, please speak slowly and quietly, in a soothing voice.

"Meditating on the lotus of your heart, in the center is the untainted,
the exquisitely pure, clear, and sorrowless, the inconceivable, the unmanifest, of
infinite form, blissful, tranquil, immortal, the womb of Brahma."
—Kaivalya Upanishad[3]

Chakra Deities Visualization

Muladhara Chakra

Lord Brahma

For your visualization of the root chakra, I suggest you first refer to page 125 for a picture of Lord Brahma. Then close your eyes and place your attention on an imaginary location about a foot in front of your heart. As you do this, your eyes, mind, and body will relax. Now, keeping your eyes closed and in that restful position, use your imagination (not your eyes) to envision a small, beautiful, radiant form of the deity Lord Brahma appearing about two feet before you at eye level. This form is made of pure light. Imagine this deity has some weight and corporeality, and he is real and alive.

Lord Brahma is seated on a pink lotus. Each of his four faces points to a cardinal direction. He carries the sacred Vedic texts in one hand. In his second hand, he holds rosary beads, symbolizing time. In his third, he bears a ladle that feeds the sacrificial fire, and in his fourth, a water pot symbolizing a primordial vessel from which all creation emanates. His four mouths create the four Vedas. His beard is white, designating sage-like experience. He wears a white garment, matted hair, an ornate gem-studded belt, and a golden crown encrusted with gems. Gold bracelets adorn both his upper arms and wrists. A flower garland and many gem-laden gold necklaces encircle his neck.

As you view this image, increase its light and radiance. Then double its brilliance and make the image even more vibrant and real. Now double the radiance again and begin to merge with the deity. Visualize yourself fully uniting and one with Lord Brahma, a divine enlightened being within you. Feel what it is like to be Lord Brahma, the deity that created the universe, who can see in all directions and who created everything with his mind. Your body is filled with Lord Brahma's light. Sense the power of Lord Brahma within, and imagine you can create anything. Feel what it is like to be the creator of your life and your destiny.

Now imagine that you are installing this figure of Lord Brahma in your first chakra at the base of your tailbone. Review the image on page 120 for a location of that chakra. Know that Lord Brahma is now permanently established in your root chakra.

Speak audibly the following mantra in a commanding voice and then silently repeat the mantra several times while imagining the mantra is vibrating at the base of your spine, at the first chakra:

OM DANG DANG DAKINI BRAHMANE LANG LANG LANG NAMAHA[4]

Phonetically pronounced:

ohm duhng duhng dahkini bramanay luhng luhng luhng nuhmaah

Now speak audibly in a commanding voice: "Within voidness, I arise as Lord Brahma. I am one with the universe, and my love fills all beings with love. We are all one."

Svadhishthana Chakra

Lord Vishnu

To begin your visualization of the pelvic chakra, you may first refer to page 132 for a picture of Lord Vishnu. Then close your eyes and place your attention on the imaginary, restful location about a foot in front of your chest. Relax your eyes and keep their attention at that same spot, with eyes remaining closed. Then, without using your eyes, envision a small, beautiful, radiant form of Lord Vishnu appearing about two feet before you at eye level. This form is made of pure light. Picture Vishnu with some weight and corporeality—real and alive.

Vishnu stands perfectly erect and symmetrical. His complexion is blue and he has four arms. He wears an elaborately draped yellow sarong and is bare-chested with a curly mark on the left side of his chest. A pink scarf, bordered in gold, is wrapped around his upper arms, and gold bracelets adorn his wrists. He wears a flower garland around his neck, jewel-bedecked earrings, and many gem-studded necklaces. A gold diadem ornamented with gems and a peacock feather decorates his head. He holds a lotus flower in his lower left hand, gold mace in his lower right hand, conch shell in his upper left hand, and gold discus in his upper right hand. He radiates pure light, like the sun.

Now increase the light and radiance of that image. Double its brilliance and make the image even more vibrant and real. Now double the radiance again and begin to merge with the deity. Visualize yourself fully united and one with Lord Vishnu. Feel what it is like to be Lord Vishnu, the maintainer of the universe, who, by its very nature, preserves all life in creation. Imagine yourself as a divine enlightened being who incarnates in various forms to vanquish evil and destruction and to restore good and light. Feel your body filled with the brilliance of Lord Vishnu's magnificence as you dream the universe into being. Feel yourself to be the maintainer of creation.

Now envision installing this figure of Lord Vishnu in your second chakra at your sacrum. See the image on page 128 for a location of that chakra. Know that Lord Vishnu is now permanently established in your pelvic chakra.

Speak audibly the following mantra in a commanding voice and then repeat the mantra silently several times while imagining this mantra is vibrating at your sacrum, at the second chakra:

OM RANG RANG RAKINI VISHNU VANG VANG VANG NAMAHA

Phonetically pronounced:

ohm ruhng ruhng rahkini vishnu vuhng vuhng vuhng nuhmaah

Now speak audibly in a commanding voice: "Within voidness, I arise as Lord Vishnu. I preserve and maintain integrity in creation. I honor all beings, and we all honor each other in truth."

Manipura Chakra

Lord Rudra

To begin your visualization of the navel chakra, you may refer to Figure 11c on page 139 for a picture of Lord Rudra. Then close your eyes and place your attention on the imaginary restful location about a foot in front of your chest. Relax your eyes and keep their attention at that spot. Then picture a small, fierce, fiery, shining form of the deity Lord Rudra appearing about two feet in front of you at eye level. This form is made of pure light. Imagine Rudra with some weight and corporeality—real and alive.

Rudra, whose name means "to cry or howl," is the fierce, destructive force in the universe—the personification of sorrow and terror, and the eliminator of evil and ignorance. He is seated in lotus posture on a bull. He has three eyes and two arms, and his face appears stern. His skin is vermillion, but appears white because his body is smeared with holy ash. He is wrapped in a tiger skin, his hair is matted, and his forehead bears a crescent moon. The Ganges River emerges from his topknot. Marks of triplet smears of holy ash adorn his forehead, neck, and arms. Multiple prayer necklaces made of rudraksha seeds encircle his neck and wrists. Cobras wrap around his head and arms. In one hand he holds a trident, and in the other, a double-sided drum.

Now increase the light and radiance of Lord Rudra's image. Double its brilliance and make the image even more vibrant and real. Now double the radiance again and begin to merge with the deity. Envision yourself fully united and one with Lord Rudra. Feel what it is like to be Lord Rudra, the destructive power in the universe, which annihilates all ignorance. Your body is filled with the shining form of Lord Rudra. Sense his destructive power within you as your mind is purified and ignorance is eliminated. Feel yourself as the divine enlightened being who, like fire, consumes all that needs elimination.

Now imagine that you are installing this figure of Lord Rudra in your third chakra at your navel. See the image on page 136 for a location of that chakra. Know that Lord Rudra is now permanently established in your navel chakra.

Speak audibly the following mantra in a commanding voice and then repeat the mantra silently several times while imagining this mantra is vibrating at your navel, at the third chakra:

OM LANG LANG LAKINI RUDRA RANG RANG RANG NAMAHA

Phonetically pronounced:

ohm luhng luhng lakini roodraa ruhng ruhng ruhng nuhmaah

Now speak audibly in a commanding voice: "Within voidness, I arise as Lord Rudra. I now transform all fantasy, ignorance, and selfishness into truth, wisdom, and compassion. I honor myself."

Anahata Chakra

Lord Isha

To visualize the heart chakra, you may first refer to page 147 for a picture of Lord Isha. Then close your eyes and place your attention about a foot in front of your chest. Relax your eyes and keep their attention at that spot. Then imagine a small, radiant, pure white form of Lord Isha appearing about two feet in front of you at eye level. This image is made of divine light—bright and shining white like millions of moons. Picture Isha with weight and corporeality—real and alive.

Isha or Ishvara, whose name means "God," is the benevolent form of Lord Shiva. Seated in lotus posture on a tiger skin, floating above the ground in levitation, he has three eyes and two arms. His beautiful calm face radiates serenity. His two hands make gestures of dispelling fear and granting boons. He wears a crescent moon on his forehead, a tiger skin covering his body, and his hair is matted. The Ganges River emerges from the topknot on his head. Multiple prayer necklaces made of rudraksha seeds encircle his neck and wrists. His body is smeared with triplet marks of holy ash on his forehead, neck, and arms. Cobras wrap around his arms and his crown. A flower garland hangs from his neck.

Now increase the pure white light and brilliance of the image of Lord Isha. Double its radiance and make the image even more dazzling and real. Now double the brightness again and begin to merge with the deity. See yourself fully united and one with Lord Isha, filled and surrounded with his shining form. Sense what it is like to be Isha, emanating infinite love power that dispels fear. Feel yourself as this divine enlightened being who strengthens concentration and grants wisdom. Experience your heart as the center of pure stillness and oneness. Feel within your heart Lord Isha's supreme yoga power—omniscient, omnipresent, omnipotent, infinite, eternal, and absolute. Feel what it is like to watch over and protect all living beings.

Now envision you are installing this figure of Lord Isha in your fourth chakra at your heart. See the image on page 142 for that chakra's location. Know that Lord Isha is now permanently established in your heart chakra.

Speak audibly the following mantra in a commanding voice and then repeat the mantra silently several times while imagining this mantra is vibrating in your heart, at the forth chakra:

OM KANG KANG KAKINI ISHAN RUDRA YANG YANG YANG NAMAHA

Phonetically pronounced:

ohm kuhng kuhng kakini eeshaan roodrah yuhng yuhng yuhng nuhmaah

Now speak audibly in a commanding voice: "Within voidness, I arise as Lord Isha. I am love as divine power. I embrace the healing energies of forgiveness, and I release the need for human, self-determined justice. I am filled with loving-kindness, and I am at peace."

Vishuddha Chakra

Lord Sadashiva as Ardhanarishvara

To begin your visualization of the throat chakra, you may first refer to page 161 for a picture of Lord Sadashiva as Ardhanarishvara. Then close your eyes and place attention on the location about a foot in front of your chest. Relax your eyes and keep their attention at that same spot. Then envision a small, benevolent, radiant form of the deity Lord Sadashiva as Ardhanarishvara appearing about two feet before you at eye level. This form is made of pure light. Imagine the deity with some weight and corporeality—real and alive.

Sadashiva has a white complexion and five faces: smoke, yellow, vermilion, white, and deep red. Four of these faces look toward each of the four cardinal directions, and the fifth face is turned upwards. He has three eyes in each face and 10 arms. Dressed in a tiger skin, his body is ash-smeared. Snakes and rudraksha beads circle his neck and wrists. In each of his faces, his third eye is open but his two other eyes are closed in deep meditation. In nine of his hands, he holds a trident, axe, sword, thunderbolt, fire, great serpent, bell, goad, noose, and his tenth hand is in a gesture of dispelling fear.

In the throat chakra, Sadashiva's form is merged with his consort, known as Shakti or Gauri. So the right side of his body is male and left side is female. She is golden color, dressed in a sari, bedecked in jewelry with a crown on her head. Her hand is in a gesture of granting boons. Since Shiva's vehicle is the bull and Shakti's is the lion, the vehicle for Sadashiva as Ardhanarishvara is half-bull, half-lion.

THE BIG BOOK OF CHAKRAS AND CHAKRA HEALING

As you are envisioning this deity, increase the light and radiance of the image. Double its brilliance and make it more vibrant and real. Now double the radiance again and begin to merge with the deity. See yourself fully united and one with Sadashiva as Ardhanarishvara. Feel what it is like to be this deity, which represents nondualism, which unifies the masculine and feminine aspects of the universe. Imagine yourself as this divine enlightened being, which integrates disparate energies into oneness. Your body is now filled with the radiance of Sadashiva as Ardhanarishvara. Feel within you the power of creative expression that rises as a result of perfect divine union of male and female energies—perfect union of supreme consciousness with divine power. Sense that the third eye of Sadashiva is granting you divine knowledge and bliss consciousness.

Now imagine you are installing this figure of Sadashiva as Ardhanarishvara in your fifth chakra at your throat chakra. See the image on page 156 for its location. Know that Sadashiva as Ardhanarishvara is now permanently established in your throat chakra.

Speak audibly the following mantra in a commanding voice and then repeat the mantra silently several times while imagining this mantra is vibrating in your throat, at the fifth chakra:

OM SHANG SHANG SHAKINI SADASHIV HANG HANG HANG NAMAHA

Phonetically pronounced:

ohm shuhng shuhng shakini saadaashiv huhng huhng huhng nuhmaah

Now speak audibly in a commanding voice: "Within voidness, I arise as Lord Sadashiva as Ardhanarishvara. I now surrender my personal will to divine will. I am calm, serene, and pure, with a melodious and commanding voice."

You may also recite audibly this "Pancha Brahma Sadashiva Mantra," which honors the five faces of Sadashiva and has been translated into English:[5]

"I take refuge in the First Born, verily I bow to the First Born. Do not consign me to birth after birth. Guide me beyond birth. I bow to the Causer of birth. I bow to the Noble One, the Eldest; to the Best, to Rudra and to Time. I bow to the Incomprehensible, to Strength, to the Causer of various forces, and to the Extender of Strength. I bow to the Subduer of all beings, and to the One who kindles the Light. I bow to those not terrible and those who are terrible, and to those who are both terrible and not terrible. Everywhere and always, Sarva, I bow to all Thy Rudra forms. May we know that Supreme Person and meditate on that Great God. May Rudra impel us! Ruler of all knowledge, Master of all beings, Commander of all study and devotion, that God Auspicious to me, be He just so, the Ever-Auspicious OM."

Ajna Chakra

Lord Parashiva

To visualize the brow chakra, first close your eyes and place your attention about a foot in front of your chest. Relax your eyes and keep their attention at that spot. Then imagine a small, radiant, pure golden form of a cosmic egg appearing about two feet in front of you at eye level. Visualize this egg as the seed from which the entire universe is hatched. This image is made of pure golden light—brilliant and shining like the Sun. Picture this cosmic egg as real and alive. Hiranyagarbha means "golden egg of creation." It is the transcendental form of Lord Shiva, known as Parashiva.

Parashiva is beyond duality—transcendental, supreme, absolute, unbounded, unlimited, omniscient, omnipresent, omnipotent, endless, beginningless, beyond duality, free from limitation, pure, whole, and one. Parashiva's mantra is OM, and he is the hum of creation that gives rise to the entire universe.

Now increase the pure golden light and brilliance of this golden egg. Double its intensity and make the image even more dazzling and real. Now double the brightness again and begin to merge with the golden egg. See yourself fully united and one with Parashiva as this golden egg. Feel what it is like to be this golden egg of creation, filled with radiance, pure, whole, and complete. Imagine that you are yourself this divine enlightened transcendental being that underlies the entire universe and gives rise to it. Experience the unity and oneness of your being, which is one and one only—without a second. Your body is filled with the radiant, formless, absolute power of Parashiva. Feel within you Parashiva's transcendental cosmic consciousness, beyond all duality.

Now envision that you are installing Parashiva in your sixth chakra at your pineal gland. See the image on page 169 for a location of that chakra. Know that Parashiva is now permanently established in your brow chakra.

Speak audibly the following mantra in a commanding voice and then repeat the mantra silently several times while imagining this mantra is vibrating in your third eye, at the sixth chakra:

OM HANG HANG HAKINI JNANADATA SHIV AUM AUM AUM
NAMAHA

Phonetically pronounced:

ohm huhng huhng hakini gyan uh daata sheev owm owm owm nuhmaah

Now speak audibly in a commanding voice: "Within voidness, I arise as Lord Parashiva. I seek only the truth. I now see the world with wisdom and insight."

After completing this meditation, lie down and rest for about 10 minutes.

Chakra Visualization to Purify the Elements

An ancient Tantric practice to purify the elements *(bhutas)* in your subtle body is called the Bhuta Shuddi Chakra Meditation. This method, which employs visualization along with repetition of *bija* (seed) Tantric mantras, purifies the *samskaras* (seeds of desire) that operate in conjunction with the elements.

Please refer to pages 88 and 90, Figures 7e and 7f, where you will see the root, pelvic, navel, heart, and throat chakras are related to the five elements of earth, water, fire, air, and ether, and the brow and crown chakras relate to mind and God. The crown chakra, related to divine Spirit and pure consciousness, is the precursor that gives rise to the advent and unfolding of mind, space, air, fire, water, and earth (in that order, from subtlest to grossest).

Please record these words onto your phone or computer so you can practice this guided meditation with eyes closed, ideally in a darkened room. When you make your recording, speak slowly and quietly, in a soothing voice.

Before practicing Bhuta Shuddhi meditation, please refer to pages 94–95 to identify the kshetram points, where you will be placing your attention during this meditation, and also refer to the pictures and descriptions of the deities that embody the element you will invoke during the meditation:

Muladhara: Indra (earth element) on page 124.

Svadhishthana: Varuna (water element) on page 131.

Manipura: Vahni (fire element) on page 139.

Anahata: Vayu (air element) on page 146.

Vishuddha: Ambara (ether element) on page 160.

Ajna: OM (mind) on page 171.

Sahasrara: Ardhanarishvara (God/Goddess) on page 196.

Muladhara

To purify the earth element in your muladhara chakra, place your attention on the perineum, the space between your anus and genitals. Then let the mantra LANG [phonetically pronounced luhng] arise in your mind quietly and effortlessly. Imagine the mantra starting to vibrate from within your root kshetram point at the perineum. Allow the mantra to pulsate its repetition easily and effortlessly, not as a clear pronunciation, but as a faint idea, at a speed that feels natural to you, while keeping your attention at the perineum. At the same time, allow your awareness to imagine earth, solidity, form, and the sense of smell at the root kshetram at the perineum. Visualize the form of the deity Indra in your mind's eye as a radiant being of light, and place that deity in the area of the root kshetram. At the same time, know that every part of your body is the temple of God, even the area where waste is eliminated.

Svadhishthana

To purify the water element in your svadhishthana chakra, place your attention on the pelvic kshetram at the genital area. Then let the mantra VANG [phonetically pronounced vuhng] arise in your mind quietly and effortlessly. Imagine the mantra starting to vibrate from within your pelvic kshetram point at your penis or vagina. Allow the mantra to pulsate its repetition easily and effortlessly, not as a clear pronunciation, but as a faint idea, at a speed that feels natural to you. Keeping your attention on the genital region, allow your awareness to imagine water, flow, fluidity, and the sense of taste at that pelvic kshetram. Envision the form of the deity Varuna in your mind's eye as a beautiful fluid deity made of water, and place that deity in the area of your genitals. At the same time, know that every part of your body is the temple of God, including the area where sexual intercourse occurs.

Manipura

To purify the fire element in your manipura chakra, place your attention on the navel kshetram at your navel. Then let the mantra RANG [phonetically pronounced ruhng] arise in your mind quietly and effortlessly. Feel the mantra starting to vibrate from within the kshetram point at your navel. Allow the mantra to pulsate its repetition easily and effortlessly, not as a clear pronunciation, but as a faint idea, at a speed that feels natural to you. As you maintain your attention at the navel kshetram, allow your awareness to imagine blazing flames of fire in dynamic motion, and the sense of sight located there. Visualize the form of the deity Vahni in your mind's eye as a radiant, glowing deity made of brilliant flames, and place that deity in the area of your navel. At the same time, know that every part of your body is the temple of God, including the area of the body where digestion of food occurs.

Anahata

To purify the air element in your anahata chakra, place your attention on the heart kshetram at your chest. Then let the mantra YANG [phonetically pronounced yuhng] arise in your mind quietly and effortlessly. Sense the mantra starting to vibrate from within the kshetram point at your heart. Allow the mantra to pulsate its repetition easily and effortlessly, not as a clear pronunciation, but as a faint idea, at a speed that feels natural to you. At the same time, let your awareness imagine the lightness and motion of air and the sense of touch and feeling as it flows in and through your heart kshetram. Envision the form of the deity Vayu in your mind's eye as a radiant, translucent, vibrating, shining deity made of air, and place that deity in the area of your heart. At the same time, know that every part of your body is the temple of God, and the heart is the throne of God's pure unconditional love.

Vishuddha

To purify the ether element in your vishuddha chakra, place your attention on the throat kshetram at your neck. Then let the mantra HANG [phonetically pronounced huhng] arise in your mind quietly and effortlessly. Experience the mantra starting to vibrate from within the kshetram point at your throat. Allow the mantra to pulsate its repetition easily and effortlessly, not as a clear pronunciation, but as a faint idea, at a speed that feels natural to you. At the same time, keeping your attention on the throat kshetram, allow your awareness to imagine at that point the emptiness and void of outer space, the nothingness that has the potential of becoming everything, and the sense of hearing. Visualize the form of the deity Ambara in your mind's eye as a transparent, motionless, still, and profoundly silent deity made of nothingness, and place that deity in the area of your throat. At the same time, know that every part of your body is the temple of God, and the throat is the seat of God's perfect creative expression.

Ajna

To purify your mind in your ajna chakra, place your attention on brow kshetram at the point between your eyebrows. Then let the mantra OM [phonetically pronounced ohm] arise in your mind quietly and effortlessly. Feel the mantra beginning to vibrate from within the kshetram point at your forehead. Allow the mantra to pulsate its repetition easily and effortlessly, not as a clear pronunciation, but as a faint idea, at a speed that feels natural to you. At the same time, see the glowing, brilliant, blazing white Sanskrit letter ॐ vibrating in your mind's eye and place that letter at the point of your brow kshetram. Then feel that the vibrating mantra OM begins spreading throughout your head. Notice OM vibrating in the area where your pineal gland is located, at the center of your head, where your mind, emotions, intellect, and ego are seated. Experience that all the elements of ether, air, fire, water, and earth arise from mind, which arises from OM. Know that OM is the seed sound vibration that gives birth to the entire cosmos. Allow all those elements to be absorbed back into OM, and what remains is stillness. At the same time, know that every part of your body is the temple of God, and your third eye is center of illumination, divine wisdom, and supreme knowledge.

Sahasrara

To purify your consciousness in your sahasrara chakra, place your attention on the crown chakra just above your head. Imagine pure, profound, eternal, beginningless, endless, unmanifest, transcendental silence and pure awareness at the bindu point at the center of the crown chakra. See the crown chakra as the doorway to pure consciousness itself. Step through that doorway and visualize your ego, intellect, mind, emotions, and body being drawn deeper and deeper into the silence. Imagine that deep silence absorbing all the aspects of individuality. As all the elements get absorbed into the silence, they simply disappear and vanish into nothingness, and what remains is oneness and wholeness. Feel waves of ecstatic bliss cascading downward from the bindu point like a waterfall that covers, fills, and permeates every atom of your entire being with pure euphoria, elation, and rapture. At the same time, know that every part of your body and subtle body is the temple of God, and your crown chakra is the center of pure, transcendental, absolute bliss consciousness.

Returning to the Root Kshetram

Now it is time to ground your experience by returning to your root kshetram, step by step.

First allow your awareness to return to the ajna kshetram at the spot between your eyebrows and repeat the mantra OM mentally for about 20 to 30 seconds.

Then return your attention to the vishuddha kshetram and the element of ether at your throat and repeat the mantra HANG silently for about 20 to 30 seconds.

Next return to the anahata kshetram and the air element at the center of your chest and repeat the mantra YANG mentally for about 20 to 30 seconds.

Then become aware of the manipura kshetram and the element of fire at your navel and mentally repeat the word RANG for about 20 to 30 seconds.

Next place your attention on the svadhishthana kshetram and the water element at your genital area and repeat the mantra VANG silently for about 20 to 30 seconds.

Finally return to the muladhara kshetram and the element of earth at your perineum and mentally repeat the mantra LANG for about 20 to 30 seconds.

After completing this meditation, lie down and rest for about 10 minutes.

Chapter Twenty-Four

THE POWER OF
MEDITATION

*"During meditation you behold divine visions, experience
divine smell, divine taste, divine touch, hear divine Anahata sounds.
You receive instructions from God. These indicate that
the Kundalini Shakti has been awakened."*
—*Sri Swami Sivananda*[1]

The best way to raise kundalini is through personal instruction from a
true spiritual master. Such a teacher can best guide you through the delicate requisite meditation practices. In addition, by reading some of my
books—*Divine Revelation, Awaken Your Divine Intuition, Exploring Meditation,*
and *Ascension*—you can learn more about meditation and higher consciousness.
You can also use my guided meditation CDs or downloadable guided meditations,
available at *www.drsusan.org*.

Here you will learn two simple meditations to lift your awareness and awaken
kundalini gently and safely. These methods derive from an ancient practice called
yoga nidra, from the Sanskrit roots *yoga* (inner communion) and *nidra* (sleep),
a simple yet profound technique for deep relaxation, rejuvenation, physical and
mental healing, greater intelligence, and spiritual awakening. It can prevent or
overcome psychosomatic disease, release tension, reduce pain, overcome fatigue,
and tranquilize the body and mind.

Yoga nidra has been scientifically proven to reduce the metabolic rate, heart
rate, and blood pressure. Brain wave activity changes from beta to alpha or theta,
indicating a relaxed, meditative state. The sympathetic nervous system reduces its
activities. Blood lactate, correlated with stress, is reduced. Skin resistance, associated with relaxation, increases.

The pranic currents flowing through the body are deeply harmonized by yoga nidra, particularly by rotating awareness through different body parts, which revitalizes the body and improves health.

"When sankalpa (desires) and vikalpas (fancies and imagination) are rooted out, then one is influenced no more by karma. When sankalpa and vikalpa are removed by constant yogic practice, the ever-blissful state of yoga nidra dawns."
—Adi Shankaracharya[2]

Getting Ready

You can practice yoga nidra in any comfortable posture. We recommend either a comfortable seated position or lying on your back in *savasana* (see below) on an exercise mat or blanket on the floor. Wait at least one hour after meals. Wear comfortable, loose clothing. Practice in a room that is clean, insect-free, quiet, dimly lit, and well ventilated. Keep your body still as possible during the entire practice.

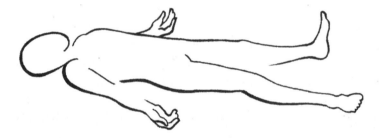

Figure 23a. Sava Asana.

Resolution

The *sankalpa* (resolve or resolution) is a prayer or goal to achieve during meditation. This is a short statement impressed on your subconscious mind during the practice, a way to remove negative blockages and resolve internal conflicts. For best results, the sankalpa is made with strong willpower and deep feeling.

You can ask for anything that will enhance your life, such as deep relaxation, divine contact, divine communication, health, success, spiritual awakening, or prosperity. You might say something like, "I AM creative and dynamic in my work," or "I AM filled with joy," and so forth. Make sure the statement is worded positively, not negatively. In other words, do not say, "I will not get sick." Instead say, "I AM perfectly healthy." You may also add, "I AM now relaxing completely but will stay awake during the practice."

Say your sankalpa audibly before and after yoga nidra. Persist with the same sankalpa daily until it brings results.

Eventually you can attain the state called *kalpa vriksha* (wish-fulfilling tree), when your sankalpas are so powerful that they always bear fruit. This arises when hrit chakra is fully open.

The instructions for yoga nidra are spoken aloud by a teacher, leading a student or group of students into guided meditation. Therefore, to practice this form of meditation alone, you must first record these instructions onto your computer or your phone. Then when you are ready to meditate, simply play the recording. Or you can order a Chakra Yoga Nidras CD from the website *www.drsusan.org*. The remainder of this chapter contains the instructions. Record only the sections in quotations. Speak the instructions very slowly onto the recording, and pause when you see three dots: . . .

Body and Cosmic Awareness

During this first meditation your awareness is drawn to various body parts. This withdraws perception from the outside world, induces deep relaxation, releases tension, awakens unbounded awareness, and brings consciousness to one-pointedness (*bindu*).

"Let us begin by lying down in sava asana and getting so comfortable that you do not need to move again. Adjust your clothing, move your head, scratch yourself, and get comfortable in every way. Close your eyes and keep them closed during the entire practice. Place your arms beside your body with palms upward. Straighten your legs and place them slightly apart. Relax fully and completely . . .

"Become aware of your entire body. Imagine your body becoming heavier and heavier, as though it were sinking into the ground. Your body is merging into the ground. Feel the heaviness of your right leg . . . your left leg . . . your right arm . . . your left arm . . . Feel heaviness in your entire body . . .

"Now become aware of your breathing. Notice your breath moving in and out. Breathe in slowly and completely . . . Now breathe out . . . Breathe in again . . . And out . . . Become aware of just your breathing. Nothing exists but your breathing now . . .

"Repeat your sankalpa [resolution] with feeling and intensity. Feel your entire body vibrating with the repetition of your sankalpa. Say the sankalpa three times with deep feeling from your heart . . . Your intention is to remain alert during this meditation . . .

"Now you will begin to rotate your awareness throughout the body. Either feel the sensation in each part of the body, or create a mental picture of that part of the body. Or mentally name that part of the body once. Remain alert and awake during these instructions, without straining.

"Now become aware of your lips . . . nostrils . . . eyes . . . ears . . . forehead . . . eyebrows . . . space between the eyebrows . . . temples . . . cheeks . . . chin . . . jaw . . . neck . . .

"Now notice your right shoulder . . . right upper arm . . . right lower arm . . . right wrist . . . right palm . . . right-hand thumb . . . second finger . . . third finger . . . fourth finger . . . fifth finger . . . all right fingers together . . .

"Now become aware of your left shoulder . . . left upper arm . . . left lower arm . . . left wrist . . . left palm . . . left-hand thumb . . . second finger . . . third finger . . . fourth finger . . . fifth finger . . . all left fingers together.

"Notice your shoulders . . . chest . . . stomach . . . lower abdomen . . . hips . . . right thigh . . . right knee . . . lower leg . . . ankle . . . top of right foot . . . right sole . . . big toe . . . second toe . . . third toe . . . fourth toe . . . fifth toe . . . all right toes together . . . Feel your left thigh . . . left knee . . . lower leg . . . ankle . . . top of left foot . . . left sole . . . big toe . . . second toe . . . third toe . . . fourth toe . . . fifth toe . . . all left toes together . . .

"Now become aware of your back. Notice your shoulders . . . upper back . . . lower back . . . waist . . . hips . . . buttocks . . . back of right leg . . . back of left leg . . . entire lower body . . . entire upper body . . . whole body . . .

"Now place your body in the room . . . Become aware of the building you are in . . . Then notice the town or city . . . Be aware of the state or province . . . Expand your awareness to the entire nation . . . Become aware of your continent . . . .

"Now become aware of North America . . . South America . . . Europe . . . Africa . . . Asia . . . Australia . . . the entire Earth . . . the Moon . . . the Sun, radiating light . . . the solar system . . . the galaxies . . . clusters of galaxies . . . the entire physical universe . . . your own unbounded awareness . . . your physical body . . .

"Now place your attention on the space between your eyebrows and notice if any images come into your mind . . . Continue to notice the space between the eyebrows . . .

"Now repeat your sankalpa again aloud three times, with deep feeling . . .

"Now it is time to come out of the meditation . . . Slowly move your hands . . . move your legs . . . become aware of being in the room . . . Notice the sounds around you. Give gratitude for your experience and then open your eyes, slowly."

Chakra Awareness

This second yoga nidra increases awareness of the chakras, thereby gently awakening kundalini energy. It is helpful to first prepare by studying Figures 8a and 8b on pages 94–95 to locate the chakra points. Also, take time to study the chakra illustrations in Part II of this book. The best way to do this is to color the drawings with markers, colored pencils, or paints. Order my book *Color Your Chakras* from Amazon or from your local bookstore.

"Lie down on your back in savasana and close your eyes. Get so comfortable that you have no need to move. Place your arms beside your body with palms facing up. Place your legs and feet slightly apart.

"Keep your eyes closed, but look at an imaginary point about one foot in front of your chest . . . Imagine that you are immersed in that space . . . Sink deeper and deeper into that space . . . You are sinking deeper and deeper . . . sinking deeper into the space in front of your chest . . .

"Now become aware of your breathing . . . While inhaling, imagine you are pulling air in through your navel . . . While exhaling, imagine you are pushing air out from your navel . . . Breathe slowly and rhythmically . . . Become aware of this breathing process . . . in through your navel . . . out through your navel . . . Notice your breathing . . .

"Now imagine you are breathing through your chest . . . Pull the air in through the center of your chest . . . Push the air outward and upward through your chest center . . . Notice your breath . . .

"Imagine you are breathing through your nose . . . Imagine the breath drawing in through your nostrils . . . notice the air breathing out through your nostrils . . . Notice breathing through your nostrils . . .

"Now repeat your sankalpa at least three times aloud. Say it with feeling, from your heart . . .

"Do your best to imagine that you see your own body from outside, or that you see your entire body through a full-length mirror . . . See your entire body . . . your feet . . . legs . . . thighs . . . abdomen . . . chest . . . arms . . . hands . . . nose

. . . eyes . . . brow center . . . face . . . entire body . . . Your whole body is reflected in the mirror . . .

"Now become aware of the chakras and kshetram within your body. Place your attention on muladhara, the root kshetram. For men, this is between your legs, in the area of the perineum, between your anus and genitals. For women, it is deep within your vagina, in the area of the cervix . . . Do your best to feel the sensation of this kshetram . . . Now place your attention at the base of your spine, at your tailbone and feel the location of this chakra . . .

"Now notice the svadhishthana chakra, in the sacral area of the spine, above the tailbone . . . Place your attention at the kshetram in the pubic bone on the front of your body . . . For men, notice the root of the penis . . . For women, become aware of the clitoris . . .

"Now become aware of the manipura kshetram in your navel . . . Place your awareness in your spine just behind the navel to locate manipura chakra . . .

"Place your attention in the anahata kshetram in the center of your chest, between your nipples . . . Then become aware of your spine in the area directly behind this kshetram and locate anahata chakra . . .

"Notice your vishuddha kshetram, at the area of your Adam's apple in your throat . . . Become aware of the spine directly behind that point to locate the vishuddha chakra . . .

"Place your awareness in the center of your head at ajna chakra, in the region of the pineal gland . . . Now become aware of the point in the forehead between your eyebrows . . .

"Now become aware of the bindu kshetram at the top and back of your head . . .

"Allow your awareness to pierce through your skull and notice the sahasrara, like an umbrella or crown over your head . . .

"Now repeat this process in reverse. Place your attention again on bindu . . . then brow point . . . then third eye chakra . . . then throat chakra . . . throat kshetram . . . heart chakra . . . heart kshetram . . . navel chakra . . . navel kshetram . . . pelvic chakra . . . genital kshetram . . . root chakra . . . perineum kshetram . . .

"Now do your best to visualize the chakras. Let us begin with the first chakra, muladhara. As each chakra is mentioned, imagine that someone is lightly pressing that chakra with a thumb. Then do your best to see, feel, or hear what is in the chakra. Notice whatever color, deity, or items are contained in the chakra. Let us now begin.

"First become aware of the muladhara root chakra at the base of your spine . . . Find it in your body and see, feel, or hear what is inside of it . . .

"Now become aware of the svadhishthana pelvic chakra in the sacral area of the spine . . . Find it in your body and see, feel, or hear what is inside of it . . .

"Next become aware of the manipura navel chakra in the lumbar area of your spine . . . Find it in your body and see, feel, or hear what is inside of it . . .

"Notice the anahata heart chakra in the thoracic portion of your spine . . . Find it in your body and see, feel, or hear what is inside of it . . .

"Become aware of the vishuddha throat chakra in the cervical spine at your neck . . . Find it in your body and see, feel, or hear what is inside of it . . .

"Now notice the ajna third eye chakra at the pineal gland in the middle of your head . . . Find it in your body and see, feel, or hear what is inside of it . . .

"Now become aware of the bindu point at the top and back of your skull . . . Find it in your body and see, feel, or hear what is inside of it . . .

"Now notice the sahasrara as a radiant crown or umbrella above your head . . . Find it and see, feel, or hear what is inside of it . . .

"Now place your attention on the ajna kshetram, in your forehead between your eyebrows. Notice any sensory experiences that you might have . . . Now ask yourself one question: 'Who am I?' Then let go and allow the answer to come to you without any effort . . .

"Now repeat your sankalpa three times aloud . . . Become aware of your breath . . . Now notice your entire body and any physical sensations . . . Become aware of your surroundings and notice any noises . . . Slowly move your body and stretch your muscles . . . Slowly open your eyes when you feel ready."

"Then say the following affirmation audibly, with eyes open: 'I AM alert. I AM awake. I AM in control. I AM divinely protected by the light of my being. Thank you God, and SO IT IS.'"

EPILOGUE

The mysteries of kundalini and the chakra energies are eternally unknowable. The only way to start to understand them is by direct experience. Those who have experienced them say they are incomprehensible. Therefore, they remain an enigma. Your only true guide on your kundalini journey is your inner guru.

By opening your heart to Spirit and experiencing the true nature of being, you can begin to fathom the unfathomable. The divine presence within you is the source of all knowledge, all mantras, all chakras, and all kundalini. You are that source. Trust in yourself and allow your heart to open in full bloom to its highest, fullest, and best potential. Live in the heart of Spirit and dwell in the house of the Lord. That is your birthright and your mission.

Be at peace in divine love.

ACKNOWLEDGMENTS

Many people have contributed to this book. Therefore, I want to give appreciation to those who have brought it to fruition. Foremost, I want to thank Jeff and Deborah Herman, who remain loyal friends and guides throughout the decades. I give gratitude to Mike Lewis, who originated the idea for the book. I am very thankful to Michael Pye and Laurie Kelly, who have continued to support me year after year. Thanks to Peter Turner, Kathryn Sky-Peck, and Jane Hagaman, and everyone else at Red Wheel/Weiser, who have worked so diligently to bring this book to press.

I wish to give special thanks to those who have assisted my quest to explore kundalini and the chakras, including: Harold and Gladys McCoy, Janet DiGiovanna, Danny Rubenstein, Linda Hayden, PJ Worley, Rian Leichter, Bill Moser, Curt De Groat, Nimueh Rephael, George Fitzgerald, and many others. Most of all, I want to express appreciation to my spiritual mentors: Maharishi Mahesh Yogi, Amritananda Mayi, Babaji Raman Kumar Bachchan, Peter and Ann Meyer, the immortal Babaji, and all the inner teachers. Without these brilliant guiding lights, I would have no comprehension of subtle energies.

NOTES

Introduction

1. Isherwood, *Ramakrishna and His Disciples*, pg. 265.
2. John 20:22.
3. Deuteronomy 34:9.

Chapter 1

1. Muktananada. *Kundalini*. From Cousens, *Spiritual Nutrition*, pg. 51.

Chapter 2

1. Jung, Carl, and J. Hauer. *Kundalini Yoga*. From Cousens, *Spiritual Nutrition*, pg. 51.
2. Genesis 1:26.
3. I Corinthians 3:16.
4. Luke 17:20–21.
5. Doctrine and Covenants 93:33-35. Wilson, *World Scripture*, pg. 143.
6. Qur'an 15:29. Wilson, *World Scripture*, pg. 141.
7. Mahaparinirvana Sutra 214. Wilson, *World Scripture*, pg. 140.
8. Genchi Kato. Wilson, *World Scripture*, pg. 142.
9. Adi Granth, Wilson, *World Scripture*, pg. 142.
10. Chandogya Upanishad, 6:8:7. Wilson, *World Scripture*, pg. 414 and 140.
11. John 1:1.
12. Greene, Brian, interview, Internet website.
13. Dhammapada 1:1, 2. Perry, *A Treasury*, pg. 484.

Chapter 3

1. Aitareya Aranyaka, 2:3:4.
2. *Hatha Yoga Pradipika*, chapter 2:3.
3. Aranya, *Yoga Philosophy,* Yoga Sutras 3:40, pg. 346.
4. Aranya, *Yoga Philosophy*, Yoga Sutras 3:39, pg. 346.

Chapter 4

1. Kaushitaki Upanishad, 3:2.
2. Luke 8:47.
3. Luke 6:19.
4. *www.nccaom.org*
5. *www.healthcmi.com*
6. *themindunleashed.com*
7. *www.sciencedirect.com*
8. *upliftconnect.com*

Chapter 5

1. Sivananda, Sri Swami, *Kundalini Upanishad*, Internet website.
2. Krishna, Gopi, *Dawn of a New Science*.
3. Hatha Yoga Pradipika, 4:17.
4. Genesis 3:1.
5. Hatha Yoga Pradipika, 3:100.

Chapter 6

1. Katha Upanishad, 1:3.3.
2. Vidyaranya, *Pancadasi*, 3:22.
3. Brihadaranyaka Upanishad, 5:3.22.
4. Kapila, *Samkhya-darsana*, 5:114.
5. Taittiriya Upanishad, 2:2-3.
6. Taittiriya Upanishad, 2:4.
7. Taittiriya Upanishad, 2:5.
8. Brihadaranyaka Upanisad, 5:3.7, Shankara's commentary.
9. Yogindra, Vedanta sara, Section 13.

10. Taittiriya Upanishad, 2:4.
11. Shankaracharya, *Vivekacudamani*, 208.
12. Ibid., 211.
13. Mundaka Upanishad, 11:2.9-10.
14. Maitrayana Brahmaya Upanishad, 2:6.

Chapter 7

1. Taittiriya Upanishad, 2:7.
2. Creative Commons Attribution 3.0 Unported license (CC BY-3.0), Dennis Nilsson.
3. Brihadaranyaka Upanishad, 3:5.1.
4. Chandogya Upanishad, 3:6.2.2-3.
5. Bhagavad Gita, 13:19.
6. Bhagavad Gita, 4:13.
7. The Avadhuta Gita, 4:15.
8. Aiyar, *Thirty Minor Upanishads*, Yogatattva Upanishad, 2:3-4, Goswami pg. 68.
9. Taittiriya Upanishad, 2:6.

Chapter 8

1. Genesis 28:12.
2. Revelation 1:20.
3. Shakespeare, *As You Like It*, act 2, scene 7.
4. Eckhart, Meister, Internet website.
5. Plato, Internet website.
6. Pascal, Penseés, 72.
7. Zohar, Vol. 1, Beresheet A, Section 1.
8. Aranya, *Yoga Philosophy,* Yoga Sutras, 1.2. pg. 7.
9. John 1:1.

Chapter 9

1. Sat Cakra Narupana, 11.
2. Vasu, *The Siva Samhita*, 5:64-65, pg. 64.

Chapter 10

1. Sat Cakra Narupana, 16.
2. Vasu, *The Siva Samhita*, 5:76-78, pg. 66.

Chapter 11

1. Subramanian, *Saundaryalahari of Sankaracarya*, 40, pg. 22.
2. Vasu, *The Siva Samhita*, 5:81-82, pg. 67.

Chapter 12

1. Katha Upanishad, 1:6.17.
2. Vasu, *The Siva Samhita*, 5:85, 86, 88, pg. 67-68.

Chapter 13

1. Thirumoolar, Thirumandiram, 1843.
2. Aranya, *Yoga Philosophy,* Yoga Sutras, 44-45.
3. Khandogya Upanishad, 4:8.1.1, 3.
4. Bhagavad Gita, 10:11, 20.
5. Mundaka Upanishad 2:2.2. *World Scripture*, pg. 142.
6. Maitrayana Brahmaya Upanishad, 6:27, *Yoga Philosophy*, pg. 348.
7. Taittiriya Upanishad, 1:2.1.

Chapter 14

1. Subramanian, *Saundaryalahari of Sankaracarya*, 37, pg. 20-21.
2. Sat Cakra Narupana, 30, 31.

Chapter 15

1. Maitrayana Brahmaya Upanishad 6:21.
2. John 4:14.
3. Judges 15:19.
4. Maitrayana Brahmaya Upanishad 6:21.
5. Taittiriyaka Upanishad 1:6.1, 2.

Chapter 16

1. Matthew 6:22.
2. Subramanian, *Saundaryalahari of Shankaracharya*, 36, pg. 20.
3. Vasu, *The Siva Samhita*, 5:111, 115, 117. pg. 71–72.

Chapter 17

1. Nityananda, *Sky of the Heart*, Sutra 28.
2. Aranya, *Yoga Philosophy*, Sutras, 3:3.
3. Bhagavad Gita 6:19-21.

Chapter 18

1. Muktananda, *Shree Guru Gita*, 57, 58.
2. Muktananda, *Shree Guru Gita*, preface.
3. Muktananda, *Shree Guru Gita*, 32-33.
4. Muktananda, *Shree Guru Gita*, 13-14.

Chapter 19

1. Sat Cakra Narupana, 44.
2. Sat Cakra Nirupana, 49.
3. Vasu, *The Siva Samhita,* 5:153-154. pg. 78.

Chapter 20

1. Krishna, *Kundalini*.

Chapter 21

1. Gheranda Samhita 3:16.
2. Hatha Yoga Pradipika, 4:68.

Chapter 22

1. Hatha Yoga Pradipika, Saraswati, pg. 18.
2. Hatha Yoga Pradipika, 2:2.

3. Hatha Yoga Pradipika, 2:41-42.
4. Bhagavad Gita 4:29.
5. Hatha Yoga Pradipika, 2:15-16.
6. Hatha Yoga Pradipika, Saraswati, pg. 189.

Chapter 23

1. *www.sos.org*
2. *en.wikiquote.org*
3. *chaplaincyinstitute.org*
4. *https://chidananda4444.wixsite.com/indianmeditation*
5. *shivadarshana.blogspot.com*

Chapter 24

1. Sivananda, *Kundalini Yoga*, Internet website.
2. Venkantanathacharya, *Yogataravali*, Saraswati pg. 768.

BIBLIOGRAPHY

Books

Aiyar, K. Narayanaswami, trans. *Thirty Minor Upanishads, Including the Yoga Upanishads*. Santarasa Publications.

Aranya, Swami Hariharananda, *Yoga Philosophy of Patanjali*. Calcutta, India: University of Calcutta, 1963.

Avalon, Arthur. *Tantra of the Great Liberation*. New York: Dover Publications, 1972.

Baker, Dr. Douglas. *Esoteric Healing*. Herts. England: Douglas Baker, 1975.

Bernard, Theos. *Hindu Philosophy*. New York: Philosophical Library, 1947.

Besant, Annie. *The Bhagavad-Gita*. Adyar, Madras, India: Theosophical Publishing House, 1973.

Chang, Dr. Stephen T. *The Tao of Sexology: The Book of Infinite Wisdom*. San Francisco, Tao Publishing, 1986.

Cousens, Gabriel. *Spiritual Nutrition and The Rainbow Diet*. San Rafael, California: Cassandra Press, 1986.

Cozort, Daniel. *Highest Yoga Tantra*. Ithaca, NY: Snow Lion, 1986.

Evans-Wentz, W.Y. *Tibetan Yoga and Secret Doctrines*. London: Oxford University Press, 1967.

Frawley, David. *Ayurveda and the Mind, the Healing of Consciousness*. Detroit: Lotus Press, 1997.

———. *Yoga & Ayurveda: Self-Healing and Self-Realization*. Detroit: Lotus Press, 1999.

Goswami, C.L., and M.A. Sastri, *Srimad Bhagavata Mahapurana*. Gorakhpur, India: Motilal Jalan, Gita Press, 1982.

Goswami, Shyam Sundar. *Layagoya*: *The Definitive Guide to the Chakras and Kundalini*. Rochester, Vermont: Inner Traditions, 1999.

Greene, Brian. *The Elegant Universe: Superstrings, Hidden Dimensions, and the Quest for the Ultimate Theory*. New York: Random House, Vintage Books, 2000.

Hume, R.E., trans. *The Thirteen Principal Upanishads*. Oxford: Oxford University Press, 1931.

Isherwood, Christopher. *Ramakrishna and His Disciples*. Hollywood, California.: Vedanta Press, 1980.

Johari, Harish. *Chakras: Energy Centers of Transformation*. Rochester, Vermont: Destiny Books, Inner Traditions International, Ltd., 2000.

Jung, Carl, and J. Hauer. *Kundalini Yoga*. Unpublished manuscript, 1932.

Kapila. *Samkhya-darsana (Samkhya-sutras of Kapila) with Vijnanabhiksu's Commentary*. Calcutta, India: Vacaspatya Press, 1936.

Karyalaya, Gobind Bhawan. *The Bhagavadgita*. Gorakhpur, India: Gita Press, 1984.

Keshavadas, Sadguru Sant. *Sadguru Dattatreya*. Oakland, California: Vishwa Dharma Publications, 1988.

Kilner, Walter J. *The Human Aura*. Fort Lee, New Jersey: Lyle Stuart, 1983.

Krishna, Gopi. *Kundalini: The Evolutionary Energy in Man*. Shambhala Press, 1967.

———. *Dawn of a New Science*. Toronto: Institute for Consciousness Research, 1999.

Liberman, Jacob. *Light: Medicine of the Future*. Santa Fe, New Mexico: Bear & Co., 1991.

Mahesh Yogi, Maharishi. *Bhagavad Gita: A New Translation and Commentary with Sanskrit Text*. International SRM Publications, 1967.

———. *Science of Being and Art of Living*. New York: Signet, 1968.

Miller, Moshe, trans. *Zohar*. Chicago, Illinois: Fiftieth Gate Publications, 2000.

Mishra, Rammurti S. *Fundamentals of Yoga*. New York: Harmony Books, Crown Publishers, 1987.

Muktananda, Swami. *Kundalini: The Secrets of Life*. New York: Syda Foundation, 1979.

———. *Shree Guru Gita*. South Fallsburg, New York: Syda Foundation, 1981.

Müller, F. Max, ed. *The Sacred Books of the East—The Upanishads, Vol. XV*. Oxford, England: Oxford University Press, 1879 (part 1), 1884 (part 2).

Nityananda, Bhagavan. *Sky of the Heart: Jewels of Wisdom from Nityananda*. Portland, Oregon: Rudra Press, 1996.

Osho. *In Search of the Miraculous: Chakras, Kundalini & The Seven Bodies*. Essex, England: C.W. Daniel Company Limited, 1996.

Perry, Whitall N. *A Treasury of Traditional Wisdom*. Cambridge, England: Quinta Essentia, 1971.

Powell, A.E. *The Etheric Double: The Health Aura of Man*. Wheaton, Illinois: Quest, The Theosophical Publishing House, 1969.

Prabhavananda, Swami, and Christopher Isherwood. *Shankara's Crest Jewel of Discrimination*. Hollywood, California: Vedanta Press, 1975.

Saraswati, Swami Satyananda. *A Systematic Course in the Ancient Tantric Techniques of Yoga and Kriya*. Bihar, India: Bihar School of Yoga, 1981.

Satprakashananda, Swami. *The Goal and the Way: The Vedantic Approach to Life's Problems*. St. Louis, Missouri: The Vedanta Society of St. Louis, 1977.

Satyeswarananda Giri, Swami. *Babaji: The Divine Himalayan Yogi*. San Diego, California: The Sanskrit Classics, 1984.

Shankaracharya. *Vivekacudamani: A Masterpiece of Advaita Vedanta in Poetry, The Works of Shankara, Vol. X,* no date.

Sheldrake, Rupert. *A New Science of Life: The Hypothesis of Morphic Resonance*. Rochester, Vermont: Inner Traditions International, 1995.

———. *The Presence of the Past: Morphic Resonance & the Habits of Nature*. Rochester, Vermont: Inner Traditions International, 1995.

Shumsky, Susan G. *Divine Revelation*. New York: Fireside, Simon & Schuster, 1996.

———. *Exploring Meditation*. Franklin Lakes, New Jersey: New Page Books, The Career Press, 2002.

———. *Exploring Auras*. Franklin Lakes, New Jersey: New Page Books, 2005.

———. *Miracle Prayer*. Berkeley, California: Celestial Arts, 2006.

———. *How to Hear the Voice of God*. Franklin Lakes, New Jersey: New Page Books, The Career Press, 2008.

———. *Ascension*. Franklin Lakes, New Jersey: New Page Books, The Career Press, 2010.

———. *Instant Healing*. Pompton Plains, New Jersey: New Page Books, The Career Press, 2013.

———. *The Power of Auras*. Pompton Plains, New Jersey: New Page Books, The Career Press, 2013.

Silburn, Lilian. *Kundalini: The Energy of the Depths*. Albany, New York: State University of New York Press, 1988.

Sivananda, Sri Swami. *Kundalini Yoga*. Shivanandanagar, India: Divine Life Society, 1994.

Subramanian, V.K. *Saundaryalahari of Shankaracarya*. Delhi, India: Motilal Banarsidass Publishers, 1998.

Svatmarama. Pancham Sinh, trans. *Hatha Yoga Pradipika*. Allahabad, India: Sudhindra Nath Vasu, the Panini office, Bhuvaneswari Asrama, 1914.

Svoboda, Robert E. *Aghora: At the Left Hand of God*. Albuquerque, New Mexico: Brotherhood of Life, 1986.

Thera, Narada Maha, trans. *The Dhammapada*. Colombo, Sri Lanka: Vijirarama, 1972.

Thirumoolar, Siddhar, and M. Govindan, ed. *Thirumandiram: A Classic of Yoga and Tantra*. Montreal, Canada: Babaji's Kriya Yoga and Publications, Inc., 1993.

Upanishads: The Ten Principal, with Shankaracharya Commentary, Vols. I and II. Poona, India: Askekar and Co., 1927, 1928.

Varenne, J., trans. *Yogatattva Upanishad: Yoga in the Hindu Tradition*. Chicago: Univ. of Chicago Press, 1976.

Vasu, Rai Babadur Srisa Chandra, trans. *The Siva Samhita*. New Delhi, India: Munshiram Manoharlal Publishers Pvt. Ltd., 1999.

Venkatanathacharya, N.S. *Mandalabrahmanopanishad, with Rajayogabhashya of Sri Shankaracharya and Yogataravali of Sri Shankaracharya with Bhavaprakasha*. Mysore, India: Oriental Research Institute, University of Mysore, 1970.

Vidyaranya, Bharati-tirtha. *Pancadasi, with commentary of Ramakrishna*. NSP, 1935.

Vireswarananda, Swami, and Swami Adidevananda. *Brahma-Sutras*. Mayavati, Pithoragarh, Himalayas, India: Advaita Ashrama, 1986.

Vishnu-devananda, Swami. *The Complete Illustrated Book of Yoga*. New York: Three Rivers Press, 1988.

von Reichenbach, Karl. *Physico-physiological Researches on the Dynamics of Magnetism, Electricity, Heat, Light, Crystallization, and Chemism: In Their Relation to Vital Force*. New York: J. S. Redfield; Boston: B. B. Mussey & Co., 1851.

White, John Warren, and Stanley Krippner. *Future Science: Life Energies and the Physics of Paranormal Phenomena*. New York: Doubleday, 1977.

Wilson, Andrew, ed. *International Religious Foundation, World Scripture*. New York: Paragon House, 1991.

Woodroffe, Sir John. *The Serpent Power: Being the Sat-cakranirupana and Paduka-pancaka*. Madras, India: Ganesh & Co., 1973.

Woodroffe, Sir John George. *Mahanirvana Tantra*. Lodi, California: Auromere, 1985.

THE BIG BOOK OF CHAKRAS AND CHAKRA HEALING

Yogananda, Paramahansa. *Autobiography of a Yogi*. Los Angeles, California: Self-Realization Fellowship, 1981.

Yogindra, Sadananda. Col. G.A. Jacob, ed. *Vedanta-sara*. NSP, 1925.

Yudelove, Eric Steven. *The Tao & The Tree of Life: Alchemical & Sexual Mysteries of the East and West*. St. Paul, Minnesota: Llewellyn Publications, 1996.

Yukteswar, Jnanavatar Swami Sri. *The Holy Science*. Los Angeles, California: Self-Realization Fellowship, 1990.

Websites

Chidananda Blog: Enlightening Inquisitive Souls: *chidananda4444.wixsite.com/indianmeditation*

Gheranda Samhita
www.yogavidya.com

M-theory to explain the Flying Spaghetti Monster?
www.assuefazione.wordpress.com

Hatha Yoga Pradipika, online version
YogaVidya.com

Mahanirvana Tantra, online version
www.sacred-texts.com/tantra/maha/

Meister Eckhart
www.spiritualeducation.org

Plato's Secret Doctrine
www.prem-rawat-bio.org

Principal Upanishads, online version
hinduism.about.com/library/weekly/aa061301d.htm

Sat Cakra Narupana, online version
www.realization.org

Sivananda, Sri Swami; Kundalini Yoga, online version
www.dlshq.org

Kundalini Yoga, online version
www.yoga-age.com

Zohar, online version
www.kabbalah.com

Other Websites Used

www.journaloftheoretics.com

www.keelynet.com

www.orgonelab.org

www.reikiteaching.co.uk

www.nuhs.edu

www.heilkunst.com

www.ncahf.org

THE AUTHOR AND HER TEACHINGS

PHOTO BY ANGELA SHIN

Dr. Susan Shumsky has dedicated her life to helping people take command of their lives in highly effective, powerful, positive ways. She is a leading spirituality expert, highly acclaimed and greatly respected professional speaker, sought-after media guest, New Thought minister, and Doctor of Divinity.

Dr. Shumsky is a multiple award–winning, bestselling author of seventeen books, including *Divine Revelation, Ascension, Miracle Prayer, Exploring Meditation, Instant Healing, The Power of Auras, The Power of Chakras, Color Your Chakras, Awaken Your Third Eye, Awaken Your Divine Intuition, Third Eye Meditations, Earth Energy Meditations,* and her memoir *Maharishi & Me.* Her books have been published in several languages worldwide, many were #1 Amazon best sellers, several were published as audio books, and two were One Spirit Book Club selections.

Dr. Shumsky has practiced self-development disciplines since 1967. For over two decades, she practiced deep meditation for many hours daily in locations such as the Himalayas, the Swiss Alps, and other secluded areas, under the personal guidance of enlightened master from India, Maharishi Mahesh Yogi, founder of Transcendental Meditation and guru of the Beatles, Deepak Chopra, and other major celebrities. Dr. Shumsky served on Maharishi's personal staff for six of those years in Spain, Mallorca, Austria, Italy, and Switzerland. She studied New Thought and metaphysics for another three decades and became a Doctor of Divinity.

Dr. Shumsky was not born with any supernormal faculties but developed her expertise through decades of patient daily study and practice. She has taught yoga, meditation, prayer, and intuition to thousands of students worldwide since 1970 as a pioneer in the consciousness field. She is founder of Divine Revelation, a unique, field-proven technology for contacting the divine presence, hearing and testing the inner voice, and receiving clear divine guidance.

Dr. Shumsky travels extensively, producing and facilitating workshops, conferences, ocean cruise seminars, and tours to sacred destinations worldwide. She also offers teleseminars and private spiritual coaching, prayer therapy sessions, and spiritual breakthrough sessions.

All of Dr. Shumsky's years of research into consciousness and inner exploration have contributed to her books and teachings, which can significantly reduce many pitfalls in a seeker's quest for inner truth and greatly shorten the time required for the inner pathway to Spirit.

On her websites, *www.drsusan.org* and *www.divinetravels.com*, you can:

- Join the mailing list.

- See Dr. Shumsky's itinerary.

- Read the first chapter of Dr. Shumsky's books.

- Listen to free interviews, read articles, and watch videos of Dr. Shumsky.

- Find Divine Revelation teachers in various areas.

- Order books, audio and video products, downloadable files, home study courses, and laminated cards of healing affirmations.

- Order beautiful, full-color prints of Dr. Shumsky's illustrations.

- Register for telephone sessions and teleseminars with Dr. Shumsky.

- Register for one of her spiritual cruises, retreats, or tours.

When you join the mailing list at *www.drsusan.org*, you will receive a free, downloadable, guided mini-meditation plus access to the free online community group forum and free weekly teleconference prayer circle.

As a gift for reading this book, please use the following special discount code when you register for one of the spiritual cruises, retreats, or tours at *www. divinetravels.com*: CHAKRAS108.

We want to hear from you. Please write about your personal experiences of meditation and kundalini awakening, or invite Dr. Shumsky to speak to your group: *divinerev@aol.com*. If you enjoyed this book, please write a customer review on *Amazon.com*, and please order more copies and give the book to friends and family as gifts.

To Our Readers

Weiser Books, an imprint of Red Wheel/Weiser, publishes books across the entire spectrum of occult, esoteric, speculative, and New Age subjects. Our mission is to publish quality books that will make a difference in people's lives without advocating any one particular path or field of study. We value the integrity, originality, and depth of knowledge of our authors.

Our readers are our most important resource, and we appreciate your input, suggestions, and ideas about what you would like to see published.

Visit our website at *www.redwheelweiser.com* to learn about our upcoming books and free downloads, and be sure to go to *www.redwheelweiser.com/newsletter* to sign up for newsletters and exclusive offers.

You can also contact us at *info@rwwbooks.com* or at

Red Wheel/Weiser, LLC
65 Parker Street, Suite 7
Newburyport, MA 01950